W9-DIT-939

The Continuing

Presence of

Walt Whitman

The

Continuing

Presence

of Walt

Whitman

The Life after the Life

Edited by Robert K. Martin

University of Iowa Press Ψ *Iowa City*

University of Iowa Press, Iowa City 52242

Copyright © 1992 by the University of Iowa Press

All rights reserved

Printed in the United States of America

Design by Richard Hendel

No part of this book may be reproduced or utilized in any form or by any means, electronic or mechanical, including photocopying and recording, without permission in writing from the publisher.

The following essays have been previously published, in somewhat different form, and are reprinted here with permission: Thom Gunn, "Freedom for All," *Times Literary Supplement*, January 5–11, 1990, pp. 3–4; Maurice Kenny, "Whitman's Indifference to Indians," *Greenfield Review* 14 (Summer/Fall 1987): 99–113; Michael Lynch, "The Lover of His Fellows and the Hot Little Prophets: Walt Whitman in Ontario," *Body Politic* 67 (October 1980): 29–31; Ned Rorem, "A Postscript on Whitman," © 1969 by Ned Rorem, published in Rorem, *Settling the Score* (New York: Harcourt Brace, 1988), pp. 311–313. Ronald Johnson's poems first appeared in *Valley of the Many-Colored Grasses* (New York: Norton, 1969), pp. 89–98.

Library of Congress Cataloging-in-Publication Data

The Continuing presence of Walt Whitman: the life after the life / edited by Robert K. Martin.—1st ed.

    p.   cm.

  Includes bibliographical references and index.

ISBN 0-87745-366-7 (cloth: alk. paper)

   1. Whitman, Walt, 1819–1892—Criticism and interpretation.

   2. Authors and readers—United States. 3. Reader-response criticism. I. Martin, Robert K., 1941–

PS3238.C59 1992

811'.3—dc20

91-44249

CIP

96 95 94 93 92 C 1 2 3 4 5

PS
3238
.C59
1992

122893

TO MICHAEL LYNCH, 1944–1991

Contents

III   BEYOND THE BORDERS

IV   THE POETS RESPOND

Acknowledgments

Support has been provided by Concordia University. I am particularly grateful for the expert services of two research assistants, Lazer Lederhendler and Frances Slingerland. Lazer provided valuable editing skills, and Fran was a scrupulous reader of drafts and checker of facts with a keen eye for the details that I tend to miss. Both of them made this project more enjoyable.

All unspecified references to Whitman's poetry are from the *Comprehensive Reader's Edition*; citations are by line number.

Introduction

ROBERT K. MARTIN

Poets to come! orators, singers, musicians to come!
Not to-day is to justify me and answer what I am for,
But you, a new brood, native, athletic, continental, greater
  than before known,
Arouse! for you must justify me.
—Walt Whitman

Whitman counted on the future to fulfill what he had begun. He himself had provided only, he wrote in a moment of modesty, "one or two indicative words for the future" ("Poets to come," 5). The poet who sought to be a nation's bard has found his audience and his new brood not only in America but internationally. The Whitman his readers have created is as diverse as those readers themselves. But he is, as he promised, everywhere: "Missing me one place search another, / I stop somewhere waiting for you" ("Song of Myself," 1345–1346).

It sometimes seems hard to avoid the presence of Whitman—even for whose who would do without it. An almost random culling of my shelves yields four examples that testify to the range of his appeal and the ways in which he has been transformed in the generations that have followed his death. The earliest, barely a few years after his death, at a time when his poetic influence seemed least, is Kate Chopin's *The Awakening*. Chopin records her heroine's awakening to sensuality and death in a remarkable passage that, although in prose, seems to come straight out of Whitman:

The voice of the sea is seductive; never ceasing, whispering, clamoring, murmuring, inviting the soul to wander for a spell in abysses of solitude; to lose itself in mazes of inward contemplation.

The voice of the sea speaks to the soul. The touch of the sea is sensuous, enfolding the body in its soft, close embrace. (34)

The personified soul seduced into a realm of physical pleasure, the caresses of an oceanic bliss, the loss of self in a world of pure sensation that is paradoxically reached through the self—these Whitmanian touches are all strikingly present. And so is a Whitmanian rhythm, the cradling movement of the sea here embodied in the repeated present participles and the soporific sibilants.

While Chopin's passage can be traced to a number of Whitmanian "origins," including "Out of the Cradle" and section 22 of "Song of Myself," her mention a few lines earlier of Edna's age—twenty-eight—locates this text quite clearly in a line of descent from section 11 of "Song of Myself." Chopin creates Edna Pontellier in part out of the hint provided by Whitman: "Twenty-eight years of womanly life and all so lonesome." Like Whitman's respectable woman, Edna's life has been lived "aft the blinds of the window," as an observer rather than as a participant in life. Her discovery of her sexuality requires that she, like Whitman's "I," be "undisguised and naked," leaving behind the social costume that has concealed the body and hence the self. Naked in the sea, she is like "some new-born creature," at once Venus and Eve in a redeemed garden. For Chopin, Whitman pointed the way to the celebration of the body and to a liberation from social convention.

For a black poet of the Harlem renaissance of the 1920s, the heritage of Whitman was more complex. Part of the difference may lie in the impossibility for a black artist of accepting the psychological approach of a writer like Chopin—Edna's personal fulfillment is enabled by her very considerable financial means and the labor of the servant Celestine. Another part of the difference comes from the shift in Whitman's cultural position: the man who in the late 1890s was still an outlawed figure of sexual freedom had by the 1920s become the hero of the prairie nationalists. This meant that the Whitman available for Jean Toomer was already mediated by writers such as Carl Sandburg (whose *Chicago Poems* was published in 1916 and *Cornhuskers* in 1918) and Sherwood Anderson (whose *Mid-American Chants* was published in 1918). Such socially conscious writers seemed incapable of capturing the realities of working-class life as experienced by American blacks or indeed of adapting Whitman's poetics to a less naïve time. The Americanist writers of the late teens provided Toomer with a watered down, sentimentalized, and heterosexualized Whitman (albeit a Whitman that Whitman had permitted himself to be) as a poet of the land and its fertility.

Toomer was not immune to these forces, of course, in his troubled celebration in *Cane* of a return to a more "primitive," chthonic world of the South. The "Harvest Song" included in the second part of *Cane* is Whitmanian in form, even as it tries to break away from the celebratory tone of the Whitmanites. The reaper who speaks the poem is isolated, worn out by labor, beaten down, unable to communicate. The song plays variations on its principal themes, "I am a reaper" and "I hunger." Although the speaker seeks comradeship and knowledge of his brothers, he is blind and deaf. He is reduced to his pain. The poem is composed of a series of eleven stanzas, all spoken by the reaper in plain, almost exhausted language. Pauses are indicated in Whitmanian fashion by ellipses. For Toomer, the Whitman heritage, the poetry of the ordinary person, could not celebrate but only record suffering. Learning from Whitman how to organize the verse paragraph and replacing linearity with circularity and repetition, Toomer has to find his way out of the blithe celebration that constituted Whitmanism in the 1920s.

In the world of black Paris of the 1930s, poets such as Sandburg and Anderson must have seemed totally beside the point and embarrassingly provincially American. The blacks who helped forge a new artistic community under the name of négritude brought together African music and chant, European poetic tradition, and American jazz. Léopold Sédar Senghor, the greatest of these writers, adapted Whitman for his purposes. Senghor makes use, certainly, of Whitmanian techniques such as the long line and the catalog or multiple random example—a device of metonymy rather than metaphor—but they are transformed by a verbal richness and an imagination nourished by surrealism. Consider his brilliant "A l'appel de la race de Saba" (1936), in which a sense of diversity hidden by colonial sameness brings the power of the proper name to new vigor:

> Car nous sommes là tous réunis, divers de teint—il y en
>   a qui sont couleur de café grillé, d'autres bananes d'or
>   et d'autres terre de rizières
> Divers de traits de costume de coutumes de langue;
>   mais au fond des yeux la même mélopée des
>   souffrances à l'ombre des longs cils fièvreux
> Le Cafre le Kabyle le Somali le Maure, le Fân, le Fôn le
>   Bambara le Bobo le Mandiago
> Le nomade le mineur le prestataire, le paysan et l'artisan
>   le boursier et le tirailleur (61)

It is only the following line, with its weak didacticism, "Et tous les travailleurs blancs dans la lutte fraternelle," that takes away some of Senghor's power to both borrow from and build on the example of Whitman. It was the American poet's New York, mediated by the Harlem renaissance, that helped to form Senghor's ecstatic response ("Nuits d'insomnie! ô nuit de Manhattan!") to the city. If some lines seem surreal ("J'ai vu le ciel neiger au soir des fleurs de coton et des ailes de séraphins et des panaches de sorciers"), others capture an erotic and violent rhythm in the beating of the nocturnal heart that seems like that of an updated Whitman.

For my last example I skip the 1960s, not because my shelves would yield no suitable examples but indeed because they would yield both too many and those too well known. Two of the essays in this volume address themselves to this period—David Eberly's remarkable exploration of the Whitman/Frank O'Hara relation and Amitai Avi-ram's challenging reexamination of Whitman and Ginsberg. But Whitman has a way of turning up in unlikely places as well as likely ones. The first chapter of David Plante's 1985 novel *The Catholic* includes a long passage from "I Sing the Body Electric." Plante's account of a young man's coming out in Boston in the 1960s is framed as a conflict of two rhetorics, one Catholic and the other gay. It is not that the Catholic discourse allows no place for sexuality; in this Franco-American education the homoerotic masochism of the Jesuit Relations has pride of place alongside the domestic sentimentality of *Atala*. But a hatred of the body prevails and requires a Whitman to transform that body, to make it into "a country with its own special gravity." To find that country, Daniel makes love to Charlie. Whitman's voice, his celebration of love between men, is enabling for Plante's hero as it has been enabling for gay readers since Whitman's own lifetime. Like no one else, Whitman suddenly reveals a new world of experience, one that he offers not only without shame but with allurement. Whitman's poetry seems the path to erotic exploration and the discovery of a new identity. For Plante, however, Whitman's powerful vision must be handled with care, since it can easily replace the hatred of the body with a cult of the body. Investing everything in the fetishized body parts of "The Body Electric," Daniel cannot face the fact that Henry "was a young man not much different from me." He has imagined all desire as universal love (as Whitman sometimes seems to urge) and thus repeated the error of his childhood which would see all desire as faith. The côté of religion and the côté of homosexuality turn out to be similar in the end. And, having discovered the body, he can never really renounce it, as the novel's ending suggests: "I imagined I heard someone in the room, heard a movement or a voice. A thrill spread over the surface of my skin. I looked out and listened. There was someone in the room, and, if I waited, he would come just close enough to the bed for me to see him in the dark." Even for this sophisticated writer who must remake his Whitman to acknowledge doubts about the eschatology of sex and indeed the notion of identity, Whitman remains an originating force. Once read, he will not go away.

Not all readers have been positive, of course. Amitai Avi-ram, in an important essay, argues that the conventional view of Whitman's "liberatory" poetics is illusory, that Whitman replaces the body with a discourse of the body. This volume also includes a very angry account by Maurice Kenny of Whitman's ignorance and misrepresentation of the native people of North America. While I think Kenny's account is wrong in many ways and certainly unfair to Whitman, I feel it is important to include it here as an indication of the response that one Native American poet has to Whitman. Kenny's account is partial as well as angry, and a poem that he names but does not quote, "Yonnondio," offers a partial counterweight in its dirge for the disappearance of Indians and their cultures, leaving only "a wailing word . . . borne through the air for a moment," a line that Hart Crane remembered as he attempted to reassess Native American history in *The Bridge*. It is of course precisely because of Whitman's unique position in the culture, his undisputed role as the central figure of American poetic history, that Kenny must answer him with such bitterness. Whitman was aware of the extent to which the Native American was, even in the appellation "Indian," a product of a European imagination. As Whitman told Thomas Donaldson,

> Indians! I suppose we are never to get rid of that word! . . .
> It is as much a misnomer as the word "American." These
> people deserved a higher, a more distinct and a more mean-
> ing name, one relating to their aboriginal or pre-Columbian
> times, one which would be significant that they were the
> possessors and owners of the continent prior to the advent
> of the Europeans. (Donaldson, 264)

There is more than a trace of an American version of "Orientalism," in Edward Said's sense, in Whitman's response to the Native American, and yet his unabashed celebration of the young chief's "superb physique" does not reduce the Indian to a mere animal, unless all admiration for physical beauty is suspect. Whitman made of the living American Indian an object of beauty and desire; in so doing he worked against the nostalgic plaint for a lost culture that dominated American literature of the period. Kenny seems to think only American Indians are seen as pure body, but he is surely forgetting many passages in *Leaves of Grass*, including Whitman's remarkable celebration of his young (white) man: "A gigantic beauty of a stallion, fresh and responsive to my caresses" ("Song of Myself," 701).

The refusal to acknowledge Whitman's sexuality has to a considerable extent permitted critiques of Whitman that might be answered, or at least diminished in intensity, if they were placed in the context of his sexuality. I bought a second-hand copy of the reprinted 1860 edition of *Leaves of Grass*, which bore the angry pencil marks of its previous owner. To Whitman's, "I proceed, for all who are, or have been, young men, / To tell the secret of my nights and days," she countered, "But I am not a young man." Apparently feeling excluded and not understanding the purpose of the "Calamus" poems, she took Whitman's assurances of universality as false, arrogant claims. There may be some of that in them, but there is also much to offer to all readers. For Irene Karjala, writing in the wake of French critic Hélène Cixous and theories of *écriture féminine*, "Whitman's fluid intersubjective body/text displays a consciousness which runs counter to masculine values" (91). She sees in Whitman a feminist textuality in a "male" text. Anglo-American feminists, as poet Alicia Ostriker's essay demonstrates, express their relationship to Whitman in more pragmatic terms, saying as Ostriker does, "He permitted love."

Protean, elusive, slippery, Whitman is everywhere and nowhere at once. An unavoidable presence, he still arouses anger, envy, and debate one hundred years after his death. The essays gathered here attempt to provide some introduction to the multiple responses that Whitman continues to evoke. There is enough Whitman, it seems, to go around. As George Hutchinson suggests in his essay on African-American poet Langston Hughes, there is no single "Whitman tradition," even if Hughes might have thought in those terms, since the response to Whitman is mediated through a host of factors including race, history, class, nationality, gender, and sexuality. What Whitman seems to have provided for readers of varied backgrounds and allegiances is a sense of *enablement*. Whitman helped make it possible to be a woman poet, a gay poet, a black poet, partly because he saw himself not as a model but as an enabler: "He most honors my style who learns under it to destroy the teacher" ("Song of Myself," 1236).

Whitman thought of himself above all as an *American* poet, even as he perhaps simplified or ignored the problems in that identity for Native Americans or blacks. But Whitman did help forge an identity both *for* and *of* Americans. As I have suggested above, that identity could be rendered in largely bathetic terms as it was in the early years of this century and threatens to become once more in recent films based on Whitman's life or poetry. Nonetheless, it also offered a sense of opportunity and an important first instance of postcolonial writing in America. Emerson had perhaps proclaimed it, but it was Whitman who *wrote back*. His mark was placed not only on writing in America but on larger patterns of self-conceptualization. Jimmie Killingsworth sees in Whitman a tension between the singularity of the individual and the multiplicity of expressiveness that he identifies with a national image of selfhood. Whitman, of course, has always had readers beyond the boundaries of America. Many of them, from his first English admirers to more recent ones, have been gay men or lesbians and have identified Whitman with the possibilities of homosexual self-expression (Whitman's role as at once a national and a gay poet demonstrating exactly the kind of tension Killingsworth suggests, one that was built into Whitman's own strategies for a subversive use of commonplace discourse, as Michael Moon's recent book has shown so clearly).

For the Portuguese poet Fernando Pessoa, also gay, Whitman meant in part an "Atlantic spirit," as Maria Irena Ramalho de Sousa Santos shows, even though the sea that really held Whitman's imagination, unlike Hart Crane's, was the Pacific. As she also shows, the line between Whitman's celebration of world democracy and that of an American imperial world order was a very fine one: in that sense Whitman's heritage is still fraught with danger. Pessoa, the ultimate modernist, was (not unlike T. S. Eliot, as James Miller has shown) drawn by the doubleness of Whitman's vision, his intense sense of Self joined with the dissolution of the Self. For Pessoa's critic and translator Susan Margaret Brown, this divergence ultimately became for Pessoa the source of the splitting of his self into separate personas, a situation that enabled the most anti-Whitmanian of them to engage in a fruitful debate with his Whitman tradition.

One aspect of Whitman criticism that has changed most dramatically in recent years has been the consideration of his role as a gay poet. It is not that this was unknown before, merely that the knowledge of it was largely suppressed even as the creators of the American literary canon wrote (in many cases) their own sexuality into their reception of Whitman. Newton Arvin in 1938, stressing Whitman's role as a "Socialist poet," nonetheless argued that his poetry and politics had a basis in his sexuality: "He translated . . . his . . . emotional experience into a political, a constructive, a democratic program" (275; my ellipses play down Arvin's self-torture as he strove both to say and not to say what he felt). F. O. Matthiessen, who was shocked by the outrageousness of Arvin's lover, Truman Capote, left homosexuality out of *American Renaissance*, except by implication (especially strong in his use of Eakins's *The Swimming Hole* as an illustration), although he did describe the poet's body in section 5 of "Song of Myself" as passive and hence "vaguely pathological and homosexual," countering this with the thought that Whitman's "fluidity of sexual sympathy made possible [his] fallow receptivity to life" (535). Although Whitman entered the American canon in part through the efforts of gay critics such as Arvin and Matthiessen, he was then subject to a homophobic critical examination that diluted or frankly eliminated the homosexual content of his work.

It was Whitman's readers who preserved Whitman from many of the Whitmanites, in an emerging network of critical and artistic response. Eric Savoy traces the panicked reaction of the younger Henry James and its eventual resolution into the warm sympathy of the later James, a critical itinerary that speaks for James's own biographical trajectory as well. James's simultaneous terror and attraction, which anticipate Hopkins's, speak of the power that Whitman held for his gay readers who knew what was often publicly denied. At a time when the homosexual sensibility, under the pressures of domestication and state terror, was moving to the margins defined by the very dandy Whitman so overdeterminedly claimed not to be ("No dainty dolce affettuoso I / Bearded, sun-burnt, grey-neck'd, forbidding . . ." ["Starting from Paumanok," 233–234]), gay readers grappled with a complex heritage. Although the view of Frank O'Hara as a surrealist poet may indeed be in part the result of a critical tactic that has operated to render him "safe," David Eberly's study shows how difficult his coming to terms with Whitman was—the apparently serious old man meeting the flaming young queen. In some senses that dilemma is always there, although gay and lesbian writers and artists of a variety of allegiances have had to reckon with Whitman's presence and model. He could be part of an American lyric tradition for composers as different as Ned Rorem and John Adams or part of a reaction against abstraction for David Hockney, recalling, as insistently as he does, not the death but the life of the author.

Sexual radicalism is a larger part of American life, even if sometimes a privileged site for homosexual self-expression, as Michael Moon and Michael Lynch remind us. Lynch's modest title belies the important connections he draws between Whitman and the "hot little prophets," the feminist and socialist community at Bon Echo. A major contribution to the history of radicalism in Ontario, Lynch's piece reminds us of Whitman's place in a larger struggle over issues of gender, class, and economics. It makes one want to know more about similar communities, such as those centered around Traubel in Philadelphia or Mosher in Maine. The radicalism of the World War I period, so abruptly brought to an end by the war and its euphemistically termed "mobilization" of opinion, is not very different from the struggles now beginning again under the pressure of AIDS, as Michael Moon suggests. The fear of disease has been enlisted as an excuse for the prohibition of sex and the renewed marginalization of gay men, prostitutes, and intravenous drug users. Whitman's courage, his relentless drive for honesty about sexuality, his own "promiscuity" that still strikes such terror into the American public need to be recuperated now, even as we can no longer accept traditional fixed definitions of sexual identity.

The process of revision that has worked to make Whitman "safe" for the classroom—at the same time that a film such as *Dead Poets Society* reminds us that pederasty/pedagogy is always threatening to a homosocial, homophobic culture—began with Whitman himself, as Alan Helms shows in his moving commentary on "Live Oak with Moss," a sequence that was later dismembered to become part of "Calamus." Whitman was always crafty, playing with the limits of the sayable, retreating when he was found out (as by John Addington Symonds), and he worked hard to construct a public image for himself that was based on both his role as the American national poet and his role as the "secret" gay poet.

Whitman's discourse of sexuality drew upon the dualisms of his day, even as he sought to bring them into balance by consciously mentioning the female along with the male, although rarely with any conviction if the context is erotic. When I began writing about Whitman in the early 1970s I used the language of essentialism, since that was the language I had learned along with a politics of group identity and group rights. Like most gay critics of my generation, I sought to understand my sexuality through the lenses of the civil rights movement. This essentialism was responsible for some of the univocal thinking that made me believe there was a single gay tradition, from which blacks were apparently absent, and a single gay way of living. I would be embarrassed by such naïveté today. What I do not regret is my insistence on the ways in which the reading and appropriation of Whitman had been part of a cultural politics of disenfranchisement and silencing. While I can no longer think of Whitman as *the* gay man, a concept that I now see must be much more fully historicized than I was prepared to do in 1975, I still see Whitman as a challenge to a set of cultural values that includes homophobia as well as a terror of the body. The panicked response I received from cultural figures such as Robert Boyers is evidence enough that the nerve I had touched was raw. Whitman still continues to challenge our assessment of our sexuality and the ways we organize it. He still refuses the tyranny of the family and compulsory heterosexuality.

This volume seeks to be an intervention and not merely a reflection. Literary reputation is always the result of a negotiation between perception and construction. I have no illusions, therefore, about the ability of any of the contributors to discover the "real" Whitman—indeed, one can wonder if Whitman could have found it, despite his repeated claims that he had done so.

Reading is always an act of rewriting. This is obviously true for the poet or composer, which is one reason I am so glad to have contributions from artists including Alicia Ostriker, Thom Gunn, and Ned Rorem, as well as those whose work is less well known, such as David Eberly and Michael Lynch. But I think it is true of all writing, whether critical or "creative." Surely our critical efforts are, at their best, like the finest of conversations with those we care about—affectionate, passionate, occasionally angry, and mattering more than anything in the world. Every dinner party is at least potentially a symposium and every interlocutor potentially a lover. My Whitman will not be yours, for he will be produced out of his texts and my reading, an act informed by my own shaping texts. Describing a heritage is always also enabling another one.

What I have wanted to avoid in this volume is a pious memorial. "The ceremonies were short," Donaldson reports of Whitman's funeral (274). This is not a book intended to look backward as much as forward; it is a book intended above all to understand not a response that took place or even has taken place but one that continues to take place, a constant invention and reinvention, a writing and rewriting that echo Whitman's own text of *Leaves of Grass*, of which there can never be a single authoritative edition. Resisting his own reification even as he polished his image, celebrating mutability even as he sought expression for his *real* self, Whitman was indeed a bundle of contradictions, an earnest Victorian and a postmodernist. I conclude the volume therefore with another poet, another set of poems, poems that, as Ed Folsom so wonderfully indicates, talk *with* and not *to* Walt Whitman. Ronald Johnson's collages work marvelously well to evoke Whitman's own acquisitive nature, his gathering of scraps here and there for the crazy quilt of his never-masterwork.

These poems begin with Whitman, but they also look forward, re-create another Whitman perhaps more real than the one we thought we knew, as Liszt or Reger can perhaps reveal Mozart to us. I have wanted from the inception of this project to avoid a study of "influence," and I am delighted to report that neither Harold Bloom nor his formulation appears often in these pages. As has often been said by now, his agonistic model of influence is too Freudian, too heterosexual, simply too *male* (if I may be essentialistic for a moment). Whitman does not compete with his readers and lovers; he is there for them to love, quarrel with, and eventually rewrite. He is and will be what we have made and will make of him.

I

Reading the Nation

Reading Gay America

Walt Whitman, Henry James,

and the Politics of Reception

ERIC SAVOY

The rise of gay and lesbian literary studies since the 1980s has not only prompted revisionist readings of the American canon but also has enabled the reconfiguration of connective pathways—the powers of influence and the dynamics of reception—that constitute literary history. Until quite recently, any attempt to trace ideological connections between the garrulous, democratic Walt Whitman and the loquacious, fastidious Henry James would have been unthinkable. In his attempt to broaden the history and theory of homosexuality, Michael Moon stresses the need "to resist the . . . literary-historiographical conventions which have tended to keep Whitman and James apart . . . and, in so doing, have tended to reify such conventional distinctions as those between fiction and poetry, between producers of popular and elite culture" ("Disseminating Whitman," 250). Moon recuperates the Whitman-James connection for gay literary history by charting in their writing "the model of abjection and rescue between higher-class man and lower-class boy" (260).

I am not immediately concerned with Whitman's and James's shared thematics; rather, my focus is on the complex and contradictory positions that James occupies in relation to Whitman early and late in his career and on the discursive symptoms of the conflict between affiliation and detachment that trouble his reception of Whitman. Examining James's responsive moments—the discourses of (re)evaluation and the intertextual sites of allusion or reinscription—permits us to reconstruct both the incitements and the obstacles to homosexual self-affirmation in the late nineteenth century. If a major goal of current gay and lesbian scholarship is to historicize the homosexual subject—to move beyond social constructionist paradigms—then careful attention to the politics of reception yields a surer grasp of the *specific* shapes of anxiety, the historical dimensions of the closet, as well as the particular impulses to move beyond isolated secrecy toward the collective project of an alternative literary tradition.

The Architecture of Secrecy

Eve Kosofsky Sedgwick has reprimanded the critical industry on Henry James for its "repressive blankness," its refusal to inquire into the asymmetries of gendered desire: "For James, in whose life the pattern of homosexual desire was brave enough and resilient enough to be at last biographically inobliterable, one might have hoped that in the criticism of his work the possible differences of different erotic paths would not be so ravenously subsumed under a compulsorily . . . heterosexual model" (*Epistemology*, 197). One of the most useful responses to Sedgwick's call for gay and lesbian commentary on Henry James, I believe, is to explore the discourses in which he negotiates his position in a homosexual tradition in Anglo-American literature. James's responses to writers who were constructed as male-identified by an emerging gay reading community are shaped by indirection, evasion, circumlocution: if James resists compulsory heterosexuality by inscribing affiliation with gay writers—and I believe this is the case—then, in response to panic, he almost invariably subverts the resistant affiliation. Characteristically, too, James tends to distance himself emphatically from troubling writers early in his career and then to revise his position by the turn of the century. James's competing discursive impulses of affiliation and detachment, revelation and erasure of homosexual identity are similar to Whitman's, although more discreet. As Sedgwick argues, "To situate Whitman properly in the history of male homosocial institutions . . . is made difficult not only by the strongly erotic charge of secretiveness and exhibitionism in his personality, but [also] by the shiftiness and historical occlusion of male homosexuality in the nineteenth century" ("Whitman's Transatlantic Context," 112).

The discourses in which James negotiates his position in (relation to) gay writing can be described as a textual architecture which houses—that is, conceals and reveals, fearfully guards and coyly signifies—the secrets of sexual identity and subcultural affiliation. Unlike Maggie Verver's allegorical pagoda in *The Golden Bowl*, which remains "consistently impenetrable and inscrutable," the prevailing architectonics of sexual secrecy in James's critical writing are sometimes disrupted by oblique gestures or coded references that (intentionally) select a gay-identified readership. This point will emerge more clearly, perhaps, if the text as secretive structure is compared to other forms of nineteenth-century architecture. In an intriguing article, Richard Rodriguez employs "grammar" as a metaphor to signify the structural affinities between the discourse of the gay and lesbian subculture and the urban architecture which it inhabits. The function of these related grammars, he argues, is to accommodate both a self-protective secrecy and the impulse toward disclosure.

The urban phenomenon that provides Rodriguez with his central "text" is the renovation of Victorian San Francisco, a project which gay men began in the 1970s. If gay culture may be represented metaphorically as a grammar, then it ironically found itself inhabiting "the architectural metaphor for the family"—ironic because no other architecture in the American imagination is more evocative of compulsory heterosexuality than the Victorian house. The connection between these apparently disparate grammars is the structural "space" of secrecy: "to grow up homosexual is to live with secrets and *within* secrets" (58), secrets that are closely guarded within the family home; preserving secrecy in adulthood requires a commodious architecture. If the Victorian house is a metaphor for American domesticity, for patriarchal confidence that binds generations together, or for the ideology of compulsory heterosexuality, then the reverse side of its daylight optimism is, of course, secrecy: this house is also associated "with the Gothic—with shadows and cobwebby gimcrack, long corridors" (59). The grammar of the gay city, Rodriguez concludes, borrows metaphors from the discursive *violation*, the disclosure of this dark secrecy. "'Coming out of the closet' is predicated upon family laundry, dirty linen, skeletons" (58)—is predicated, in other words, upon metaphors within metaphors within metaphors, a labyrinthine discourse of indirection.

Rodriguez's reading of the Victorian house as a site of conflict between secrecy and its violation provides a useful point of origin or analogue for a parallel reading—a reading of the representation of the American city by gay writers whose hermeneutics of self precluded a frank or direct affiliation with an emerging gay tradition, yet whose discourse curiously aligns itself with that of the gay precursor. What, then, are the functional paths of affiliation and reinscription within this tradition? Harold Bloom's hetero(phallo)centric model, which links influence to competition, emphasizes that the subsequent writer employs a corrective swerve to reinscribe the received text while making space for the self; it does not account for the peculiar dynamics of the gay literary tradition. Instead of the Bloomian anxiety of influence—the "misreading of the prior poet, an act of creative correction that is . . . necessarily a misinterpretation" (30)—it is infinitely more accurate to speak of the pervasive influence of anxiety, which arises not from the filial fear of literary preemption but rather from the fraternal recognition and definition of the (proscribed) desiring self in the reception of the prior text. It is equally important, I would argue, to problematize and to historicize our concept of anxiety. Nineteenth-century male-identified male writers responded in complex ways to literary traces or encodings, however oblique, which resonated with their own sexuality, however repressed. The conflicting impulses of writerly attraction and horrified self-recognition, prompting simultaneously a reinscription *of* and an emphatic distancing *from* the received homotext, certainly signify anxiety, but the critic must avoid applying a twentieth-century model of subjective hermeneutics to the nineteenth-century writer's strategies of self-explanation, of negotiating the limits of the possible. Perhaps the most useful site for a critical examination of nineteenth-century anxiety is the reception of Walt Whitman by highly conflicted Anglo-American writers, particularly Henry James.

Recuperating the Jamesian text is necessary for the fuller construction of gay literary history. Its attendant difficulties arise not only from the persistently heterosexist orientation of Jamesian biography and the tortuous discretion of James's discursive paths but also from the difficulty of imag(in)ing how James explained himself to himself. It is highly unlikely that he thought of or named himself in the current idiom. It will never be possible to (re)construct a gay identity for Henry James in the way one can for Walt Whitman because of the semantics of caution that characterizes his text and because of James's likely destruction of any biographical evidence in his great bonfire of 1909, which reenacted the silencing strategy employed in such works as *The Wings of the Dove* and "The Aspern Papers." ("His act," observes Leon Edel, "was consistent with his belief that writers were themselves responsible for clearing the approaches to their privacy" [437]). However, those documents that have survived—particularly James's extensive correspondence late in his life with such young men as Rupert Brooke, Hendrik Andersen, and Howard Sturgis—reveal the fairly direct articulation of homoerotic desire. In any case, I am less concerned with biographical demonstration or with James as a psychosexual "case" than I am with the Jamesian text and its tactics of affiliation with and cautious distancing from a recoverable, identifiable, gay literary tradition. The search for this kind of evidence responds to Sedgwick's call for the opening up of "a different and less distinctly sexualized range of categories" (*Epistemology*, 188) on the contested ground of nineteenth-century masculinity. It attempts also to situate in gender politics the prevailing secrecy of James's discourse, the qualities of which have been defined most perceptively by Hugh Kenner:

> His geomancer's response to impalpabilities—tones and airs, surfaces and absences—inaugurated a poetic of the mute . . . , a poetic of eschewals and refrainings, working round the margins of a voiceless theme, a theme voiceless because not yet public, not yet specified. . . . James's effort to articulate such matters within the shape of the formal English sentence yielded the famous late style, where subject and verb are "there" but don't carry the burden of what is said. Other syntactic structures do that. Behind [this] . . . persists the voice that pursued so intently so many refusals and eschewals, and built so magisterially suspensions and resolutions out of things only half-named. . . . (16–17)

James's paradoxical effort to "articulate" from the marginal space of what Kenner calls "a voiceless theme" provides an entry into the curious tension between affiliation and distance in James's response to received gay writing. The general paradigm is temporal: James read self-identified gay texts at the outset of his career, responded with unusually negative intensity, and then reconsidered his position late in life around the turn of the century. This is as true of his readings of Pater and Whitman as it is of Flaubert and other French novelists who did not contribute to a gay literary tradition but who were nonetheless seen as immoral by the youthful and morally earnest Henry James. James's peculiar combination of attraction to "decadent" literature and his inscription of horrified revulsion is a striking instance of Sedgwick's concept of "homosexual panic." Sedgwick argues that as "'the homosexual' became available as a descriptive category" in the nineteenth century, homophobia came to function as an "immensely potent tool . . . to set proscriptive and descriptive limits to the forms of male homosocial desire"; homophobia thus delineates "a space, and perhaps a mechanism, of domination" (*Between Men*, 87). While Sedgwick is concerned with the regulatory consequences of homosexual panic, the effect of homophobia on *heterosexual* men, I wish to resituate it among writers like James who were essentially male-identified in their orientation but, to the extent that they recognized this impulse in others and in themselves, attempted concealment. This, I think, enables a new reading of James's early response to Walt Whitman.

Robert Martin's revisionist account of Whitman's reception provides two points that illuminate the context in which James read and, in effect, constructed Whitman. The first is his observation that "prior to Whitman there were homosexual acts but no homosexuals. Whitman coincides with and defines a radical change in historical consciousness: the self-conscious awareness of homosexuality as an identity" (*Homosexual Tradition*, 51–52). The second is that Whitman's homosexual readers "immediately sensed the possibility of community" (50). Building on Martin's exploration of Whitman's search for a signifying lexicon, Richard Dellamora maintains that Whitman "calls into being a community of readers and poets . . . [and] likewise devises a range of terms for desire between men" (86). James's response to such Whitmanian "devising" is—in his 1865 review of *Drum-Taps* for the *Nation*, written when James was twenty-two—entirely panicked and resistant. Applying Emersonian definitions of "the real poet" who "extracts [life's] latent meaning and holds it up to common [read: universal] eyes," James dismisses Whitman's "prolonged muscular strain," the "wanton eccentricities" of his language, and his "monstrous" attitude as "an offense against art" (*Literary Criticism: Essays*, 629, 632). Building to a peak of pique, James insists that

to become adopted as a national poet, it is not enough to discard everything in particular and to accept everything in

general, to amass crudity upon crudity, to discharge the un-
digested contents of your blotting-book into the lap of the
public. You must respect the public which you address; for
it has taste, if you have not. It delights in the grand, the heroic, and the masculine; but it delights to see these concep-
tions cast into worthy form. (633)

It is significant that the terms of James's disapprobation—
"wanton," "eccentric," "monstrous," "crude"—coincide with
and modify a perhaps more fatal attraction to "the muscular," to
a "delight in . . . the masculine." I acknowledge that such a
reading of a young, anxious, divided James would be somewhat
forced against the will of the subject without the contextualizing
supplement of James's late and entirely revisionist response to
Whitman.

(Re)reading Gay America

The background against which we must read James's late
(re)construction of Whitman is the evolution of Whitman's reception by gay men in the years between 1865 and 1898, particularly
in England. Dellamora insists that "the physical expressiveness
and ardent feeling for other men evident in Whitman's work . . .
makes him available . . . *as the signifier* of male-male desire in a
new form of sexual-aesthetic discourse"; the tendency of writers
like Hopkins and Swinburne, he suggests, is to stand "in admiring but troubled relation" to Whitman (87). Sedgwick argues not
only that "*Leaves of Grass* operated . . . as a conduit from one
man to another of feelings that had, in many cases, been private
or inchoate" but, more importantly, that "photographs of Whitman, gifts of Whitman's books, . . . admiring references to
'Whitman' . . . seem to have functioned as badges of homosexual recognition, were the currency of a new community" (*Between Men*, 205–206).

Living in England and connected to such enthusiastic readers
of Whitman as John Addington Symonds, Henry James could
not have avoided attaching a gay signifier to the "currency" of

the Whitmanian signifier in the emerging discourse community. It is fascinating to read, in this context, James's series of short articles entitled "American Letters," published between March and July of 1898. In reviewing a collection of Whitman's letters to Peter Doyle, issued significantly under the title *Calamus*, James coyly suggests that "the little book appeals . . . to the Whitmanite already made" and confesses his surprise in the event that it "failed of power to make a few more" (*Literary Criticism: Essays*, 662). My reading of this passage detects James employing the term "Whitmanite" as an encoded signifier capable of being decoded by a discriminating readership while eluding others, as well as James suggesting the interpellative power of Whitman's letters to call "a few more" gay men to subjective self-recognition and perhaps subcultural affiliation. Such a reading considers the possibility that late in life Henry James became a resistant writer, that he employed what Foucault would call a "reverse discourse" by which "homosexuality began to speak on its own behalf, to demand that its legitimacy . . . be acknowledged" (101). As Sedgwick observes, "the men who were more or less firmly placed on the proscribed end of the homosocial spectrum" were "united powerfully by proscription and . . . worked powerfully to claim and create a difference—a difference beyond proscription" (*Between Men*, 202). Most intriguing, perhaps, is James's conclusion: Whitman's inscriptions to his friend "of what they both saw and touched" constitute a "record" which "remains, by a mysterious marvel, a thing positively delightful. If we ever find out why, it must be another time. The riddle meanwhile is a neat one for the sphinx of democracy to offer" (*Literary Criticism: Essays*, 662). James defers the disclosure of Whitman's "riddle" to "another time," to some utopian futurity, and if James has deployed the code of the "Whitmanite," with its impulse toward discreet interpellation, he also respects the privacy of the self, for the architectonics of his text accommodate the ultimate secrets and refusals that make Whitman "the sphinx of democracy."

In revising his stance on Whitman, Henry James distances himself from his youthful anxiety and reconstructs his subjectivity: in a letter written in 1903, he refers to his 1865 essay as "the little atrocity I . . . perpetrated on W. W. in the gross imper-

tinence of youth"; his characteristic response to these "abomina-
tions of my early innocence" is the impulse to "destroy them
wherever I spy them" (Allen, *Solitary Singer*, 578–579). For
James, coming to a different perspective on Whitman was intri-
cately involved in the larger matter of his return to America in
1904, and I want to explore the ways in which Whitman figures
or signifies in the intertextual dynamic of James's inscription of
the American city. Evidence that Whitman was very present to
James during his American odyssey is provided by Edith Wharton's autobiography, which argues that "James thought [Whit-
man] . . . the greatest of American poets." Wharton recounts an
evening in which James read aloud from Whitman—"his voice
filled the hushed room like an organ adagio," she recalls—and
concludes by suggesting that "James's admiration of Whitman,
his immediate response to that mighty appeal, was a new proof
of the way in which, above a certain level, the most divergent
intelligences walk together like gods" (186).

The product of James's American tour of 1904–1905 was a
group of texts that continue his obsession with the architecture
of secrecy. Versions of Richard Rodriguez's Victorian house are
of course anticipated by prior texts—the vaguely sinister apart-
ment of Mme. de Vionnet in *The Ambassadors* and Fawns in *The
Golden Bowl*; these are structures of unreadability, analogous to
the fine discretion of the characters whom they accommodate.
But James's return to America after a twenty-year absence demanded the confrontation of hidden identity and the "reading,"
however tentative, of the formerly unreadable self. If "The Jolly
Corner" allegorizes the hermeneutics of the self in a mansion of
many apartments or provides an architecture in which secrecy is
embodied in the form of a haunting ghost, then one might say
that *The American Scene* provides an architecture, or more precisely an architectonics, for a larger cultural secrecy. The text
turns on or constructs tropes around the question of relation:
specifically, the relation of the present to the past but, more generally, the relation of James's observer—cast sometimes as "the
repentent absentee" but more frequently as "the restless analyst"—to a seemingly transformed American city. If the architecture of *The American Scene* is unified by the trope of reading, by

which the "restless analyst" attempts to read "the overscored tablet" (88) of New York, then I suggest that this trope of reading contains another: the trope of the anxious, closeted Henry James reading the text of Whitman. New York is the site of reading, of intertextuality, of a problematic affiliation with Whitman; the Victorian house that is *The American Scene* is haunted by the ghost of Whitman, who, like the ghost in "The Jolly Corner," will be confronted obliquely through the allusive (elusive?) paths of the intertext.

At every turn in New York, James inscribes a vision of the power of the American city that reinscribes—in order to affirm, to qualify, or to correct—Whitman's in "Crossing Brooklyn Ferry." At the outset, James focuses the multiple aspects of New York—"the extent, the ease, the energy, the quantity and num-ber of all notes scattered about" (72)—in the "symbol" of the "great circling and plunging, hovering and perching sea-birds, white-winged images of the spirit, of the restless freedom . . ." (73). This bird's-eye view repeats the Whitmanian image of the gull, which signifies both the power of the city and the futurity of the poetic gaze:

> I . . . Watched the Twelfth-month sea-gulls, saw them
>   high in the air floating with motionless wings,
>   oscillating their bodies,
> Saw how the glistening yellow lit up parts of their
>   bodies and left the rest in strong shadow. (27–29)

The endless procession across the East River is for Whitman a wholly positive sign of American energy; for James, the "bigness and bravery and insolence" of the scene are a "type of dauntless power" (74). Crucially, both Whitman and James represent the darkening of the American prospect: Whitman's optimistic, democratic vista is mitigated by "the dark patches" which, in "Crossing Brooklyn Ferry," signify primarily sexual repression; James finds a cause in technological progress, in which the "vast white page" of the city awaits "the black overscoring of science" (75). The connection between "dark patches" and "overscoring" lies in James's sense that the Whitmanian dream of America—signified, always erotically, by the "clear loud voices of young men"—is subverted by America's unquestioning belief in progress at the cost of humane values. In an ironic rewriting and reversal of Whitman's "ferry-boat or public assembly" in which the poet is called "by [his] nighest name," James experiences only alienation in the city, in which "the assault of the turbid air seemed all one with the look, the tramp, the whole quality and *allure*, the consummate monotonous commonness, of the pushing male crowd, moving in its dense mass." The American Utopia has become, in this incipient moment of modernism, the Unreal City.

Another crucial connection between "Crossing Brooklyn Ferry" and *The American Scene* is the relationship between that which cannot be written and that which cannot be read. For Whitman, the unsayable—the absence of a discourse of desire—has political implications: "We understand then do we not? / What I promis'd without mentioning it, have you not accepted?" (98–99) is perhaps the "darkest patch" in the Whitman text, the failure to articulate the democratic vista. This failure to write the American character resonates significantly with James's failure to read it. "What [signified] meaning," he ponders, "can continue to attach to such a term [signifier] as the 'American character'? . . . It is as if the syllables were too numerous to make a legible word. The *il*legible word, accordingly, the great inscrutable answer to questions, hangs in the vast American sky . . . belonging to no known language, and it is under this . . . ensign that he travels and considers and contemplates" (121–122).

Finally, if New York is for Whitman a page on which to inscribe the dream of American futurity, a page on which "dark patches" fall to subvert inscription, then New York is for James a "copious tell-tale document" which exhausts the reader. The loss of Whitman's dream of America "may be read . . . all the way from river to river and from the Battery to Harlem, the place in which there is most of the terrible town" (99). *The American Scene* is, in Ezra Pound's words, "a creation of America" that gestures toward a tradition of alien perspectives from Crèvecoeur to de Tocqueville. More important is the reading that is enabled when *The American Scene* is contextualized in relation to James's late writings on Whitman, secrecy, and the ghosts of former selves.

In this particular constellation, *The American Scene* allegorizes the reading of the city, which contains an inner signifying pattern of reading and reinscribing gay America. The ample architecture of *The American Scene* personalizes the political, enabling recognition and detachment, pleasure and anxiety, moments of discreet subcultural affiliation and moments of panic, sorrow, and loss.

Langston Hughes and

the "Other" Whitman

GEORGE B. HUTCHINSON

By the "other" Whitman in my title I have in mind two distinct but related concepts. One comes from the title of an article published by Leandro Wolfson in 1978, "The Other Whitman in Spanish America," in which Wolfson criticizes the continued adoration of Whitman in Latin America, pointing out the inaccuracies in the Hispanic view of the North American poet. This "other" Whitman has been debunked and/or repressed (depending upon how you look at it) in the United States since the 1950s as part of the effort to bring his poetry into the academy during an era of formalism, hostility to political writing or propaganda, and emphasis upon confessional aspects of poetry. It was felt that Whitman had to be saved from his disciples as well as from the criticism of scholars who found his work to lack "form."

The second concept I have in mind is closer to Borges's, that of Whitman as a poetic "other" to all of us for the very reason that he is each one of us when we respond to his call, a ubiquitous signifier always slipping in and out of our embrace, an ecstatic moving always outside our attempts to fix a position for him. This "other" Whitman will always elude us because his otherness is fundamental to his own textual production. It is this more radical and mercurial otherness that has made him the most diversely appropriated American poet. For some reason, in Whitman's mirror many "others" to white, patriarchal American culture have seen themselves; the process of translating his voice has helped them to find their own. Langston Hughes certainly attested to this effect in his own career.

The association of Hughes with Whitman, I suspect, is less than obvious to most readers. If Whitman is often singled out as the archetypal (white male) American poet, Hughes's experiments with black-based idioms and aesthetic principles rooted in blues ballads and spirituals have had an incalculable effect upon the development of a distinctive African-American poetics. Yet, like Sterling Brown after him, even in writing his "folk" poems Hughes considered himself to be following out the implications of Whitman's poetic theory (Rampersad, 1:146). At various points in his long career, Hughes put together no fewer than three separate anthologies of Whitman's poetry (one of them for children), included several Whitman poems in an anthology on *The Poetry of the Negro*, wrote a poem entitled "Old Walt" for the one hundredth anniversary of *Leaves of Grass*, and repeatedly—in lectures, newspaper columns, and introductions—encouraged black Americans to read his work. He called Whitman "America's greatest poet" and spoke of *Leaves of Grass* as the greatest expression of "the real meaning of democracy ever made on our shores." Feeling that Whitman had been ignored and, in current parlance, marginalized by the custodians of culture, Hughes indeed attempted in his own way to canonize the poet he considered "the Lincoln of our Letters" (*Chicago Defender*, July 4, 1953).

The poems Hughes most liked are not the ones most taught today. For example, "Ethiopia Saluting the Colors," which has been called racist in content and hackneyed in form, Hughes praised as "the most beautiful poem in our language concerning a Negro subject" and included it in *Poetry of the Negro*. His collaborator Harry T. Burleigh (an important black composer) even set the poem to music. "Song of the Open Road" and "Song of the Answerer" were two of his other favorites. Hughes admired the public poems that dramatized the singer's egalitarian ubiquity, his ability to permeate social boundaries, and his role as multiversal "answerer," which accounted, in Hughes's view, for Whitman's ability to portray black people realistically.

In "Song of the Answerer"—a poem that has rarely attracted the notice of scholars—the answerer knows that "Every existence has its idiom, every thing has an idiom and tongue . . . / He says indifferently and alike *How are you friend?* to the President at his levee, / And he says *Good-day my brother*, to Cudge that hoes in the sugar-field, / And both understand him and know that his speech is right" (31, 34–36). The egalitarian message and the specific reference to the black field-worker would have attracted Hughes at once. But two other characteristics also stand out. First is the importance of respecting the "idiom" of each existence. The answerer is able to resolve this idiom into his own tongue, which he then bestows upon people, who then translate that tongue back into their own even as they translate the answerer himself. "The English believe he comes of their English stock, / A Jew to the Jew he seems, a Russ to the Russ, usual and near, removed from none" (45–46). Whitman also allows for the possibility of multiple translations and thereby answers the objections of those, such as Doris Sommer, who claim that he tries to make us all equal by making us all mirror images of himself. On the contrary he demands that each of us make him a mirror image of *our* selves. As Hughes saw it, "his poems contain us all. The reader cannot help but see his own better self therein" (Perlman et al., 98). Whitman's specular answerer acts as a mediator between plural identities, reconciling pluralism with union—"One part does not counteract another part, he is the joiner, he sees how they join" (33). Hughes insisted that, in his masked performances, Whitman was able to project a voice, ventriloquistically, outside his own socially constructed role within American culture, a voice that resonated in the sensibilities of a tremendous range of writers throughout the world (*Chicago Defender*, Aug. 1, 1953).

Though precipitated by the specific ideological and social conflicts in which Whitman was immersed in the years leading up to the Civil War, the evident drive in the poems toward a resolution of those conflicts opens up a liminal, antistructural arena in which the very self is dismembered as it escapes all formulae. This semiotic shattering of the unity of the self in the process of textual production is matched by the exceedingly multivalent, overdetermined quality of Whitman's poetic language, the quality which helps account for its "translations" into so many different social contexts. On top of even these factors is the function of the unnamed second person within the very type of poems Hughes most admired—those like "Song of the Answerer" and "Song of the Open Road."

One reason Whitman's poetry has resonated in the sensibilities of black American writers is that in certain of his poems he uses the condition of the slave as representative of the condition of his audience. The "you" of his songs, if it is to apply to *all* readers, must apply to slaves, those most graphically denied the right to self-determination. The poem "To You (Whoever You Are)" at times seems directly addressed to a slave:

> None has done justice to you, you have not done justice
>   to yourself,
> None but has found you imperfect, I only find no
>   imperfection in you,
> None but would subordinate you, I only am he who will
>   never consent to subordinate you,
> I only am he who places over you no master, owner,
>   better, God, beyond what waits intrinsically in
>   yourself. (14–17)

Arguably, Whitman here distills the specific oppression of black people in the antebellum United States into a metaphor for the hidden condition of all people—"you, whoever you are." But his slave is not just any slave—his slave is the *most* enslaved, the one rejected by all others and even by himself or herself. Eschewing pity for admiration and love, the poet projects upon his reader, as by a shamanistic charm, a spiritual freedom that will ensure self-fulfillment: "The hopples fall from your ankles, you find an unfailing sufficiency, / Old or young, male or female, rude, low, rejected by the rest, whatever you are promulges itself" (44–45). A poem such as this virtually begs for appropriation to an African-American frame of reference.

Hence, Hughes was not simply in *the* Whitman tradition (although he may have been happy with such a characterization); rather, he practiced an African-American–based poetic syncretism that Whitman's answerer explicitly invited: "The words of the true poems give you more than poems, / They give you to form for yourself poems, religions, politics, war, peace, behavior, histories, essays, daily life, and every thing else, / They balance ranks, colors, races, creeds, and the sexes" (75–77). The very nature of Hughes's absorption of Whitman was inevitably shaped by his "racial" identity and historical placement. In fact, it appears that by moving him toward an appreciation of the poetry of the common people, insisting on self-trust, and teaching "straying" from the teacher-poet himself, Hughes's demonic Whitman encouraged black cultural self-identification.

The very years in which Hughes grew close to the urban black community (having grown up largely removed from it) while determining to make his living as a poet were those in which he was most intensely under the spell of Whitman, as Arnold Rampersad's biography shows. Moreover, at a critical point in his life, when leaving the United States for Europe and Africa on a merchant ship, he threw overboard every book he owned except *Leaves of Grass*. "I had no intention of throwing that one away," he wrote in a passage from his autobiography (Rampersad, 1:72). By the time he returned to America, Hughes had determined what his vocation would be. His absorption of Whitman was as thorough as that of any other North American poet of his generation. Even in describing the blues to Carl Van Vechten to help him with a preface to *The Weary Blues*, Hughes would slip effortlessly into a cadence, a mixture of idioms, and even the exact phrasing of "old Walt," stealing Whitman's evocation of sexual desire: "In the Gulf Coast Blues one can feel the cold northern snows, the memory of the melancholy mists of the Louisianna [*sic*] low-lands, the shack that is home, the worthless lovers with hands full of gimme, mouths full of much oblige, the eternal unsatisfied longings."

Hughes was the first African-American poet to sense the affinity between the inclusive "I" of Whitman (which Whitman claimed as his most important innovation—"the quite changed attitude of the ego, the one chanting or talking, towards himself and towards his fellow humanity" ("A Backward Glance," 564) and the "I" of the blues and even of the spirituals. The result of Hughes's appropriation of this triply descended "I" is amply demonstrated in one of his first published poems, "The Negro Speaks of Rivers":

I've known rivers ancient as the world and old as the
    flow of human blood in human veins.

My soul has grown deep like the rivers.

I bathed in the Euphrates when dawns were young.
I built my hut near the Congo and it lulled me to sleep.
I looked upon the Nile and raised the pyramids above it.
I heard the singing of the Mississippi when Abe Lincoln
    went down to New Orleans, and I've seen its muddy
    bosom turn all golden in the sunset. (*Weary Blues*, 51)

Though Hughes would later, for the most part, turn away from the Whitmanesque style of free verse, the example of Whitman's break with traditional definitions of the poetic, his attempts to achieve an orally based poetics with the cadence and diction of the voice on the street, at the pond-side, or at the pulpit, provided a partial model for the young black poet looking for a way to sing his own song, which would be at the same time a song of his people.

Furthermore, Whitman's conception of the relationship between poet and community was fundamentally that in which Hughes came to believe: "In vain," Whitman had written, "will America seek successfully to tune any superb national song unless the heartstrings of the people start it from their own breasts—to be return'd and echoed there again." Hughes would not have to wait for the people to start the song from their breasts; it was ready-formed in the spirituals and blues, which he could justly regard as the most American of song genres available to modern poets. Moreover, these forms embodied the very sort of call-and-response pattern for which Whitman seemed to be asking. It would take Hughes's example (and later that of Zora Neale Hurston and Sterling Brown) to transform the dialect tradition into an uncompromising revelation of the folk-based African-American expressive arts, with a range, a flexibility, and a precision that had not yet found their way into poetry.

The "Epilogue" (later entitled "I, Too") of Hughes's first book, *The Weary Blues*, can be read in part as a signifying riff on "old Walt's" songs, forthrightly challenging American rituals of incorporation and exclusion while more subtly playing off of Whitman's "I Hear America Singing" with a dark minor chord.

> I, too, sing America.
> I am the darker brother.
> They send me to eat in the kitchen
> When company comes . . . (109)

In the American family home, the "darker brother," disowned by white siblings, has been cast out of the common room to servants' space, where he nonetheless grows strong. The poem prophesies the transforming force of the black singer's particular challenge—on the basis of his own aesthetic standards—for the humanization of the white American audience: "They'll see how beautiful I am / And be ashamed,— / I, too, am America." In this epilogue to his first collection—a poem with which he often concluded his poetry readings—Hughes registers his own distinctive poetic identity as both black and American. Simultaneously, he protests a *community*—even *family*—relationship with those across the color line and makes his claim as an heir to Whitman.

His second volume, *Fine Clothes to the Jew*, would show an even more radical break than *The Weary Blues* with past "literary" models by relying more exclusively upon the blues matrix for its aesthetic. Ironically, while the book was being blasted in the black press on genteel grounds and such intellectuals as W. E. B. Du Bois and Benjamin Brawly speculated that Hughes was pandering to the prurient interests of white folks, Hughes was invited to speak to the Walt Whitman Foundation about his poetry. Here, according to his biographer, he described "modern free verse, and his own work, as descending from Whitman's great example" (Rampersad, 1:146), an admission T. S. Eliot and Amy Lowell declined to make. At the same time, he emphasized his reliance upon the black folk tradition, which he characterized as the source of some of America's most distinctive aesthetic achievements. His very descent from Whitman demands difference from him, but difference within an American field. Hughes's liminal status—between white and black intellectual communities— freed him to explore new African-American literary forms.

Hughes had come to Whitman by way of such midwestern rebels as Carl Sandburg prior to the twenties. His was in most respects the democratic "transnationalist" and socialist Whitman pushed by Horace Traubel and other early disciples in the United States, followed by such influential figures as the French unanimist Léon Bazalgette, whose hagiographical study, *Walt Whitman*, had an enormous impact throughout Europe and Latin America, finally reacting back upon left-wing "cultural nationalists" in the United States. *Whitmanisme*, as the French called it, was a pervasive intercultural phenomenon (Betsy Erkkila) that embraced anti-imperialists in Europe (Romain Rolland) and the United States (*The Seven Arts* circle), as well as India (Rabindranath Tagore) and Latin America (José Martí, Rubén Darío) (see Grünzweig). The Hispanic reception of Whitman deserves particular attention here, for Hughes's connections with writers in the Caribbean and Latin America (and in Spain during its Civil War) were important in his career.

Whitman's influence upon such influential poets and revolutionaries as José Martí and Pablo Neruda is generally well known. Even as these socially engaged writers fought imperialism, they looked toward Whitman as a great New World forebear, the champion of democracy, social justice, and national self-determination. Fernando Alegria's account of the image of Whitman he'd had as a student at the University of Chile before

World War II is broadly representative: "Whitman era el defensor de la libertad del espíritu, el enemigo de prejuicios, el orgulloso sostenedor de la pureza y excelencia de la faena artística, el cantor de la juventud, de la vida en contacto con la naturaleza, el hermano mayor de los trabajadores, el romántico apóstol de los perseguidos y explotados" (9–10). Such views of Whitman have remained very strong to this day and have even come back to influence North American writers such as June Jordan, who has recently championed him as a "white father" whom reactionary college professors in the United States have repressed.

Jordan's view is quite similar in this respect to Hughes's, as his 1946 essay "The Ceaseless Rings of Walt Whitman" makes clear: "Many timid poetry lovers over the years have been frightened away from his *Leaves of Grass* . . . because of his simplicity. Perhaps, too, because his all embracing words lock arms with workers and farmers, Negroes and whites, Asiatics and Europeans, serfs and free men, beaming democracy to all, many academic-minded intellectual isolationists in America have had little use for Whitman, and have impeded his handclasp with today by keeping him imprisoned in silence on library shelves" (96–97). Knowing that Whitman's name had been invoked in movements for social change, Hughes claimed that *Leaves of Grass* had literally helped millions of people struggling against oppression around the world.

North American critics have generally dismissed Latin American interpretations of Whitman as naïve, overly politicized, or insufficiently attuned to Whitman's craftsmanship. These dismissals can be attributed not only to the North Americans' more accurate knowledge of a poet's life but also to the ways in which critical trends within the United States have shaped the academic readings of *Leaves of Grass* and to the way in which literature has been institutionalized. In the revaluation of Whitman which coincided with his rising status within English departments, the earlier left-wing, populist, politically engaged, prophetic, and "public" Whitman (espoused by such figures as Eugene Debs, Clarence Darrow, and Emma Goldman when Hughes was young) was debunked along with his disciples, while the private, relatively apolitical poet was discovered beneath the yawping pose.

Whitman's academic reputation grew as the work of critics such as Gay Wilson Allen, James E. Miller, and Edwin Haviland Miller in the 1950s and 1960s succeeded in differentiating the weaker, supposedly more prophetic verse from the stronger, more aesthetically satisfying "poetry." The interpretive shift contributed significantly to the developing appreciation of Whitman's work but had the effect of devaluing, even suppressing, many of those elements of *Leaves of Grass* which had done most to gain Whitman a broad international following and which most appealed to Hughes. This may partly account for our difficulty in recognizing the close relationship between Whitman and African-American poetry. Precisely the elements that scholars found in Whitman as they established him in university curricula were the elements Hughes deprecated in other modern poets: linguistic "difficulty" or apparently willful obscurity, literary allusiveness, and private confession—qualities professors love to explore but that often alienate "common" readers (and that one rarely finds in Hughes's work).

The legendary Whitman Hughes encountered in Latin America was also ubiquitous among writers in Spain during its civil war; Whitman was a heroic personage to such poets as Federico García Lorca and Miguel de Unamuno, not to mention Neruda who also fought for the antifascist cause. These are all people whom Hughes knew in Spain. García Lorca became one of Hughes's favorite poets; indeed, Hughes translated the play *Bodas de Sangre* and some of the gypsy ballads, and he intended to translate *The Poet in New York* at one point. The "Ode to Walt Whitman" in this book-long poem functions as what one translator calls "a synthesis, climax, and solution to the underlying theme of the book" (Jaen, 81). But what is more intriguing about *The Poet in New York* is the connection it draws between the spirit of Whitman and black American culture. In this poem, black people emerge as those who, still expressing the elemental passions and desires of humanity, hold out the hope of realizing Whitman's dream.

At the end of "Ode to Walt Whitman," Whitman's spirit is to be carried on by a black American child who will "announce to the whites of the gold / the coming of the reign of the wheat," a veiled allusion to *Leaves of Grass* (as quoted in Craige, 79). Indeed, throughout *The Poet in New York*, the suggested revolt of African-Americans against an oppressive, dehumanizing, and mechanistic civilization seems the only hope of realizing the sort of society of which Whitman had dreamed. A host of themes and images interrelate Whitman and the black people of Harlem: the ability to dream (one of Hughes's constant themes), the power of "blood," erotic energy, closeness to nature, water and beach imagery, a valuing of community, and a subversive threat to socioeconomic oppression. The "Ode to Whitman" initiates a turn in the poem as a whole toward the speaker's reconnection with nature, accompanied by a growing sense of hope and community. This shift is signified in part by the increasingly musical and incantatory style, which reaches its apogee in the optimistic closing section, "*Son* of the Negroes in Cuba." The poem must have hit Hughes with great force, for he had earlier convinced Nicolás Guillén of Cuba to use folk-based *son* lyrics as a basis for poetry. Of course, by the mid-thirties the main thrust of Hughes's poetry had already been determined, but what I would like to emphasize is an intertextual field connecting Whitman, Hughes, García Lorca, and such Latin American poets as Guillén, a field which considerably alters our vision of "American" poetry and the relationships between its "black" and "white" avatars. As late as 1965, when the separatist Black Arts Movement was gaining steam, Hughes wrote a show called "Tell It to Telstar" in which he combined excerpts from Whitman with songs and spirituals of black America.

The nature and history of Langston Hughes's relationship to Whitman complicate the project of developing sweeping theoretical models for the complex interplay between what at any given time might be constituted as particular radical traditions in the United States, for the centers of these traditions do not hold. Authors are not unitary figures inhabiting fixed cultural coordinates but are often liminal voyagers upon open roads, transgressors of even our latest pieties. This is not necessarily because they were in fact living freer than we give them credit for or because of some timeless, transcendent property but because of the subversive, overdetermined quality of poetic signification itself, because of the tendency of artists to straddle thresholds of social difference, which may be fundamental to their roles, and because of the multiple ways in which authors have been received on their textual journeys.

Whitman's Indifference to Indians

MAURICE KENNY

In vision and language Walt Whitman is America's Homer. His hero, however, was not the Greek classic—the noble individual of high birth—but the cumulative average. Bulk vastness and superlatives of "great" and "greatness" were his guidons. He was certainly a democratic nationalist, a flag waver. He was the poet of the ordinary person—butcher, baker, candlestick maker but not of the Indian chief. He sang of the bus driver, the factory hand, the mechanic, the farmer, the ferryman of Brooklyn but not of the feathered warrior.

Whitman sang electrically of nature; he created poems of the industrial boom in America and its dynamics which thrust the nation into leadership of world powers, secure in might and wealth but diseased with guilt. Everything which was American found a phrase in his verse, even the "common street prostitute":

"When I mix with these interminable swarms of alert, turbulent, good-natured, independent citizens, mechanics, clerks, young persons—at the idea of this mass of men, so fresh and free, so loving and so proud, a singular awe falls upon me" ("Democratic Vistas," 388).

Whitman wrote profusely of the woodcutter, the sailor, the frontiersman, the pioneer, the emigrant, generals such as Grant and Sheridan and Custer, and the army recruit, green and raw, courageous and wounded, stammering in his European accent in the new land of opportunity, sent West to protect the bulging population which was a target for feathered arrows.

Whitman's common man became the common soldier decidedly happy with "beans and hay." He became Whitman's noble man, embraced and paeaned for both his endurance and inherent stupidity. A job was a job—and killing Indians was a job, and jobs could not be found in the large eastern cities. He rigorously served under his new flag, and Whitman prodded him to glory. Everything which fell under Whitman's ken moved his poetic spirit: the lightning of the new skies and new horizons; the death of presidents; Denver, "queen city of the plains"; the "common earth, the soil"; William Cullen Bryant; the Battle of Gettysburg; Niagara Falls. He wrote America and America was his true hero, his Ulysses: "I Hear America Singing."

Everything America produced or which produced America was allowed a pentameter in Whitman's work—but only rarely the American Indian, the indigenous native to the land, what the Native American sons and daughters know as Mother Earth.

And yet Whitman was truly fascinated with Indian words and names and copied out many within an essay entitled "Slang in America": "Miss Bremer found among the aborigines the following names: *Men's*, Horn-point; Round-Wind; Stand-and-look-out; The Cloud-that-goes-aside; Iron-toe; Seek-the-sun; Iron-flash . . ." (576). It is certainly understandable that anyone, especially such an imaginative and enthusiastic poet as Whitman, would find these names fascinating, but why as "slang in America"? How do they differ from John the Baptist or Richard the Lion-Hearted? As with these two English equivalents, the names pointed out particular characteristics of the person's nature, prowess, or accomplishments, obviously a fact Whitman failed to recognize.

Whitman gained employment as a minor clerk in 1865 in the Indian Bureau of the Interior Department in Washington, D.C. This employment was of short duration. He was soon dismissed by his puritan superior, James Harlan, who recoiled from the purloined pages of the *Leaves of Grass*. Harlan believed the book was indecent and fired the "good gray poet." It would be expected that while Whitman was employed in this office he would have become acquainted with and acutely aware of the federal government's calculated plan to exterminate the Indians. The worthless treaties were at his fingertips; the recorded injustices perpetrated upon Indians were under his naked eyes; documents and letters of unscrupulous officials prodding the extermination of the "savages" most certainly would have been familiar to him. The horrifying slaughter of innocent Cheyenne and Arapahoe women and children at the infamous Sand Creek Massacre occurred only the preceding November of the year he took this employment. As many eastern liberals were greatly distressed by this mass murder, how was it that Whitman ignored those death cries? In the essay "An Indian Bureau Reminiscence," he wrote most clearly of his tenure there:

After the close of the Secession War in 1865, I work'd several months (until Mr. Harlan turn'd me out for having written "Leaves of Grass") in the Interior Department at Washington, in the Indian Bureau. Along this time there came to see their Great Father an unusual number of aboriginal visitors, delegations for treaties, settlement of lands, &c.—some young or middle-aged, but mainly old men, from the West, North, and occasionally from the South—parties of from five to twenty each—the most wonderful proofs of what Nature can produce, (the survival of the fittest, no doubt— all the frailer examples dropt, sorted out by death)—as if to show the earth and woods, the attrition of storms and elements, and the exigencies of life at first hand, can train and

fashion men, indeed *chiefs*, in heroic massiveness, imper-
turbability, muscle, and that last and highest beauty consist-
ing of strength—the full exploitation and fruitage of a human
identity, not from the culmination-points of "culture" and
artificial civilization, but tallying our race, as it were, with
giant, vital, gnarl'd, enduring trees, or monoliths of separate hardiest rocks, and humanity holding its own with the
best of the said trees or rocks, and outdoing them. . . .

Let me give a running account of what I see and hear
through one of these conference collections at the Indian
Bureau, going back to the present tense. (577–578)

Herewith he describes certain chiefs and their "outfits" which
certainly take his eye's attention.

Let us note this young chief. For all his paint, "Hole-in-the-
Day" is a handsome Indian, mild and calm, dress'd in drab
buckskin leggings, dark gray surtout, and a soft black hat.
His costume will bear full observation, and even fashion
would accept him. His apparel is worn loose and skant
enough to show his superb physique, especially in neck,
chest, and legs. (578)

Sounds as if he's attempting to describe a horse on the block. The
descriptive catalog continues:

Though some of the young fellows were, as I have said,
magnificent and beautiful animals, I think the palm of unique
picturesqueness, in body, limb, physiognomy, etc., was
borne by the old or elderly chiefs, and the wise men. (578,
emphasis added)

This shockingly insensitive running account utterly fails to see
a single human quality other than a sensuousness in these men,
young or old, who had traveled far to the Capitol to bargain for
their lives, lands, liberty, culture, and survival with the "Great
Father." How could this alleged democratic humanitarian look
only at the "loose and scant" attire and discover merely the flesh
of these "magnificent and beautiful animals" without some sense

of shame for his connotative observation? He did not describe the young recruit or his superior officers in such terms, in such sensuous language. But then the recruit and Grant and Custer were not *animals*, nor had they survived as the fittest by their own natural wiles but by selective breeding and the slaughtering wars, wars that raged across Europe for hundreds of years not so much for the "survival of the fittest" but for the spoils those wars offered. Whitman failed to see the lines of suffering and anxiety in the faces of these men; he failed to hear their quick heartbeats; he failed to feel any emotion with the exception of a hedonistic fancy or possible appetite. But his estimate hardly differed from that of his contemporaries. Even General George Custer admired the physiques and prowess of these "beautiful animals." For the larger part of his own creative life, Whitman was considered by both society and most of the literati as a "criminal monster," an outlaw of sorts. How is it he did not recognize kindred spirits— his counterparts in the Indian chiefs, warriors, or "wise men" who were also labeled "criminal monsters"? In another essay, "Some Diary Notes at Random," he described a ninety-four-year-old black slave he had known as a young boy in Long Island as "cute." Whitman claimed later in life to be an abolitionist.

In 1879 Whitman traveled west into southeastern Colorado to Fort Lyon, a mere horse ride from the site of the Sand Creek Massacre. Writing of his trip to Fort Lyon in *Specimen Days*, he fails to record that infamous slaughter:

> Between Pueblo and Bent's fort, southward, in a clear af-ternoon sun-spell I catch exceptionally good glimpses of the Spanish peaks. We are in southeastern Colorado—pass im-mense herds of cattle as our first-class locomotive rushes us along. . . . We pass Fort Lyon—lots of adobie houses—lim-itless pasturage, appropriately fleck'd with those herds of cattle . . . a belated cow-boy with some unruly member of his herd—an emigrant wagon toiling yet a little further, the horse slow and tired—two men, apparently father and son, jogging along on foot—and around all the indescribable *chiaroscuro* and sentiment (profounder than anything at sea) athwart these endless wilds. (220)

No sign of a village of tipis, no buffalo in his sight, no plumed warrior, no woman tending child, no elder instructing youth, and certainly no bloody massacre grounds which were a fistful of miles away from his locomotive window. His published works contain not a whisper or suspicion of sympathy for those so brutally murdered and mutilated, including women and children, so that one day those immense herds of cattle might fleck that sea of grass at such places as the Chivington Ranch, located in slight approximation to his "first-class locomotive."

Although such silence about their fate might indicate his acquiescence in the planned extermination of all Indians in the Americas, Whitman does on occasion describe the red "savage" in a heightened understanding of, at least, the costume:

Their feathers, paint—even the empty buffalo skull—did not, to say the least, seem any more ludicrous to me than many of the fashions I have seen in civilized society. I should not apply the word *savage (at any rate, in the usual sense) as a leading word in the description of those great aboriginal specimens,* of whom I certainly saw many of the best. ("An Indian Bureau Reminiscence," 579, emphasis added)

What he gives with one hand he takes away with the other.

And on another trip to the city of New Orleans:

One of my choice amusements during my stay in New Orleans was going down to the old French Market, especially of a Sunday morning. The show was a varied and curious one; among the rest, the Indian and negro hucksters with their wares. For there were always fine specimens of Indians, both men and women, young and old. I remember I nearly always on these occasions got a large cup of delicious coffee with a biscuit, for my breakfast, from the immense shining copper kettle of a great Creole mulatto (I believe she weigh'd 230 pounds). (*Prose Works,* 1:606)

The utterance of a typical American tourist traveling in foreign lands. This paragraph sounds as if Whitman were attending the farmers' market browsing for fresh summer tomatoes or early ears of corn, not consorting with human beings even though he's thoroughly fascinated with the color and gaiety of the French Quarter as any tourist would be.

Whitman produced a few minor poems concerning Indians. He recorded the deaths of both Red Jacket and Osceola. In "Red Jacket (from Aloft)," he writes:

> Upon this scene, this show,
> Yielded to-day by fashion, learning, wealth,
> (Nor in caprice alone—some grains of deepest
> meaning,)
> Haply, aloft, (who knows?) from distant sky-clouds'
> blended shapes,
> As some old tree, or rock or cliff, thrill'd with its soul,
> Product of Nature's sun, stars, earth direct—a towering
> human form,
> In hunting-shirt of film, arm'd with the rifle, a half-
> ironical smile curving its phantom lips,
> Like one of Ossian's ghosts looks down.

Ossian, of course, was a legendary Gaelic bard of the third century often denounced as the pure fakery of James Macpherson when he published the collection *Fingal*. Red Jacket was sixty-three years old when Whitman was born and so to him Red Jacket and his deeds during the American Revolution could hardly be considered "legendary." Red Jacket's skill as a warrior was minimal. He was teased by both Cornplanter and Joseph Brant for his cowardice in battle and failure to attend the battles. His importance to the Iroquois Confederacy and to the British, especially during the American Revolution, was as an orator and politician. How odd that in this verse Red Jacket stands "arm'd with the rifle" and not the quill. Surely Whitman would have known these salient facts concerning Red Jacket, who in his time was widely acclaimed as an Indian leader. It supports the fact that Whitman was an uncritical Rousseauian romanticist, not well up on current events, or an outright racist; his collected writings seem to suggest all three at varying times.

Osceola doesn't fare much better than Red Jacket in the "good gray poet's" verse:

> Painted half his face and neck, his wrists, and back-
> hands,
> Put the scalp-knife carefully in his belt—then lying
> down, resting a moment,
> Rose again, half sitting, smiled, gave in silence his
> extended hand to each and all,
> Sank faintly low to the floor (tightly grasping the
> tomahawk handle,)
> Fix'd his look on wife and little children—the last:
> (And here a line in memory of his name and death.)
> ("Osceola," 5–10)

In an epigraph Whitman states that Osceola died of "a broken
heart." Most historians agree he died of malaria or possibly from
being poisoned or from maltreatment. Later his head was cut off
and placed on display in the Medical Museum. At the time of his
death Osceola was thirty-four and Whitman was nearing twenty.
A U.S. marine was the poet's informant, a boy he'd met one day
in Brooklyn.

He wrote "Yonnondio," an Iroquois lament, and in the poem
"The Sleepers" he devoted a passage to an Indian "squaw,"
though she was a somewhat supernatural being who appeared
before his mother: "She remember'd her many a winter and
many a summer, / But the red squaw never came nor was heard
of there again" (115–116). Whitman was obviously, I hope, unaware that the word "squaw" was a derogatory term that referred to a woman's reproductive organs. It did not signify an Indian woman as such. And there are other scattered passages, but
Whitman basically held the "doomed" Indian as not a fit subject
for verse: Indians neither produced nor were produced by Whitman's hero, America, and merited only a veiled apparition or
pitiful elegy.

Whitman, however, immortalized General George Armstrong
Custer in the elegy "From Far Dakota's Cañons," within which
Custer died "bearing a bright sword in thy hand, / Now ending
well in death the splendid fever of thy deeds" (20–21)—deeds
such as killing Indians manipulated through surprise attacks for
self-aggrandizement and for the federal government. As a poem

it is not successful; as an elegy it borders on the maudlin; as history it is about as accurate as Keats attributing the discovery of the Pacific Ocean to Cortés.

In his collection of daily jottings, *Specimen Days*, Whitman noted in August 1881 his viewing of John Mulvany's painting of Custer's fall at the Little Big Horn. The poet lamented, pathetically, that he had but an hour to spend in thought before this "vast canvas" with "swarms upon swarms of savage Sioux, in their war-bonnets, frantic . . . driving through the background, through the smoke, like a hurricane of demons" (275). Mulvany's painting, *Custer's Last Rally*, was "all native, all our own, and all a fact" (276). It was American, not native in an indigenous sense. Only America could produce a spectacular event of such heroic proportions. Whitman, apparently, was a proponent of the manifest destiny bilge of the earlier decades and still of his current day. While there is no overt condemnation of Indians, there is also no understanding of what the "rally" was all about. His was a simple case of hero worship and adulation of the legendary boy-general and his glossy curls. Perhaps Whitman had read too many penny novels. "Custer (his hair cut short) stands in the middle, with dilated eye and extended arm, aiming a huge cavalry pistol" (276). In the elegy "From Far Dakota's Cañons," the poet had Custer's hair "flowing" and portrayed the general "leaving behind [him] a memory sweet to soldiers." This does not sound like the "Hard-backsides" or "Iron-ass" many of those soldiers remembered. There is some doubt that his own men, such as Marcus Reno or Fred Benteen, would retain a "sweet" memory of the suicidal young general who had been labeled a murderer of his own soldiers by his staff.

Even in 1876, strangely, in America many important authors did not accept the fact that Custer brought about his own defeat and demise in the direct attack on the Lakota (Sioux) and Cheyenne peaceful encampment at Little Big Horn on that hot June morning. Most sensible historians today conclude that Custer was in total error when foolishly attacking this encampment which outnumbered his troops. This fact had been repeatedly spelled out to the general by various scouts in his command. As Mari Sandoz suggests in *The Battle of the Little Bighorn*, 1876 was an election year and killing Indians in the Far West could easily catapult his missile-star high in the skies before the eyes of the American public about to select, nominate the next candidate for president. His aim in this attack, *not* battle, was to revive the American sentiment. His last major campaign was in 1868, eight years prior to the Little Big Horn. The public is fickle and prone to forgetfulness. He needed headlines and consequently brought along his own newspaper reporter. Knowing full well the odds against him, knowing also the American public's deep desire for heroism and heroes, he chose to attack an encampment of nearly 10,000 Indians with a handful of soldiers—many raw recruits, some drunk on whiskey, and many frightened and angry that their commander would knowingly lead them to their deaths. The daredevil never faltered. He marched his men into glory, into history, and into Whitman's imagination ready and willing to accept the boy-general as hero and champion of the people, his "average bulk." All nations are in need of cultural heroes, hence, Ulysses and Aeneas, Virginia Dare of Roanoake and George Washington. Custer had his Homer, his Virgil in Whitman; however, not only are the poem and the essay both inaccurate, they also are creatively weak in execution and language and do not survive as a major work of art befitting the honor of epic. Nor is Custer a proven cultural hero. He did not save the day, let alone the men under his command. What he accomplished, apart from his demise, was to start a controversy which continues to rage to this moment.

Whitman describes, again in *Specimen Days*, an extended trip to the Far West in autumn of 1879. The poet, while traveling the plains among the ghosts of legendary chiefs, never mentions the historical fact that those lands were once inhabited by Indians. The word "Indian" is not used. Strange.

I cannot but wonder where Whitman's thoughts lay at the Camp Grant Massacre or the Sand Creek Massacre or the flight of the Nez Percé. How is it that Geronimo, Roman Nose, Crazy Horse, and Chief Joseph were not fit subjects for epics, great warriors and heroes to their people which they indeed are? Whitman was not the only major poet of his day to slight these heroes. Whittier, Emerson, Lowell, and Lanier all ignored them.

But Whitman's life-style, thought, poetic vision, and sympathies were with the common American, so he could be expected to hold strong feelings for the plight of a mighty race of human beings crushed under the impervious foot of the imperialism of mechanical progress. Not until the twentieth century did poets fully realize the essential value and quality of that culture so readily put to the gun.

It is a tragic loss that the American Indian did not prove a fit subject for Whitman's powerful poetics. Perhaps Whitman, with all his shoulder-power, might well have composed a truly immortal epic. He lived during the momentous time of the Plains Nations and the deaths of the Woodland Nations. Obviously, for whatever personal reasons, Whitman closed his ears and shut his eyes to the Indians' death cries. Much to literature's and history's loss, he turned his back on American tragedy.

Sitting Bull, Rain-in-the-face, Black Kettle, Roman Nose, and their brothers and sisters still await a courageous poet to recreate their lives and deeds, their monumental strengths and successes, and their suffering in verse, for the eyes and ears of the world. Perhaps their own living sons and daughters will take up the pen. Whitman's indifference failed them.

Power ceases in the instant of repose; it resides in the moment of transition from a past to a new state, in the shooting of the gulf, in the darting to an aim. This one fact the world hates, that the soul becomes . . .
—Ralph Waldo Emerson

The limits of language, as of reality itself, are not rigid but fluid. Only in the mobile and multiform word, which seems to be constantly bursting its own limits, does the fullness of the world-forming logos find its counterpart. Language itself must recognize all the distinctions which it necessarily effects as provisional and relative distinctions which it will withdraw when it considers the object in a new perspective.
—Ernst Cassirer

Tropes of Selfhood

Whitman's "Expressive Individualism"

M. JIMMIE KILLINGSWORTH

In *Habits of the Heart: Individualism and Commitment in American Life*, the best-selling study of national character as revealed through hundreds of interviews with contemporary Americans, Robert Bellah and four distinguished coauthors are the latest generation of American social scientists to find in Walt Whitman a representative voice for selfhood in the United States. Like the first generation, which included William James, these cartographers of the soul are attracted by the poet whose great theme was what he believed to be simultaneously (and ironically) most common and most precious—"myself":

I resist anything better than my own diversity,

.   .   .   .

This is the grass that grows wherever the land is and the
water is,
This is the common air that bathes the globe.

This is the breath of laws and songs and behaviour,
This is the tasteless water of souls . . .
("Song of Myself" [1855], 347, 358–361)

Within himself, Whitman felt "the current and the index" of
human life, in the general as well as in the particular. In his first
great poems, published in 1855 and inspired by the physical
strength of a robust middle age, he put his secret intuitions onto
the record of public life in an attempt to live out the Emersonian
dictum that, in speaking his inmost thoughts, he would make
universal sense. Trusting inner resources, he proclaimed in "Song
of Myself": "These are the thoughts of all men in all ages and
lands, they are not original with me, / If they are not yours as
much as mine they are nothing or next to nothing" (353–354).

The poet's confidence in the sympathy of readers was hardly
unflagging, however, even in the early poems. By 1860, "Calamus" would record the downward turn of selfhood, the crisis of
identity, the alienation of the isolated individual, the anxious homosexual in a predominantly heterosexual culture: "I wonder if
other men ever have the like out of the like feelings?" he would
ask (see Killingsworth, 102). Throughout his life, through the
flow and ebb of extensive sympathy and defensive withdrawal,
Whitman would continue to ask the big questions that, despite
methodological sophistication and ever-deepening specializa-
tion, still haunt the social sciences: "What is a man anyhow?
What am I? and what are you?" ("Song of Myself" [1855], 390).

Bellah and his colleagues and James before them have, in one
sense, rescued Whitman from his isolation. For them, the Whitmanian "I" has come to represent a prototypical relationship between self and society. However, the honor of being a representative person, an Emersonian hero, is compensated negatively by
the requirement that the self sacrifice its proud "diversity," the

very thing which resists "anything better." Fitting Whitman into a category has meant neglecting the power of his poetic language to transform categories, indeed, to overwhelm them. What Ernst Cassirer has said of dogmatic metaphysical systems may be applied just as well to the categories theorized in the social sciences: "Most of them are nothing other than . . . hypostases of a definite logical, or aesthetic, or religious principle. In shutting themselves up in the abstract universality of this principle, they cut themselves off from particular aspects of cultural life and the concrete totality of its forms" (82). Dealing with what Cassirer calls "the problem of signs"—the question of how a sign like "I" relates to and interpenetrates the multiform realities that it represents—is for social psychology a matter of looking "backward to its ultimate 'foundations'" in mental life; Whitman's poems, on the other hand, engender an attitude of discovery that looks forward, pressing language toward a "concrete unfolding and configuration in . . . diverse cultural spheres" (105). In poetic language, Whitman discovered a fluidity that denied the trivialization of selfhood, that broke through the limits imposed by too tight a system, and that curved back upon its source. Indeed, he found that expression of the self tended to erode and reformulate that which had been expressed. Like Emerson before him, he realized the "one fact the world hates, that the soul becomes."

According to the scheme developed in *Habits of the Heart*, history has produced two distinctively modern attitudes of the self toward society at large, utilitarian individualism and expressive individualism. In contrast to the earlier republican and biblical versions of autonomous selfhood, both utilitarian and expressive individualism are seen as failures, for they undermine the connection between person and community. In the view of Bellah and his coauthors, the utilitarian and the expressivist lose sight of historical tradition and subsequently view community as merely an environment of personhood. This ahistorical psychic isolation produces a chronic lack of social commitment in contemporary American life.

Utilitarian individualism is the characteristic attitude of the

"self-made" woman or man. Utilitarians may allow their personal goals to be defined by external standards—better salaries
and bigger houses or progress up the social ladder—but they are
motivated exclusively by the drive for individual success. The
great predecessor of the utilitarian outlook, according to Bellah,
is Benjamin Franklin, particularly as he appeared in his own
Autobiography. The difference between Franklin and modern
utilitarian individualists is that he tempered his drive for success
with a measure of republican idealism, which his cultural de-
scendants lack altogether. The legacy of his famous list of practical virtues has thus become the cult of professionalism, the
sixty-hour workweek, the fast fortune, dressing for success, and,
ultimately, conspicuous consumption.

Expressive individualism, like its utilitarian cousin, is preoc-
cupied with success, but the expressivist longs to break even
more completely with community, trusting internal, intuitive
measures of achievement instead of accepting external standards.
Whereas for the utilitarian individualist success is merely a tech-
nical matter of finding the right means to a preestablished end,
the expressivist tries to extract both means and ends from the
inner sources of body, heart, and soul. For Bellah, Whitman is
the cultural prototype of expressive individualism. His legacy in
our times—which, like Franklin's, has lost its republican moor-
ings—is the therapeutic search for identity and the overthrowing
of communities based on kinship and regional or national identity in favor of homogeneous "life-style enclaves," the ubiquitous support groups of our age, gatherings defined by special
interests and expressive styles of behavior rather than by shared
traditions or political goals. How, Bellah seems to ask, could
Whitman's democratic personalism have come to this?

Despite this conservative tendency to valorize figures from the
past at the expense of contemporary Americans, however, it is
quite possible to argue that Whitman made some progress toward the completed image of modern expressivism quite on his
own. At times he reached points where his expressiveness came
to threaten not only the basis for community but also the very
concept of the individual. Exploring the tensions inherent in expressive individualism, the poet found himself, like many of our

contemporary expressivists, on the very brink of selfhood, the place theorized by the sociologist Erving Goffman and by the deconstructionists, for whom there is no foundational self at all but, in Bellah's words, "merely a series of social masks that change with each successive situation," an "absolutely empty, unencumbered and improvisational self" (80).

Bellah argues that Whitman's idea of success "had little to do with material acquisition": "A life rich in experience, open to all kinds of people, luxuriating in the sensual, as well as the intellectual, above all a life of strong feeling, was what he perceived as a successful life" (14). Whitman's homosexuality, in this reading, represents one "way in which he rejected the narrow definition of the male ego dominant in his day" (15). If we extend this line of reasoning, accounting for the rhetorical as well as the expressive aims of the poems, we come to see "Calamus" as an encouragement for like-minded men to join him in ignoring the "plaudits in the capital," to follow him down "paths untrodden," bypassing the impositions of class, region, and economic condition—much as he himself had done in choosing his friends from among young intellectuals and working-class men in the late 1850s—and forming an enclave of comrades bound by the sentiment and expression of "manly love."

If we use Bellah's interpretive line as a critical tool, however, we must allow that such an enclave could have but a weak effect on the political life and social commitment of the individual members. Its chief character, the persona of the "tenderest lover," is too malleable, too ephemeral, too promiscuous, too concerned with image and appeal to inspire communal action. In "Are You the New Person Drawn toward Me?" the speaker wards off a would-be disciple with this admonition:

> Are you the new person drawn toward me?
> To begin with take warning, I am surely far different
>   from what you suppose;
> Do you suppose you will find in me your ideal?
> .   .   .   .
> Do you suppose yourself advancing on real ground
>   toward a real heroic man?

Have you no thought O dreamer that it may be all maya,
illusion? (1–3, 8–9)

In like manner, Whitman would fend off John Addington Symonds, a homosexual who sought a political ally, and he would snub the advances of his female admirer Anne Gilchrist with these words: "Dear friend, let me warn you somewhat about myself—& yourself also. You must not construct such an unauthorized & imaginary ideal Figure, & call it W. W. and so devotedly invest your loving nature in it. The actual W. W. is a very plain personage, & entirely unworthy such devotion" (*Correspondence*, 2:170). Of course, the "actual" Walt Whitman in these biographical instances could well be read as yet another expressive trope, fulfilling within other contexts the need of the self for defense against external social demands.

In the very concept of expressive individualism, then, there is a deep tension which in his poems and public life Whitman freely tested. Individualism favors singularity, but expression favors multiplicity, diversity. Except in its most radically expressive phase, individualism is a foundationalist concept, placing the certain inner self at the center of an uncertain world. Expression tends to dislocate every center, to undermine every foundation, including the self, and to impinge, for example, upon the private self of the "Calamus" poet, rooting out either a confession of his true nature or stimulating yet another evasion, yet another mask. As the self is expressed, it is transformed, yielding by turns the "tenderest lover" of the "Calamus" poems, the "friendly and flowing savage" of "Song of Myself," or the "very plain personage" of the letters.

In "O Living Always, Always Dying," which was originally grouped in "Calamus," the speaker chants, "O to disengage myself from those corpses of me, which I turn and look at where I cast them, / To pass on, (O living! always living!) and leave the corpses behind" (5–6). Living, in this trope, is a transcendental act of expression, shedding the old self as the new self emerges. In its final placement in the "Whispers of Heavenly

Death" cluster, the poem strikes a bold contrast with its companion, "A Noiseless Patient Spider," which in a superb figure relates the soul to an "isolated" spider launching filaments out of itself, seeking among the surrounding spheres a "ductile anchor" for its "gossamer thread." While the spider-soul stands at the center of expressive life, the snake-soul of "O Living Always, Always Dying" sheds the self with each new expression, leaving behind an empty and discarded skin, a mere corpse.

Whitman thus demonstrates a division within the category of expressive individualism. The self may remain more or less secure and thereby realize expressions as its products. Or it may with each strong expression utterly refashion its very basis for being. If it is continually re-expressed—or if expression becomes an end in itself—the self loses its status as a substance and becomes the empty cipher "I" that semioticists have described as the sign most clearly disconnected from any stable referential base. "What is the reality to which *I* or *you* refers?" asks Émile Benveniste. "It is solely a 'reality of discourse'" (218–219). Whitman himself approached this extreme reduction of "myself" to a linguistic reality in a now-famous latter-day reflection on his poems: "I sometimes think the Leaves is only a language experiment—that it is an attempt to give the spirit, the body, the man, new words, new potentialities of speech" (*American Primer*, viii–ix).

In light of the tension between foundationalist individualism and the antifoundationalist tendency of tropic expressiveness, what can we identify as the sources of selfhood for expressive individualism in general and for Walt Whitman in particular? Three possibilities arise in *Leaves of Grass*. The first is the body, attention to which brings forth a kind of physical individualism, such as that of the libertine. The second is the soul, the intuition, the unconscious, which produces psychic individualism or egotism. The third is language, the poem, the text, or tropic individualism. In Whitman's poetry, if not in every instance of expressive individualism, all three sources are invoked, often simultaneously. Unlike the deconstructionists, who insist that individuality is always undone in its own making and thereby discharged into a consuming network of intertextuality, Whitman never completely uncouples tropic individuality from physical and psychic sources.

In the 1850s he seems indeed to have generated tropic power by seeking language adequate for expressing the demands of the robust body and the corresponding shapes of soulful fantasy. The tropes of "Song of Myself" are especially dazzling as a result of this interior interchange. In section 5, for example, we find the physical self addressing the "other I am," the soul, seducing the unconscious, and liberating an orgasmic flow of language that wraps in ambiguity the conventional gender relations of body and soul: ". . . you settled your head athwart my hips and gently turn'd over upon me, / And parted the shirt from my bosom-bone, and plunged your tongue to my bare-stript heart" (88–89).

Language provides the negative principle of the poem, playing Shiva the destroyer to the soul's and body's Brahma the creator. The body is erotic and as such demands intercourse with others. The Emersonian soul is republican and seeks communion through the sympathetic imagination. The text obliges with its fluent "I am" but insists as well upon distinction, upon "not." The tropes of selfhood require continual differentiation:

> People I meet, the effect upon me of my early life or the
> ward and city I live in, or the nation . . .
> These come to me days and nights and go from me
> again,
> But they are not the Me myself. (67, 73–74)

And what is the "Me myself" if not a poem resisting the reading of others?

> Apart from the pulling and hauling stands what I am,
> Stands amused, complacent, compassionating, idle,
> unitary,
>
> .   .   .   .
>
> Looking with side-curved head curious what will
> come next,

> Both in and out of the game and watching and
> wondering at it. (75–76, 78–79)

Language is the medium that provides distance, the detachment in the attitude of these lines. Writing creates the space
wherein the self becomes free from the demands of the body and
the power of the soul to overwhelm the senses and to drive
loving observation into self-absorbed reverie. In the strongest
poems of *Leaves of Grass*, the demands of body and soul merge in
images of the fantastic, delightfully recorded by the writer standing "Apart from the pulling and hauling . . . / . . . amused, com-
placent, compassionating, idle, unitary . . . / Looking with side-
curved head curious what will come next."

Not only in the energetic bursts of the 1855 "Song of Myself"
but also in the later poems, in which the force of physical life is
somewhat withdrawn, Whitman celebrates the de-centering and
re-creative power of poetic language. "Passage to India" (1874) is
among the best examples. In his old age Whitman told Horace
Traubel, "There's more of me, the essential ultimate me, in that
than in any of the poems. There is no philosophy, consistent or
inconsistent, in that poem . . . but the burden of it is evolution—
the one thing escaping the other—the unfolding of cosmic purposes" (Traubel, 1:156–157). The poem begins with a celebration
of the soul's power to set the foundations for material progress.
Centuries before the transatlantic cable was laid in 1866—"The
seas inlaid with eloquent gentle wires"—the self, here in its
guise as the Emersonian oversoul, established its networks of
sympathetic union across the seas and over the lands. The actual
placing of the cable, like the building of the Suez Canal and the
transcontinental railroad—all the spanning accomplishments of
Whitman's era—is but a late realization of the connections pio-
neered by soulful meditation. Even with these realizations, the
soul will not rest:

> After the seas are all cross'd, (as they seem already
> cross'd,)
> After the great captains and engineers have
> accomplish'd their work,

> After the noble inventors, after the scientists, the
>   chemist, the geologist, ethnologist,
> Finally shall come the poet worthy of that name,
> The true son of God shall come singing his songs.
>   (101–105)

Ironically, the soul of this "true son of God" is self-surpassing. The soul that had been the foundation for material progress has come by the poem's conclusion to be the principle by which that progress is discounted, surpassed, erased. In wiping the slate clean, the troping self risks all, even its own status as a foundation for further invention, further realization:

> Sail forth—steer for the deep waters only,
> Reckless O soul, exploring, I with thee, and thou
>   with me,
> For we are bound where mariner has not yet dared to go,
> And we will risk the ship, ourselves and all. (248–251)

Bellah's homage to Whitman, the attribution of paternity in the lineage of expressive individualism, fails to do justice to the range and the political value of the Whitmanian self. The sociologist's conservative reading particularly neglects the linguistic root of antifoundationalist expressivism. In like manner, William James honored Whitman with metaphysical oversimplification, finding in the poet the very type of "healthymindedness," the tendency toward a radical openness whose mysticism is large and whose democratic embrace contains multitudes (81–83). But Whitman's poems eloquently protest such reduction; even if reduction takes breadth as its theme, its net effect is a conceptual narrowing.

It is not especially surprising that the Whitman of the poems resists the Whitman of the social scientists. To say that they fall short is not to slander James and Bellah—for who could exhaust the meanings of the best poems?—but is instead a comment on the different politics of poetry and the social sciences. Poems like Whitman's have their own social agenda. They aim to explode just the kind of categories that the social sciences work to build, explanatory frameworks that make life stand still, solid structures in the uncertain sweep of history.

Whitman's expressivism arose in opposition to the flatness and meanness that had overwhelmed the republican spirit. Developed in the mood of 1848, the poems of the fifties were no doubt a "language experiment," a radical essay in consciousness, whose aim, in Whitman's own words, was "to give the spirit, the body, the man, new words, new potentialities of speech" (*American Primer*, viii–ix). As the philosopher Charles Taylor has recently suggested, in the "search to recover a language of commitment to a greater whole," Bellah and his colleagues "write as though there were not really an independent problem of the loss of meaning in our culture, as though the recovery of a Tocquevillian commitment would somehow also fully resolve our problems of meaning, of expressive unity, of the loss of substance and resonance in our man-made environment, of a disenchanted universe" (509). The so-called human potential movement—which, like Bellah, Taylor traces to Emerson and Whitman—and all other forms of sentimental, therapeutic expressivism aim to create a haven of selfhood away from the demands of commitment. In contrast to this weak strand of expressivism stands a strong form of expression that challenges the individual to test external demands against the needs of the body and to experiment with the tropes of a new life, as Whitman did in all of his best poems, perhaps most clearly in "I Sing the Body Electric" (see Killingsworth, 1–15).

Bellah gives no criteria for distinguishing between weak and strong versions of expressive individualism. Nor, for that matter, does he provide criteria for distinguishing between weak and strong republican individualism. He appears to suggest that republicanism is inherently stronger than expressivism and thus ignores the historical development of republicanism toward the aggressive and domineering practices of male, middle-class, middle-aged, heterosexual, white, and industrialist individuals. It was no doubt the emergence of this hegemony within the bosom of republican individualism that urged Whitman and other strong expressivists to look within themselves for alternatives.

In this light, life-style enclaves, which Bellah views as necessarily degenerate, take on a different aspect as well; they arise when traditional communities fail to meet the needs of certain groups. The one example discussed at any length in *Habits of the Heart* is retirement communities, which clearly fill the gap left when families no longer can or will care for their oldest members. Presumably for rhetorical reasons, Bellah waffles on the exact status of certain other groups, notably the gay and lesbian communities. Though fitting rather well the definition of a life-style enclave, these groups and others like them may represent rising forces of life-style expression that try out a political will that is destined eventually to alter the current of a more general community's mainstream. Just as there are strong and weak versions of expressivism, there are strong and weak life-style enclaves. While the weak enclave discovers its ultimate goal in adjustment to the status quo, the strong enclave is at the very least protopolitical. Like the strong poem, it encourages the individual to hold fast against contrary social demands and to remake social life according to a new image.

In his poems and in his life, Whitman embodied the waverings of the expressivist spirit, with full pendulum swings from strong to weak and back again. In moments of personal doubt and in periods of dryness he withdrew his faith from the text, leaving the poems mere vehicles for asserting a conventional soul, an I'm-ok-you're-ok therapeutic crutch. This trend is particularly noticeable in *Drum-Taps* and in certain poems of the early 1870s, when the Civil War and physical hardship had numbed the poet's body and stifled his confidence in tropic individuality—a condition chronicled in this war-struck poem:

> Quicksand years that whirl me I know not whither,
> Your schemes, politics, fail, lines give way, substances
>   mock and elude me,
> Only the theme I sing, the great and strong-possess'd
>   soul, eludes not,
> One's-self must never give way—that is the final
>   substance—that out of all is sure,
> Out of politics, triumphs, battles, life, what at last
>   finally remains?

When shows break up what but One's-Self is sure?
("Quicksand Years")

The considerable beauty of this poem depends upon the reader's identification of the expressed soul as the center of the poet's pain. The pain comes partly from grief over republican individualism, the hopes of which, for Whitman as for many others, had died in the Civil War (see Killingsworth). And the pain comes partly from the thought that the poet of "Song of Myself" and "Calamus" could stand for this reduction of expressive individualism to such an empty cipher abstractly expressed—"the theme," "One's-self," "the final substance," "the soul."

In the hundred years since Whitman's death, American social sciences have used the poet's tropes of selfhood as mere emblems for social categories—healthymindedness, expressive individualism. The suggestiveness of this work cannot be denied; the concept of expressivism, if not definitive, has a great deal of heuristic power. Moreover, through the attention of readers as prominent as James and Bellah, Whitman's place in American culture is affirmed. In many ways, the homage of social scientists is the realization of all the poet longed for—a form of canonization (in both the literary and the religious senses). "The proof of a poet is that his country absorbs him as affectionately as he has absorbed it," he wrote in 1855 in the preface to *Leaves of Grass*.

And yet *Leaves of Grass*, when read not as the product of a talkative ego but rather as a "language experiment," may seem to challenge the social theorists of the next hundred years to value the specific instance or experience in the face of the abstract category, to treat with suspicion the label, the system, the class, all that narrows, confines, or brutalizes by denying singularity, to recognize in language a creative medium that will not remain a slave to the world of referents, and to regard the ambiguity of poetic language as a means of social revitalization.

All truths wait in all things,
They neither hasten their own delivery nor resist it,

They do not need the obstetric forceps of the surgeon,
The insignificant is as big to me as any,
What is less or more than a touch?

Logic and sermons never convince,
The damp of the night drives deeper into my soul.

Only what proves itself to every man and woman is so,
Only what nobody denies is so. ("Song of Myself"
   [1855], 647–655)

Rereading Whitman under Pressure of AIDS

His Sex Radicalism and Ours

MICHAEL MOON

It was what I saw as Whitman's sex radicalism that first drew me to study his writing in earnest in the late seventies when I was coming out as a gay man. Radical in his insistence on representing a wide range of nonprocreative sexualities in his poetry, the author of *Leaves of Grass* exceeded even this already daring program by proceeding to offer himself as imaginary lover—body as well as soul, he repeatedly asserted—to the reader with a directness of appeal that I had then otherwise encountered only in relation to some of the more engaging models in the full-color nude photographs in the gay-male sex magazines I had discovered around the same time. These magazines—my particular favorite had the Whitmanian title *In Touch*—seemed to me homologous with *Leaves of Grass* in some important ways, mainly through their stagings of imaginary or uncanny relations of touch with oneself (through masturbation) or with another man or other men, in the senses both of feeling their bodies and having one's own body felt and of being emotionally stirred by these contacts and by the men who were their focus. The catch in these touching relations, both in *Leaves of Grass* and in the gay magazines, was of course that the other man—author of *Leaves of Grass* or hunky nude model—who was ostensibly offering himself to the reader as lover wasn't really there, didn't actually perform the magical metamorphosis verbally enacted by the author-speaker in Whitman's "So Long!": "(Is it night? are we here together alone? . . . I spring from the pages into your arms . . ." (54, 56).[1] Yet many of Whitman's readers—as well as many readers of gay sex magazines—seem to have had the sense and the wit, perhaps encouraged by Whitman's example in *Leaves of Grass*, not to give the attitudes expressed by the terms "really" and "actually" in the preceding sentence more than their due. The author of *Leaves of Grass* repeatedly insists that he is—in something of the same way the male model in the magazine photo is—virtually or imaginarily or uncannily available to touch and be touched by the reader.

What kind of sex-radical practice is constituted by Whitman's commitment to representing a wide range of sexual desires, prominently including homoerotic desire, and to disseminating an erotic physical presence through his writing? Even before I began graduate school, while working for awhile as an independent scholar, I tried to write about Whitman's particular brand of sex radicalism. Tracing Whitman's relations to Fourierism, to other communitarian movements, idealist and practical, to the sex-reform movements of the period, to the discourse of "Free Love" in the writings and "experiments in living" of such contemporaries of his as Stephen Pearl Andrews, John Humphrey Noyes, and Victoria Woodhull, I learned much about the history of sexuality in the nineteenth-century United States, but little of what I learned seemed very useful in my attempts to understand Whitman's practice. A couple of years ago, when I last had occasion to write about the question of Whitman's sex radicalism, I emphasized what struck me at the time as its anachronistic qualities, arguing that it derived not from the political crises around issues of the body and its regulation during the years he was producing *Leaves of Grass* (i.e., from 1855 when the book was first published until 1892, the year of his death and also the year he published the last revision of his book) but from a quite different set of sexual-political crises that had played themselves out in the decades of Whitman's youth and early adulthood, the years before he began producing the successive editions of *Leaves of Grass*.

I still think it is useful in reading Whitman to recognize this pronounced tendency in his writings to interact with a wide range of discourses of the antebellum period—strains of democratic idealism, of fraternal utopianism, of the political impulses and rhetoric of the nascent labor movement, or working-class discourses of the perils and pleasures of free association (at least for men) in taverns and boardinghouses—that in substantial part constitute his own discourse. Nevertheless, I have come to think more recently that it is at least as important in reading Whitman to acknowledge those qualities of his work that one might describe as anachronistic not because they tend backward chronologically and historically but because they tend forward, tend presciently—prophetically, if you will—to engage practices of sex radicalism that typify those of our own time, especially those that have recently become mass movements in response to the spread of HIV. One can chart the articulation of a sex-positive counter-response to sex-phobic responses to AIDS through a series of pamphlets and essays produced over the past decade, beginning with the booklet *How to Have Sex in an Epidemic* (1983) and continuing through Simon Watney's *Policing Desire: Pornography, AIDS, and the Media* (1987), Douglas Crimp's "How to Have Promiscuity in an Epidemic" (in the volume he edited entitled *AIDS: Cultural Analysis, Cultural Activism* [1988]), and Cindy Patton's "genealogy of safe sex" practices in her book *In-*

venting AIDS (1990). Whitman's representations of sexuality in *Leaves of Grass* anticipate this crucially important gay political movement in a number of ways.

The dissemination over the past few years of pro-safe-sex writing and representation in general, through books, slick and desktop-published magazines and fliers, videos, and safe-sex workshops and demonstrations, represents an elaboration and an intensification of "queer" self-representation and self-exploration that have been ongoing in various distinct and recognizable forms at least since readers began coming across *Leaves of Grass* in bookstores, having intense, including sexually intense, responses to it and writing Whitman about their feelings toward him and his work. These communications took the form of a modern, mixed-genre document that combined elements of the fan letter with elements of the love letter, the "mash note," and, in some cases, the obscene phone call or, in a somewhat different mode, the phone-sex call, both of these latter, of course, *avant la lettre*. Whitman must have been one of the first authors to receive such letters in large numbers; some of the richest of these came from his fellow writers, such as Anne Gilchrist, Bram Stoker, and Charles Warren Stoddard. Many of the most engaging letters Whitman received from "loving fans" were from admirers not of his book but of his personal presence and manner— working-class young men, especially his Civil War soldier friends (most of whom seem to have been unaware that Whitman wrote "seriously"), of the kind Charley Shively has published in his two important collections, *Calamus Lovers* (1987) and *Drum Beats* (1989).

As I began this essay by attesting, it is not only Whitman's contemporaries who had strong responses to the seductive maneuvers he makes in his writing. Last year a friend, a fellow English professor, told me that his father had once discovered him masturbating and reading *Leaves of Grass* when he was twelve years old (a scene, I suspect, that has been played out in homes all over the English-speaking world and beyond it over the past century and more). The father, almost as embarrassed as his son, felt compelled to intervene and finally stammered, "W-w-what are you . . . *reading?*" as if it were his son's literary taste that was of primary concern at the moment. A recent drawing by artist Andy Baird demonstrates a thoughtful awareness on his part of the erotic dynamics of Whitman's writing.² Baird's drawing, done in heavy, confident penstrokes, shows the upper three-quarters of the body of a late-adolescent boy who is masturbating as he looks down, tongue extended, at his erect penis. In large letters in the upper lefthand corner of the picture, beside the boy's in-clined head, the artist has inscribed Whitman's famous words, "Camerado, this is no book, / Who touches this touches a man."

I take Baird's drawing of a masturbating boy along with his quotation of Whitman as an emblematic parody of Whitman's ideal reader—one for whom mediation through the book, the printed text, has been bypassed. The scene is one in which Whit-man's words and another man's sexual pleasure seem to have found each other without benefit of the young man's having read *Leaves of Grass* (he may or may not be literate, may or may not read poetry). There is a kind of resonant redundancy to Baird's captioning a picture of a boy stroking his erect penis with the Whitman line, since it might well seem (possibly hilariously) self-evident to anyone looking at the picture, as well as to the boy in the picture, that what the boy is touching is "no book" but "a man." Whitman's announcement of the fact in the context of this picture seems in one sense even more fatuous than my friend's father's query about the title of the book he had come upon his son reading. But the Baird drawing and its caption reverberate along another axis, the one dividing/uniting man and erection in the picture and, further, dividing/uniting both of these entities from or with book. The mediating text, *Leaves of Grass*, may seem to have fallen entirely out of Baird's representation of the erotics of Whitmanian "touch"; the boy just masturbates, he doesn't read *and* masturbate. But the scene is not that simple and clear-cut. What Baird's drawing depicts is not only a boy masturbating, it is also a picture of a book that is in Whitman's words "no book," which is not only *Leaves of Grass* but any book or text that by design negates itself in the production of some kind of bodily/erotic contact between reader and author or between reader and text.

It is significant in this connection that Baird's drawing appeared in a "fagzine" or "queerzine," a kind of contributor-produced publication that has proliferated in the past few years in relation to a number of different but related gay and lesbian sex-radical movements. These movements have been primarily concerned with generating safe-sex practices and with supporting the validity of same-sex desire and behavior in general, especially in the face of homophobic constructions of AIDS as "a disease caused by gay people and their sexual behavior." "Queerzines," like *Leaves of Grass*, which may be considered to have in a sense initiated the genre, emphasize contact between reader and writer through shared desire and common concern with the affirmation of "queer" desire as well as with the exploration of various versions of safe-sex techniques.

We are accustomed to thinking of the term for the kind of writing that negates itself in the process of producing some kind of sexual connection between reader and author and/or between reader and text as pornography, a standard definition of which is writing that is intended primarily to arouse the reader sexually. Yet works like Whitman's—as well as Baird's and even the aforementioned gay pin-up magazines—suggest that this heavily reified understanding of the erotic effects of writing is thoroughly inadequate. The traditional invidious distinction between using pornography for sex and having "real" sex with another person resembles the conventional moralistic distinction between masturbation and "real," mature sex, as it also resembles the heterosexist and homophobic notion that heterosex is "real," "mature," "authentic," and homosex is not. Masturbating, masturbating while reading or looking at "pornography" (i.e., what is ordinarily understood as and often condemned for being sexual desire mediated by a text), imagining engaging in or actually engaging in sex with someone else of the same sex—these have all been considered inferior, inadequate, immature, or inauthentic in comparison with "the real thing," heterosex. What the works of Whitman and other aggressively "queer" writers suggest is that all sexuality resides "in touch," that all sexuality is mediated and textual, that there is no such thing as unmediated exchange between persons, including unmediated sexual exchange.

Sexual desires and acts between heterosexual-identified persons are of course no less mediated than similar desires and acts between other persons, although our heterosexist society has a strong stake in maintaining the pervasive fiction that the behaviors that constitute heterosexuality are natural or (to vary the metaphor considerably) "hardwired," while other behaviors are unnatural or the product of a perverse, circuitous bypassing of one's "innate" heterosexual hardware. This fiction obscures most of the ways in which many ostensibly "hetero" behaviors are in an important sense the same as "homo" ones, as in the cases of oral and anal sex and other practices that are common to both sexual orientations—indeed, an awareness of the commonality of these practices tends to erode one's sense of the fixity or stability of these supposedly definitive differences.

Historian Jonathan Ned Katz has recently demonstrated that rather than constituting a departure from a long-established sexual norm, the emergence of homosexual identities in late-nineteenth-century medical, legal, sociological, and literary writing developed hand in hand with a hardly less novel and controversial identity called heterosexuality. Whitman's writing about sex is one of Katz's most telling examples of how homo- and heterosexuality developed as complementary concepts rather than homosexuality's being derived as an oppositional term to heterosexuality, as is commonly (mis)understood. As Katz points out, for every move Whitman can be seen making in his poetry toward representing various phases of homosexual desire, as he does most extensively in the "Calamus" poems, he can also be seen making a corresponding move toward representing heterosexual desire, as he does in "Children of Adam." It has become commonplace in Whitman criticism to speak of "Calamus" as the homosexual section of *Leaves of Grass* and "Children of Adam" as the heterosexual section, but one has only to look at a representative "Children of Adam" poem such as "Spontaneous Me"—a poem which treats an indeterminably broad range of sexual behaviors, primarily in relation to the penis and masturbation—to see that Whitman conceives of heterosexuality as being as highly fragmented and as highly mediated as any other kind of sexual relations.

One hundred years after Whitman's death, it may be time to

remind ourselves of what a heavy burden of meaning he put not only on the sexualities that were emerging in his time but also on death, particularly on his own projected death. Sexuality and death are frequently represented in Whitman as standing in determinate relation to each other, but not in the terms that had long been conventional in Western European culture, especially in erotic poetry—e.g., that an orgasm is a "little death."

Beginning in the third (1860) edition of *Leaves of Grass*, at a time when he could not have imagined the mass carnage that would ensue during the years that were to follow, Whitman started explicitly specifying that it would be his own death that would finally release him from what he seems to have come to perceive as the trammels of personal identity and desire and permit him to effect through his text the general dissemination of physical affection from himself to his readers that he had been promising since 1855. The way this distribution of his bodily affections among his readers depends on the death of the poet had been at least implicit in *Leaves of Grass* from its first appearance, as in the penultimate lines of the poem Whitman later entitled "Song of Myself":

> I depart as air, I shake my white locks at the runaway
>   sun,
> I effuse my flesh in eddies, and drift it in lacy jags.
>
> I bequeath myself to the dirt to grow from the grass I
>   love,
> If you want me again look for me under your boot-soles.
>
> You will hardly know who I am or what I mean,
> But I shall be good health to you nevertheless,
> And filter and fibre your blood. (1337–1343)

This self-dispersal takes a relatively mild form; the poet seems even before death to be already disintegrated into the organic elements that compose his body. Death comes not as a shattering effect severing body from identity but as a relatively painless scattering effect, as if the countless effusions that constitute "Song of Myself" had inevitably culminated in the effusion of the poet's own "flesh," which is in turn beneficently transformed into a tonic for the reader.

In the poetry written five years later (in 1860), the seductive intentions of the poet are more openly avowed, as are what had earlier been mere intimations that his potentially physically affectionate relation to the reader crucially depended on the poet's dying. In the climactic lines of "So Long!" Whitman gives the reader permission to assume his (the poet's) death. Even if this event has not yet actually taken place, it has virtually taken place by means of the poet's publication of his poems. The best-known lines of "So Long!" are perhaps among the two or three most frequently cited passages from Whitman's writing: "Camerado, this is no book, / Who touches this touches a man, / (Is it night? are we here together alone?) / It is I you hold and who holds you, / I spring from the pages into your arms . . ." (53–57). Though endlessly quoted, these lines are almost never interpreted in context. Consider the work of suppression going on in Whitman's readers' long-established habit of quoting his seductive "moves" out of the context of the scene of his dying in which they are embedded in the text:

> My songs cease, I abandon them,
> From behind the screen where I hid I advance
>   personally solely to you.
>
> Camerado, this is no book,
> Who touches this touches a man,
> (Is it night? are we here together alone?)
> It is I you hold and who holds you,
> I spring from the pages into your arms—decease calls
>   me forth. (51–57)

The scene of the poet's sudden bodily emergence into his reader's arms, read out of context, has often been taken to be a comic gesture. Such an interpretation more or less depends on the suppression of the condition—"decease"—that in the remainder of the line is represented as enabling the poem and/or the poet's transformation from lines on a page to affectionate, embodied lover lying in the arms of and embracing the reader.

Several lines later, at the end of the poem, the poet again assumes a disembodied state, even as he reassures the reader of his enduring affection: "I love you, I depart from materials, / I am as one disembodied, triumphant, dead" (70–71).

In his capacity to pass at will into and out of being embodied, Whitman's self-representation recalls the transformative powers of the figure of the woman in section 11 of "Song of Myself." In those lines the woman is first shown "hid[ing] handsome and richly drest aft the blinds of the window," peeking out unseen at a large group of young men bathing at the shore, whom she desires singly and collectively ("Which of the young men does she like the best? / Ah the homeliest of them is beautiful to her"). In the second part of the section, she both "splash[es] in the water" with them and "stay[s] stock still in [her] room"; that is, she or some part of herself passes out of her house "unseen" into the water, while another part of herself (her body?) remains indoors. An "unseen hand" passes over the bodies of the young men; "they do not ask who seizes fast to them, . . . They do not think whom they souse with spray". In other words, a good time is had by all, "unseen" pleasuring "hand" and young men alike.

The representation of the woman's hiding "aft the blinds of the window" and her subsequent projection of a part of herself out into the midst of the bathing party—some of this is clearly echoed in "So Long!" in Whitman's representation of himself coming out "from behind the screen where [he] hid" from the reader while he (the poet) was still alive, still writing "songs," in order to "spring from the pages into [the] arms" of his reader. Whitman depicts himself performing a similar self-projection twice in his Civil War poem "The Wound-Dresser" (at lines 20 and 59). In the second of these passages, self-projection is again (as it has been in the twenty-ninth bather section of "Song of Myself") followed by the ministrations of a "soothing hand" passing over young men's bodies (in this poem it is said to "pacify" them). The brief final section of the poem reads:

> Thus in silence in dreams' projections,
> Returning, resuming, I thread my way through the
>   hospitals,

The hurt and wounded I pacify with soothing hand,
I sit by the restless all the dark night, some are so young,
Some suffer so much, I recall the experience sweet and
    sad,
(Many a soldier's loving arms about this neck have
    cross'd and rested,
Many a soldier's kiss dwells on these bearded lips.)
    (59–65)

Here, rather than representing himself evaporating into thin air
or disintegrating into the soil as he does at the end of "Song of
Myself," Whitman uncharacteristically imagines a habitation for
male-homoerotic love, locating it on his neck, where "many a
soldier's loving arms . . . have cross'd and rested," and on his
lips, where "many a soldier's kiss dwells." Aside from the more
enduring embodiments and habitations he imagines producing
in writing, the sites where love between men resides—at certain
points on the surface of the loving and beloved body—are portrayed by Whitman as being both liminal and fragile.

In "Of Him I Love Day and Night," a text that was originally
one of the "Calamus" poems but that Whitman subsequently re-
assigned to a section entitled "Whispers of Heavenly Death," the
poet dreams not of his own self-dispersal but of that of his
beloved:

Of him I love day and night I dream'd I heard he was
    dead,
And I dream'd I went where they had buried him I love,
    but he was not in that place,
And I dream'd I wander'd searching among burial-
    places to find him,
And I found that every place was a burial-place;
The houses full of life were equally full of death, (this
    house is now,)
The streets, the shipping, the places of amusement, the
    Chicago, Boston, Philadelphia, the Mannahatta, were
    as full of the dead as of the living,
And fuller, O vastly fuller of the dead than of the living;

> And what I dream'd I will henceforth tell to every
>   person and age,
> And I stand henceforth bound to what I dream'd,
> And now I am willing to disregard burial-places and
>   dispense with them,
> And if the memorials of the dead were put up
>   indifferently everywhere, even in the room where I
>   eat or sleep, I should be satisfied,
> And if the corpse of any one I love, or if my own corpse,
>   be duly render'd to powder and pour'd in the sea, I
>   shall be satisfied,
> Or if it be distributed to the winds I shall be satisfied.

Here, rather than imagining his own dissemination as he does elsewhere in his poetry, Whitman imagines a general dissemination of death through the world, beginning at the point of the disappearance and dispersal of his lover's dead body. The world he depicts has been subjected to a chiasmatic reversal, a pulling wrong-side-out with regard to life and death: having formerly "successfully" contained death, the world has become contained by death, their relation reversed, so that now "every place [is] a burial-place."

The dispersal by pulverization that the poet imagines being carried out both on his own dead body and on that "of any one I love" results in an imagined double dissemination unusual in Whitman's poetry. It may puzzle some readers that the figure of the bodies of the poet and his lover being "render'd to powder and pour'd in the sea . . . / Or . . . distributed to the winds" should be said prospectively to satisfy him. It is no ordinary notion of satisfaction that is being projected here, requiring as it does the utter disintegration of the bodies of both the lover and his deceased beloved. The impelling fantasy in these lines is one of resisting mourning by refusing to imagine either one's own or one's beloved's body securely buried but instead imagining them both pulverized and scattered to the winds. The violence of such a fantasy proceeds from the difficulty of writing about such extreme loss without yielding to the tendency to represent it in abstract and generic terms, which is itself a violent (and reductive) transformation of the loss.

Among our own contemporaries, it is artist and AIDS activist David Wojnarowicz whose work is perhaps most like Whitman's in its commitment to countering this tendency violently.[3] A passage from a 1989 essay by Wojnarowicz seems in some ways to parallel Whitman's violent resistance to "proper" burial and mourning behavior with uncanny closeness:

> There is a tendency for people affected by this epidemic to police each other or prescribe what the most important gestures for dealing with this experience of loss would be. I resent that, and at the same time worry that friends will slowly become professional pallbearers, waiting for each death of their lovers, friends and neighbors and polishing their funeral speeches; perfecting their rituals of death rather than a relatively simple ritual of life such as screaming in the streets. I feel this because of the urgency of the situation, because of seeing death coming in from the edges of abstraction where those with the luxury of time have cast it. I imagine what it would be like if friends had a demonstration each time a lover or a friend or a stranger died of AIDS. I imagine what it would be like if, each time a lover, friend or stranger died of this disease, their friends, lovers, or neighbors would take their dead body and drive with it in a car a hundred miles an hour to washington dc and blast through the gates of the white house and come to a screeching halt before the entrance and then dump their lifeless form on the front steps. It would be comforting to see those friends, neighbors, lovers and strangers mark time and place and history in such a public way. (109)

The scene Wojnarowicz finds "comforting" exceeds ordinary notions of comfort as resolutely and furiously as the scene Whitman imagines exceeds ordinary notions of satisfaction. The terms in which Wojnarowicz proposes that the component of rage in mourning be thoroughly enacted by the mourner make especially striking and salient one of the features of Whitman's poetry that is most valuable to those of us rereading it under pressure of the AIDS pandemic, and that is the way the writing can focus not only the melancholia we inevitably feel (in a more conventional poem of mourning, for example, such as "Vigil Strange I Kept on the Field One Night") but also other feelings and states that are perhaps harder to recognize and harder to avow but are indispensable to us in our current struggles with embodiment and disembodiment.

NOTES

1. Citations to Whitman's poetry in this essay are to *Leaves of Grass: A Textual Variorum of the Printed Poems.* Mandy Berry, Jon Goldberg, Dan Itzkovitz, Samira Kawash, Katy Kent, and Eve Kosofsky Sedgwick read and discussed earlier drafts of this essay with me; their generous and thoughtful responses to my ideas about rereading Whitman under pressure of AIDS were extremely helpful and stimulating, and I want to thank each of them warmly.

2. Baird's drawing appeared in *Holy Titclamps* 5 (Summer 1990): 10. As of this writing, the issue is still available for $1.00 from Boxholder, P.O. Box 3054, Minneapolis, MN 55403. The editor requests that correspondents not use the title of the magazine on the envelope.

3. John Carlin discusses what he sees as some of the connections between Wojnarowicz's work and Whitman's; Carlin does not pursue the sex-radical connections I see as being the leading ones between these two bodies of work.

II

Some Readers

A Serpent in the Grass

Reading Walt Whitman and Frank O'Hara

DAVID EBERLY

Born almost one hundred years apart, Walt Whitman and Frank O'Hara lived to chronicle their eras while exposing their most intimate selves. Both gay, they explored their sexuality and the "city of orgies, walks and joys"—Manhattan—which protected and nourished it, providing "lovers, continual lovers."[1] While Whitman anxiously sought a public exposure and approval which O'Hara shirked, both faced incomprehension and denigration of their work by many of their early readers. Both, too, produced a prodigious amount.

The similarities between these two poets are even more striking if one recalls not the portrait of the bard avuncularly contemplating what is now known to be a cardboard butterfly or the great profile by Thomas Eakins which so resembles New Hampshire's Old Man but a daguerreotype taken in the early 1840s. This portrait shows us a Whitman soon to be emended, a young dandy with walking stick and smart hat, a cosmopolitan man-about-town, news editor, and opera lover, the same "dainty dolce affetuoso" that he would later renounce. This young Whitman strongly resembles the young Frank O'Hara, smitten with New York, with its size, opportunities, and arts, with seeing and hearing so much and meeting so many, with "The latest dates discoveries, inventions, societies, authors old and new, / My dinner, dress, associates, looks, compliments, dues" ("Song of Myself," 68–69). In the midst of this profusion, Whitman portrayed himself

> Apart from the pulling and hauling stands what I am,
> Stands amused, complacent, compassionating, idle,
>   unitary,
> Looks down, is erect, or bends an arm on an impalpable
>   certain rest,
> Looking with side-curved head curious what will come
>   next,
> Both in and out of the game and watching and
>   wondering at it. ("Song of Myself," 75–79)

Whitman's self-portrayal is notably similar to O'Hara's description of himself, "Standing still and walking in New York."

Although O'Hara once acknowledged Whitman as his "great predecessor" and declared that "only Whitman and Crane and Williams, of the American poets, are better than the movies" (*Collected Poems*, 498), he was as likely to deprecate Whitman as to praise him. O'Hara, for example, could simply forget him, as he does in "A True Account of Talking to the Sun at Fire Island," in which the Sun recalls his conversation with Mayakovsky but not his relationship with Whitman. In his poem "Day and Night in 1952," O'Hara stood on its head Whitman's powerful rhetorical device of beginning lines with prepositional phrases by concluding the last thirty-three lines with the preposition "of." He hilariously mocked Whitman's hymns to American democracy and womanhood by calling to the "Mothers of America" to "let your kids go to the movies!" where if lucky enough they will be picked up and "may even be grateful to you / for their first sexual experience" (371–372), and he reduced Whitman's catalogs to a breathless listing of movie stars in "To the Film Industry in Crisis." In one of his sliest deflations of his predecessor, O'Hara satirized Whitman's great paean to autoeroticism in a few witty lines:

> Big-town papers, you see, and this great-coated tour of
> the teens
> in (oh bless me!) imagination. That's what the snow said,
> "and doesn't your penis look funny today?" I jacked
> "off." (144)

Indeed these two poets described their art in terms—and tones—that could not be more opposite. To Whitman, "The known universe has one complete lover and that is the greatest poet." This poet "knows the soul" and "drags the dead out of their coffins and stands them again on their feet." He "does not only dazzle his rays over character and scenes and passions . . . he finally ascends and finishes all . . . he exhibits the pinnacles that no man can tell what they are for or what is beyond . . . he glows a moment on the extremist verge" (*Leaves of Grass* [1855], 11–12). O'Hara conceived of the poet much differently. "You just go on your nerve," he commented in "Personism: A Manifesto," his most important statement about his art. "If someone is chasing you down the street with a knife you just run, you don't turn and shout, 'Give it up! I was a track star for Mineola Prep'" (*Collected Poems*, 498). O'Hara described "Personal Poem" as "a diary of a particular day and the depressed mood of the day," parenthetically adding that "it's a pretty depressing day, you must admit, when you feel you relate more to poetry than to life" (511). The picture of the poet which O'Hara presented in that poem, where he meets LeRoi Jones and lunches on fish and ale, gossips, ranks other writers, and decides that "we don't want to be in the poets' walk in / San Francisco even" (335), could not seem more different from Whitman's description of the poet of "beautiful blood and a beautiful brain" who "hardly knows pettiness or triviality" (*Leaves of Grass* [1855], 9–10).

But Whitman offered a number of contradictory readings of himself. The "divine" bard and literatus could also write that "What is commonest, cheapest, nearest, easiest, is Me" ("Song of Myself," 259) and portray himself as a "rude child of the people" who "eats cheap fare, likes the strong flavored coffee of the coffee stands in the market . . . likes to make one at the crowded table among sailors and work-people—would leave a select soirée of elegant people any time to go with tumultuous men" (Traubel et al., 23). While one might see O'Hara hesitating briefly before choosing a soirée or the baths, this self-description has much the same ambience as O'Hara's self-descriptions.

O'Hara also gave differing versions of his intent as a poet. In one of his earliest poems he presented a picture of himself which, despite its irony, strongly recalls Whitman's self-conception:

> And here I am, the
> center of all beauty!
> writing these poems!
> Imagine! (*Collected Poems*, 11)

Later, in "Meditations in an Emergency," he claimed to be "the least difficult of men. All I want is boundless love," and enthused, "Even the trees understand me! Good heavens, I lie under them, too, don't I? I'm just like a pile of leaves," a humorous gloss on some of Whitman's most well known lines, "I lean and loaf at my ease . . . observing a spear of summer grass." In fact, while O'Hara declared in "Meditations" that he has never "clogged" himself "with nostalgia for an innocent past of perverted acts in pastures," thus distancing himself from his precursor, he then boldly raided Whitman's grassy fields in an audacious rewriting and seized them as his own: "One need never leave the confines of New York to get all the greenery one wishes—I can't even enjoy a blade of grass unless I know there's a subway handy, or a record store or some other sign that people do not totally *regret* life" (*Collected Poems*, 97).

Confronting a poetry scene that he found as stultifying as

Whitman did his own, O'Hara sought to sabotage the rigid concept of the poem then enforced by the New Critics, who he believed had "ruined" American poetry "to a great degree" with
"certain rather stupid ideas about how, about what is the com-
portment in diction that you adopt (*Standing Still*, 12). He did so
by turning to the French dadaists and surrealists, particularly
Reverdy and Prevert, and to Mayakovsky, much as Whitman
turned to other influences when he rejected the poetic diction
of Tennyson and Longfellow. Whitman once remarked to Horace
Traubel, "I sometimes think the *Leaves* is only a language experiment—that is an attempt to give the spirit, the body, the man,
new words, new potentialities of speech—an American, a cosmopolitan (the best of America is the best cosmopolitanism) range of
self-expression (*American Primer*, viii–ix). Whitman shoveled
words into the maw of American poetry and altered it forever:
ya-honk, hanker, blab, pimple—the list is as long as a reader
chooses to make it. O'Hara, too, expanded the dictionary of
American poetic vocabulary, adding such oddities as his catalog
of "kangaroos, sequins, chocolate sodas" and "harmonicas, ju-
jubes, aspirins." These things, he wrote, "do have meaning.
They're strong as rocks" (*Collected Poems*, 15).

O'Hara demonstrated this process of language expansion in
his poem "Why I Am Not a Painter." Written as a witty answer
to a perhaps idle question, O'Hara's poem has been frequently
read as a demonstration of the similarities between the process
of painting and his own art:

> I am not a painter, I am a poet.
> Why? I think I would rather be
> a painter, but I am not. Well,
>
> for instance, Mike Goldberg
> is starting a painting. I drop in.
> "Sit down and have a drink" he
> says. I drink; we drink. I look
> up. "You have SARDINES in it."
> "Yes, it needed something there."
> "Oh." I go and the days go by
> and I drop in again. The painting

is going on, and I go, and the days
go by. I drop in. The painting is
finished. "Where's SARDINES?"
All that's left is just
letters, "It was too much," Mike says.

But me? One day I am thinking of
a color: orange. I write a line
about orange. Pretty soon it is a
whole page of words, not lines.
Then another page. There should be
so much more, not of orange, of
words, of how terrible orange is
and life. Days go by. It is even in
prose, I am a real poet. My poem
is finished and I haven't mentioned
orange yet. It's twelve poems, I call
it ORANGES. And one day in a gallery
I see Mike's painting, called SARDINES.
(*Collected Poems*, 261–262)

O'Hara has done more in this poem than illustrate the creative process of putting in and taking out—what he characterized as "I do this, I do that"—that he shared with the abstractionists who surrounded him. While the poem subtly links the two arts by comparing and finally equating sardines—not apples—and oranges, it also imprints the word *sardines* onto both the reader's individual awareness and the American collective consciousness. Who could now write a poem using the word *sardine* that would not recall O'Hara's? "All that's left is just / letters," the painter notes. "It was too much." Too much, indeed. In writing this seemingly offhand poem, O'Hara demonstrated his power to create as masterfully as Whitman himself, and in its own way the lowly sardine now takes its place among the buffalo, heifers, she-whales, ground-sharks, and bats of Whitman's bestiary to become an indelible part of our poetry.

But "Why I Am Not a Painter" also explores a more personal aspect of O'Hara's experience not only as a poet but as a gay man writing in the mid-1950s, for this poem about painting is also about appearances, about concealing and revealing reality, about identity, about "passing." These are issues that confront all homosexuals, who must decide how much of themselves they will expose to the heterosexual world which surrounds, threatens, and minimizes them. In "Why I Am Not a Painter" O'Hara writes of making an earlier poem about orange in which the word *orange* does not appear anywhere in its twelve sections, but when done he has also written a poem in which it does. Even more tellingly and paradoxically, O'Hara, who states that he has become a "real poet" in the process of writing his new poem, also claims that he has produced something that "is even in prose." This sense of contradictory doubleness, of visibility and invisibility, of being here and not here, of hiding and "coming out," forms an essential part of the experience of any homosexual in our society. "SARDINES," written so large at the start of Mike Goldberg's painting because "it needed something there," is reduced at its finish, for "all that's left is just / letters." It was, to repeat what the artist said, "too much." And yet "SARDINES" does not just vanish. It remains, to those who are made aware, in the painting's title.

In recent years a number of critics have established the specifically homosexual context of Whitman's poetry.[2] It was a subject about which Whitman was extremely sensitive and about which he wrote "Only in a few hints, a few diffused faint clews and indirections" ("When I Read the Book," 6). But Whitman, despite an extensive revision of his work, chose not to hide completely the homosexual vision and experience which so mark some of his greatest poems. As he wrote of his "Calamus" poems:

> Here I shade and hide my thoughts, I myself do not
>   expose them,
> And yet they expose me more than all my other poems.
>   ("Here the Frailest Leaves of Me," 2–3)

In them he wrote of "the institution of the dear love of comrades," stating that he had taken his pen to tell of "the two simple men I saw to-day on the pier," parting:

The one to remain hung on the other's neck and
    passionately kiss'd him,
While the one to depart tightly prest the one to remain
    in his arms. ("What Think You I Take My Pen in
    Hand?" 6–7)

This subject did not go unnoticed by Whitman's critics, who
even before had excoriated him for conceiving "such a mass of
simple filth" while declaring that he deserved "nothing so richly
as the public executioner's whip" (Helms, 262). (The vehemence
of these criticisms disguised an attack not only on Whitman's
views on the subject of sex, which could at least be alluded to,
but on the topic of homosexuality as well, which could not. The
threats of his critics were not idle ones in post–Civil War America. In the 1870s, Anthony Comstock successfully led the fight to
enact antipornography laws whose effects could still be felt by
Frank O'Hara writing eighty years later.

O'Hara faced an equally protracted, if not as virulent, reaction
against homosexuality during most of his productive years. It is
easy to forget that O'Hara was vulnerable to exposure and arrest
in New York, where gay bars were routinely raided until the
Stonewall riot in 1969, three years after his death, or that he
too was threatened by obscenity laws. Unlike Whitman, O'Hara
chose (and it must be seen as a choice) not to publish most of his
work during his life, thereby shielding himself from possible
prosecution and his poetry from emendation.

O'Hara's poetry was often criticized—and minimized—in a
code whose vocabulary signaled to its audience that the poet in
question was gay and so not to be taken as seriously as his heterosexual peers. Thus O'Hara's poetry was described as "sentimental" and compared to a "pretty girl." He was characterized
as "gay, glancing, ephemeral" and "fun, bitchy," and his work
was said to be "full of campy gossip, silly jokes." Upbraided for
"naughty-little-boy sayings," he was also marginalized as a member of a "personal cosmopolitan elite" which "most certainly," as
one critic wrote, "is not my world" (Elledge, 14–45).

To write his most intimate and sexual message, particularly in
his early years, O'Hara, like Whitman, had to resort to his own

"clews and indirections." Much has been made of O'Hara's obscurity and unreadability in poems like "Easter" and "Second Avenue," of his deliberate obfuscation of points of reference, of the surrealist nature of his work, and of his relationship to the abstract expressionist art then so prevalent. When asked to explain "Second Avenue," O'Hara could give only a fragmented version of it, offering what he called "little pieces," making it seem "very jumbled, while actually everything in it either happened to me or I felt happening" (*Collected Poems*, 49). And a lot of what happens is sexual.

In "Second Avenue" O'Hara created a dense poem whose "verbal elements," as he described them, were "intended consciously to keep the surface of the poem high and dry" (*Collected Poems*, 497) and not "wet," a word which carries a connotation more sensual than the "reflective and self-conscious" definition he gives to it. In the poem he monitors that effect by asking the poem's reader, "Is your throat dry with the deviousness of following?" (497). Such "deviousness" is rewarded in "Second Avenue" not only with a Scheherazade profusion of things seen and imagined but also with the embedded nuggets of the artist's simultaneous sexual and creative development:

Well enough. To garner the snowing snow and then
    leave,
what an inspiration! as if suddenly, while dancing,
    someone,
a rather piratish elderly girl, had stuck her fan up her ass
and then became a Chinese legend before the bullrushes
    ope'd.
Yet I became aware of history as rods stippling the dip
of a fancied and intuitive scientific roadmap, clarté et
volupté et vif! swooping over the valley and under the
    lavender
where children prayed and had stillborn blue brothers of
entirely other races, the Tour Babel, as they say, said.
I want listeners to be distracted, as fur rises when most
    needed
and walks away to be another affair on another prairie,

> yowee, it's heaven in Heaven! with the leaves falling
> like angels who've been discharged for sodomy
> and it all almost over, that is too true to last, that is,
> "rawther old testament, dontcha know." (*Collected
>   Poems*, 145–146)

O'Hara frequently used a sexually suggestive vocabulary which often became graphic. But the explicit sexual meaning of many of his passages is partially obscured in a welter of images, allusions, in-jokes, and rapid shifts, rendering it more palatable and less threatening to possibly hostile readers.

O'Hara explored his own growth more deeply in his poem "In Memory of My Feelings." Its dreamlike atmosphere of quietude resembles that of Whitman's "The Sleepers" and, like it, contains a "number of selves" which O'Hara searches for:

> The dead hunting
> and the alive, ahunted.
>
>   My father, my uncle,
> my grand-uncle and the several aunts. My
> great-aunt dying for me, like a talisman, in the war,
> before I had even gone to Borneo
> her blood vessels rushed to the surface
> and burst like rockets over the wrinkled
> invasion of the Australians. (*Collected Poems*, 253)

Their faces rise like Whitman's ennuyés, onanists, and battle-scarred, his married couples. "Beneath these lives," O'Hara wrote, in a line as compelling as any of Whitman's, "the ardent lover of history hides,"

>   tongue out
> leaving a globe of spit on a taut spear of grass
> and leaves off rattling his tail a moment
> to admire this flag. (254)

If in "The Sleepers" Whitman gathered and embraced the fragments of his dissociated self and accepted his shadow, night, in a similar way, O'Hara accepted his serpent self, admiring "this flag," an image which can only refer to Whitman's love token.

O'Hara in this penultimate section of his poem merged his identity with "a few dirty men," Norwegian sailors. (The reference to Hart Crane's lover is, I think, oblique and telling.) In doing so O'Hara achieved a remarkable vision:

> Grace
> to be born and live as variously as possible. The
>   conception
> of masque barely suggests the sordid identifications.
> I am a Hittite in love with a horse. I don't know what
>   blood's
> in me I feel like an African prince I am a girl walking
>   downstairs
> in a red pleated dress with heels I am a champion taking
>   a fall
> I am a jockey with a sprained ass-hole I am the light
>   mist in which a face appears (*Collected Poems*, 256)

This catalog is as arbitrary and inclusive as any Whitman wrote and signals to the reader O'Hara's own great claim of poetic vision within an American and homosexual tradition. Finally, it is O'Hara's serpentine self which is saved, as secure in its being as Whitman's self had been. It remains "coiled around the central figure, / the heart / that bubbles with red ghosts, since to move is to love," whose prey "is always fragile and like something, as a seashell can be / a great Courbet, if it wishes. To bend the ear of the outer world" (256).

Much like Walt Whitman, Frank O'Hara conceived of the ideal listener of the "outer world" in the most intimate terms. Describing how he wrote a poem in "Personism," O'Hara stated, "While I was writing it I was realizing that if I wanted to I could use the telephone instead of writing the poem and so Personism was born. . . . It puts the poem squarely between the poet and the person, Lucky Pierre style, and the poem is correspondingly gratified" (*Collected Poems*, 499). This hilarious description of the process of writing—and reading—as a three-way sexual sandwich resembles Whitman's equally outrageous claim on *his* reader who, along with the poet, is to be gratified:

Camerado, this is no book,
Who touches this touches a man,
(Is it night? are we here together alone?)
It is I you hold and who holds you,
I spring from the pages into your arms—decease calls
    me forth. ("So Long!" 53–57)

O'Hara's readers, however, were no faceless "camerados" and, unlike Whitman, he never had to ask, "Who is now reading this?" He knew that his readers were his friends—Grace Hartigan, Jane Freilicher, Joe LeSueur, Bill Berkson, and many others. By writing for this audience, O'Hara was able to achieve a privacy of tone which only anxiously and momentarily appeared one hundred years earlier in Whitman's "Calamus" poems:

For thus merely touching you is enough, is best,
And thus touching you would I silently sleep and be
    carried eternally. ("Whoever You Are Holding Me
    Now in Hand," 25–26)

This is as quiet and moving a moment in American poetry as any, resembling O'Hara's tribute to his lover, Vincent Warren, of whom he wrote, "when I am in your presence I feel life is strong":

the faint line of hair dividing your torso
gives my mind rest and emotions their release
into the infinite air where since once we are
together we always will be in this life come what may
    (*Collected Poems*, 349)

Walt Whitman could not risk being as explicit as his successor. Instead he could hint and hope and, frightened, withdraw: "Already you see, I have escaped from you":

For it is not for what I have put into it that I have
    written this book,
Nor is it by reading it you will acquire it,
Nor do those know me best who admire me and
    vauntingly praise me,
Nor will the candidates for my love (unless at most a
    very few) prove victorious,

> Nor will my poems do good only, they will do just as
>   much evil, perhaps more,
> For all is useless without that which you may guess at
>   many times and not hit, that which I hinted at;
> Therefore release me and depart on your way.
>   ("Whoever You Are Holding Me Now in Hand,"
>   32–38)

O'Hara never asked his readers to "release" him, foregoing their pleasurable grasp. He could literally and imaginatively telephone, visit, date, and gossip with them. He created in his poems a world in which he felt so secure in their friendship that he felt safe enough to take, as he does in one of his best-known poems, "Joe's Jacket," something in return, a token "all enormity and life," a jacket to protect him on those

> many occasions as a symbol does when the heart is full
>   and risks no speech
> a precaution I loathe as a pheasant loathes the season
>   and is preserved
> it will not be need, it will be just what is and just what
>   happens (*Collected Poems*, 330)

Wrapped around the shoulders of the poet, it is a symbol as personal and as reverberant as Whitman's plant.

NOTES

1. All quotations from *Leaves of Grass* in this article are taken from *Leaves of Grass: A Textual Variorum of the Printed Poems*.

2. For further information, see Robert Martin's *The Homosexual Tradition in American Poetry* and the essays by Joseph Cady and Alan Helms included in Krieg. Two well-researched although idiosyncratically written volumes by Charley Shively, *Calamus Lovers* and *Drum Beats*, add much detail as well as speculation.

Whispering Whitman

to the Ears of Others

Ronald Johnson's Recipe for *Leaves of Grass*

ED FOLSOM

A hundred years after his death, American poets and poets from around the world still talk about, talk to, *talk back* to Walt Whitman. It's a singular phenomenon: Whitman's persistently palpable presence commands poets to continue to talk to him (Folsom). At some point in the lives of most twentieth-century American poets, some encounter with Whitman takes place. Again and again poets come to grips with his definition of what an American poet should (and should not) be and respond to his development of the poetic line, his concepts of poetic subject and object, his prophecies about democracy. They revise him, reject him, argue with him, beseech him; they express disappointment in him, anger with him, reverence for him.

No poet worked as hard as Whitman to initiate such an intense verbal reaction. He did not conceive of himself as a poet so much as the generator of poetry: he believed it would be in the encounter with his work that poetry would occur. He saw his poetry not as meaning or as a container of meaning but as the event at which or out of which meaning is made possible. So his poems remain sites for the creation of meaning, initiators of new poems, promoters of "poets to come." Whitman was not interested in readers who succumbed easily to his authority, who settled back into the subservient role of being talked to, guided, lectured. He wanted to create with his poetry a new kind of reader, a reader for the democratic era—one who would wrestle his or her way to equality with any authority, one who would "Resist much, obey little." This new relationship of reader and writer is what the 1855 preface to *Leaves of Grass* (and much of *Leaves* itself) is finally about: Whitman initiates a poetry that releases the reader from the oppressive weight of tyrannical authority. No longer will readers "sit . . . under some due authority and rest satisfied." Emerson, too, bemoaned how "our reading is mendicant and sycophantic" (*Essays*, 268), and Whitman's project for a democratic American readership is an extension and intensification of Emerson's call for a self-reliant readership. Whitman, then, built "talking back" into the very fiber of his poetry, and in essential ways his poetry works only when it is talked back to.

The massive century-long record of how and why poets have talked back to Whitman, have responded to his challenge, is proof of the importance and validity of his project. Roy Harvey Pearce, in *The Continuity of American Poetry*, suggests that "all American poetry [since *Leaves of Grass*] is, in essence if not in substance, a series of arguments with Whitman" (57). But what is remarkable is how much American poetry has been in *substance* a record of that argument. Whitman is not only an influence, he is a presence, and this distinction defines the unique relationship poets have had with him over the past century.

Some of the fertile conversations that poets have had with Whitman have been examined before, but I would like to focus here on one that has so far received little attention: Ronald Johnson's remarkable "Letters to Walt Whitman." (Johnson's "Letters" appear at the end of this monograph.) In these poems, Johnson— a Kansas-born poet who now lives in San Francisco and who writes cookbooks as well as poetry—inscribes one of the most sustained and suggestive of all the poetic encounters with Whitman, an encounter that accomplishes exactly what Whitman hoped for: new poems gathered from *Leaves of Grass*.

Johnson's poems talk *on* with, more than they talk back to, Whitman; they literally move into Whitman's words and explore the darknesses there. Johnson's talking back is a talking with, even a talking within, Whitman. Johnson is a master at finding poems by opening up silences within other poems. In his massive *RADI OS*, he creates a long poem by literally canceling out letters of Milton's *Paradise Lost*, allowing a new poem with contemporary themes to emerge from the partially silenced full text of Milton's poem, just as *RADI OS* emerges from *Paradise Lost* if the right letters are removed. In a sense, any editing of a poem for an anthology does the same thing—each generation (and every editor) includes different selections from *Paradise Lost* to reflect changing tastes, personal needs and educational preferences, and shifting critical approaches and to emphasize themes that seem relevant to the current time. Johnson simply takes this commonplace practice a few steps into the *un*commonplace, selecting parts of words rather than sections of poems, groups of letters instead of groups of lines. His version of Milton's epic is just as meticulously accomplished as any edited version; he scrupulously acknowledges what he has deleted by allowing the proper empty spaces (once occupied by Milton's other letters) to appear on the page.

Guy Davenport—reminding us that invention "really means *finding*"—says that what Johnson writes "is not what we ordinarily call a poem" because it "incorporates in generous measure the words of other men" which he "spaces out" to create a "finely textured geometry of words," the quotations "simply a part of the world, like Wordsworth's daffodils, which the poet wishes to bring us" (Johnson, *Valley of Many-Colored Grasses*, 10–11, 13). It might be argued, of course, that to some extent all poets are doing something of the same thing whenever they write, taking the same words, the same letters used by all the poets of the past in all the poems of the past, and allowing new compositions to emerge by altering the old arrangements: thus the burden of the past, the anxiety of influence. Whitman called his own version of this process "composting"—a breaking down of the past in order to reconstruct it into the present. For Whitman, composting was a linguistic process as much as a physical one. When Whitman entitled a poem "This Compost," he was referring not just to the ecology of life cycles but to his very poem, which was itself a construct of words that had been commonly used in the poetic constructions of other poets but which he had now broken down and reorganized into a new structure. Just as he composted his past to create a present poetry that challenged inherited tradition, so do more recent poets break Whitman's poems down to create a present poetry that challenges him while recognizing and honoring him.

Johnson's approach to Whitman is strikingly Whitmanian. Johnson, too, is fascinated with the process of composting and often writes of the necessity of decay to create a fertile soil:

> a humus! (The upper strata—dry newly-
> fallen leaves, twigs, lichen
>
> .   .   .   .
>
> A middle stratum of Sprouting
> —blanched root-threads downward in a rich, dark
> mold & cotyledons curling faintly green toward light—
> Sprouting
> & Decay. Odors of rotted leaves—
>
> .   .   .   .
>
> And the under-ooze & loose loam of slug & worm.)
> (*Valley of Many-Colored Grasses*, 85)

This passage is from the poem that introduces the "Letters to Walt Whitman" in "The Different Musics" (1966–1967), where he takes Whitman's "newly- / fallen" *Leaves* and creates a "Sprouting" out of the century-long "Decay." He writes very much in the spirit of Robert Duncan, who also felt Whitman's lines melding with his own and who, when he says, "Let me join you again this morning, Walt Whitman," means for the joining to occur literally in the poetry—"Even now my line just now walking with yours"—as Whitman's rhythms and phrases and voice mingle with, inspire, and then give way to his own. Johnson begins his poems with lines from Whitman's work, then allows a new poem to emerge from the impulse of those selected lines, echoing and absorbing other words and images from *Leaves*.

It is perhaps not surprising that in addition to poetry, Johnson writes cookbooks. In both poetry and cooking he is concerned with the chemical arts of transformation, of working with original combinations of ingredients to create new meldings: his "Letters to Whitman" are recipes for preparing *Leaves* for renewed consumption. Johnson's cookbooks are composed much like his poetry: cookbooks, too, are never created out of pure inspiration but rather are collected and revised and edited from other cookbooks, the pieces borrowed and recomposed into new formulations. "A lot of the recipes in this book," Johnson says at the beginning of one cookbook, "are worn smooth as river pebbles, and I can no longer say for certain where I first clipped them, who cooked them for me, even what part of the country they came from." His many poetic sources create in his work the same sensation of diligent gathering, of "widening the common table with anything fine he could lay a hand on" (*American Table*, v, ix).

Johnson's "Letters to Whitman" are new preparations of the ingredients in Whitman's poems. An earlier poem by Johnson, "Emanations," explores this "trickling out" (L. *emanare*) of his own poems from Whitman's poems, as he begins with a quotation from "Song of Myself":

> I find I incorporate gneiss, coal, long-threaded moss,
>   fruits, grains, esculent roots,
> And am stucco'd with quadrupeds and birds all over.

These lines allow Johnson's own outstriding, an echo and an advance, as his poem emanates from Whitman's:

> I find I advance with
> sidereal motions
> —my eyes containing substance
>
> of the sun,
> my ears built of beaks & feathers— (*Green Man*, 38)

Letter 10 to Whitman celebrates how Johnson's poems are the result of his careful listening to and absorption of *Leaves*:

> I have put my ear close & close to these lips, heard them
> to the last syllable
> spun out—
>
> .   .   .   .
>
> And ever these nights of 'love-root', sweet
> calamus, embrace me, elusive, illusive, their buzz'd whisper
> ever
> at my ear.
>
> *Echoes, ripples.*
> There are Camerados, Walt—still they come.
> And nights yet to come
>
> to whisper you
> to the ears of others.

Johnson's poems are the echoes, ripples, emanations of Whitman's own poems, and he is Whitman's true camerado, whispering him still to our ears, with new emphases, new insistencies. We hear both Whitman and a Whitman echo.

In his first letter to Whitman, Johnson begins with a quotation from section 49 of "Song of Myself" where Whitman hears the "whispering" of stars and suns and grass and asks, "If you do not say any thing how can I say any thing?" So Johnson seeks out immersion in the world, attempts an identity with the things of nature to the extent that he can feel them express themselves, hearing "messages of the air / (as the air assumes tongues in its swift passage) / wreathing in sibilant expansions / outward" (*Valley of Many-Colored Grasses*, 87). He is like Gary Snyder immersing himself "up to the hips in gods" or W. S. Merwin stripping human speech to silence until he can hear the water laugh:

> Let us tunnel
> the air
>
> .   .   .   .
>
> let us burrow in
> to a susurration, the dense starlings,
>
> of the real—
> the huge
> sunflowers waving back at us,
>
> as we move
>
> —the great grassy world
>
> that surrounds us,
> singing.

Johnson follows Whitman's movement in section 5 of "Song of Myself" from God and transcendence—"Swiftly arose and spread around me the peace and knowledge that pass all the argument of the earth, / And I know that the hand of God is the promise of my own" (91–92)—to the grass and mullein. He probes into Whitman's "limitless" world of the very real, immersing himself in the soil until he hears not so much the song of the self as the song of the leaves of grass (ultimately a very similar song, as Whitman reminds us).

The rest of Johnson's letters to Whitman explore the possibilities of such a joining with the real world. Letter 5 begins with Whitman's "Earth, My Likeness" and, echoing several "Calamus" poems (including "In Paths Untrodden" and "The Prairie-Grass Dividing"), ends with a remarkable evocation of momentary unity with the natural world:

> I have lain in the open night,
>
> til my shoulders felt twin roots, & the tree of my sight

swayed,
among the stars.

I, too, have plucked a stalk of grass

from your ample prairie, Walt.

The act of talking back here involves taking a leaf from Whitman's *Leaves* and contemplating it, like Whitman with *his* prairie
grass: "The prairie-grass dividing, its special odor breathing, / I
demand of it the spiritual corresponding" ("The Prairie-Grass
Dividing," 1–2). Johnson plucks, divides, inhales Whitman's
lines, and demands of them insights and correspondences,
which become his own poems, extensions—or *in*-tensions—of
Whitman's lines.

In Letter 9, Johnson has his most probing discussion with
Whitman, questioning Whitman's notions of reality, challenging
the ease with which he seemingly could ingest the world into his
poetry. As always, the poem begins with Whitman's words:

Landscapes projected masculine,
full-sized and golden . . .
With floods of the yellow gold of the gorgeous, indolent,

sinking sun, burning, expanding the air.

But this time, instead of flowing out of Whitman's lines, Johnson's poem resists and questions:

But are these landscapes to be imagined,
or an actual
Kansas—the central, earthy, prosaic core of us?

Or is the seen always winged, an *eidolon* only to us—&
never
the certain capture
of great, golden, unembroidered

slabs?

All is Oz.
The dusty cottonwoods, by the creek,
rustle an Emerald City.

And the mystic, immemorial city

is rooted in earth.

All is Oz & inextricable,

bound up in the unquenchable flames of double suns.

What we see, Johnson senses, is *always* imagined, always an "*eidolon*" (the word again echoing Whitman, who in his late poem "Eidólons" chants the similar truth, that "All space, all time" is "Fill'd with eidólons only," that the "true realities" are "eidólons," phantoms never finally capturable. All is Oz, the imagined city, but still rooted in an actual Kansas (the Wizard of Oz, after all, turned out to be just a common Kansas huckster). There *is* an actual, then, but we never see it, only the winged self-projections of it—and we can never extricate what we see from what is. Every moment of perception is "bound up in the unquenchable flames of double suns"—the twin suns of reality and our imaginations that in concert illuminate our world. All scenes we see are lit by both the real sun and the sun we hold within us, the sun of our imagination, the sun we conceive to be a sun. Whitman suggested the same binary illumination of world and self in "Song of Myself" where, if it were not for the balancing sun of the self, the rawly illuminated world would be too much to take: "Dazzling and tremendous how quick the sun-rise would kill me, / If I could not now and always send sun-rise out of me" (560–561).

Johnson's discussion with Whitman, then, carries on one of Whitman's deepest concerns: how the poet can "indicate" to men and women "the path between reality and their souls." This, for Whitman, is the poet's whole imaginative purpose, to map out that ground below the twin suns, to give imaginative voice to nature's "dumb, beautiful ministers." (One of Whitman's favorite passages culled from his journal reading was "The mountains, rivers, forests and the elements that gird them round would be only blank conditions of matter if the mind did not fling its own divinity around them" [see *Notes*, 53].)

In Letter 4, Johnson begins with Whitman's lines about how "*The press of my foot to the earth / springs a hundred affections, / They scorn the best I can do to relate them*. . . ." He is fascinated with Whitman's sense of a world teeming with reality that the poet cannot apprehend but knows is there nonetheless: "*The bright suns I see and the dark suns I cannot see are in their place*. . . ." Here are the dual suns again, of course, and as Johnson looks at the world he is aware that we see through a lens of the mind; what we see is colored by what we see with, by what is in our minds. Our senses act as a sieve, sifting out much of what is always before us; the mesh is determined by what we know, by what categories we have been taught to perceive, and the rest is invisible to us:

I see the trees,
the blue accumulations of the air
beyond,
perceived
as through a sieve—

& all, through other, & invisible, convolutions:
those galaxies in a head

close-packed & wheeling.

But realizing this dual perception, the double suns, Johnson is aware that if he keeps his eyes open, his imagination and the world will join again and again in a mass of "new symmetries," new juxtapositions that will allow poetry to happen endlessly:

I am involved with the palpable
as well
as the impalpable,

where I walk, mysteries catch at my heels
& cling
like cockle-burrs.

My affinities are infinite, & from moment to moment
I propagate new symmetries, new

hinges, new edges.

It is appropriate that Wallace Stevens, whose poetic career was dedicated to an exploration of the tensions between rock-hard reality and fluid imagination, chose to portray the sun as Whitman, shifting and incessantly altering our perceptions of the world, fluid as fire and flame:

> In the far South the sun of autumn is passing
> Like Walt Whitman walking along a ruddy shore.
> He is singing and chanting the things that are part of
> him,
> The words that were and will be, death and day.
> Nothing is final, he chants. No man shall see the end.
> His beard is of fire and his staff is a leaping flame. (150)

The sun we see and see by is not a "real" sun at all but a character, a Walt Whitman, created somewhere on the pathway between reality and our souls. As poetic responses like Johnson's make clear, a century after Whitman's death his illumination remains intense.

Free Verse in Whitman and Ginsberg

The Body and the Simulacrum

AMITAI AVI-RAM

Walt Whitman's poetry has been called a "poetry of the body" (Killingsworth), and it is by now very much a commonplace to associate his free verse with the themes of freedom, democracy, and sexual liberation. By contrast, one tends to think of traditional English stress-syllabic meters as restrictive and to associate them with class inequalities and, to put it reductively, with Victorian prudery. These views are consistent with Whitman's own comments, and they continue to inform free verse and the resistance to traditional meters in our own age, which together constitute one of Whitman's most enduring legacies to later poets such as Allen Ginsberg. Yet traditional metrical forms, since they work by invoking in the reader a clear sense of rhythm, might more properly be called "poetry of the body." Ballads, hymns, nursery rhymes, and jingles all seem to invite in the reader a sympathetic response to their rhythms in a way that can be and often is directly reflected in movements and feelings in the body. The continuum from poetry to music to dance is patent in the case of today's rap music, which is composed generally in traditional ballad quatrains or more complex tetrameters. And what can be said for popular tetrameter forms is no less true, if subtler, in the case of the grand, high-style iambic pentameter; even a Shakespearean soliloquy is, by virtue of its mere sounds, a poetry of the body. Meanwhile, a century after Whitman's death, free verse itself has become so highly institutionalized that one may wonder whether we can continue claiming its freshness or even its liberating qualities. If Whitman's poetry is to be called a poetry of the body, it behooves one to account for the ironic fact that the traditional meters against which his free verse rebels are much more obviously "of the body."

If Whitman's poetry is poetry of the body, then what body are we talking about? And what is its relation to poetry? The loss of palpable rhythms is obvious and seems to suggest not a move closer to the body but a move further away. Is there any gain to compensate for this loss? The position taken in this essay is that Whitman's use and promotion of free verse can be understood not as a simple liberation of the body but as a shifting of the body from a realm of direct experience available through palpable and audible musical rhythms in poetry toward an imaginary item which has only a problematic relation to the body itself, a being whose existence can only be inferred by thought. What we have in Whitman is not an appeal to the body through sound but an appeal to the *idea* of the body, imagined to be lurking somewhere underneath the obscuring tissue of representation. In other words, in Whitman we have not the rhythmic body but a simulacrum of the body (Baudrillard). Although Whitman's free verse looks like and has long been taken as a gesture of rebellion against oppressive social rules, it can be understood as an instance of the simulacrum, that is, the replacement of the real thing by a conceptual image of it that can be bought and sold. As such, Whitman's free verse develops concomitantly with the dawning of some of the other features of American culture during the Industrial Revolution and since—especially the shift from actually having physical experience to talking endlessly about it in medical, scientific, and other confessional terms and the ever-increasing isolation of the individual, nowadays felt as an inevitable result of technologies such as cars and television.

The Sympathetic Reading of Whitman's Free Verse

Current views of Whitman's free verse, generally sympathetic, tend to associate it with the overriding theme of similitude. Throughout all the major poems of *Leaves of Grass* before *Drum-Taps* and in many of the later poems as well, the theme can be understood in a general way as the assertion or discovery of the commonality of all beings. All of us—men and women, rich and poor, poet and reader, self and other—are, behind the masks of difference, essentially the same, and it is that similarity that makes sympathy possible, a sympathy usually represented as erotic love and at the same time politicized as democracy. Homoerotic love is privileged in "Song of Myself," "Calamus," and elsewhere, because it is the love of beings who are visibly similar. Even apparent opposites such as animal and vegetable, animate and inanimate, and living and dead are brought into the ever-expanding realm of likeness.

The principle of this likeness is, as Mutlu Konuk Blasing has suggested, the logic of synecdoche. Everything is equivalent to everything else because everything is a part of the same whole: "I too had been struck from the float forever held in solution, / I too had receiv'd identity by my body" ("Crossing Brooklyn Ferry," 62–63). But then everything is also part of everything else, in a sort of mystic relation of parts to wholes. Hence the speaker in "Song of Myself" asks the reader immediately to identify with him—"And what I assume you shall assume, / For every atom belonging to me as good belongs to you" (2–3)—and concludes by avowing, "I contain multitudes." Indeed, the speaker in "Song of Myself" and, perhaps more indirectly and

less self-assuredly in many of the earlier poems, including "Calamus," seems to speak from the position of the Hegelian subject
who has attained the condition of the Absolute and for whom
therefore every part *is* the whole (see Blasing, 130–131; Rukeyser; and Hughes, "Ceaseless Rings"—but see his metrical
tribute, "Old Walt"). Whitman's catalogs in "Song of Myself"
and elsewhere are catalogs of types; everything observable typi-
fies the entire universe of which it is a representative part.

Not only is everything equivalent to everything else, but the
similarity of equivalence among things is hidden, lurking behind
their appearances, and must be revealed by the poet. Hence, in
"Scented Herbage of My Breast," the second poem in "Calamus," the Absolute is figured as death, and everything, including the poet and the poems themselves (the latter figured as
"leaves" or "herbage"), is at once a synecdochic representative
form and a disguise for the "real reality," death:

> Give me your tone therefore O death, that I may accord
>   with it,
> Give me yourself, for I see that you belong to me now
>   above all, and are folded inseparably together, you
>   love and death are,
> Nor will I allow you to balk me any more with what I
>   was calling life,
> For now it is convey'd to me that you are the purports
>   essential,
> That you hide in these shifting forms of life, for reasons,
>   and that they are mainly for you,
> That you beyond them come forth to remain, the real
>   reality,
> That behind the mask of materials you patiently wait, no
>   matter how long (28–34)

The idea that the similarity is hidden behind an outward show
of difference helps to explain Whitman's free-verse form within
Blasing's type of generally sympathetic reading. Although all the
lines of Whitman's poems look and sound different, surface differences conceal an essential likeness, as evidenced by the like-

ness of thought-processes from line to line—that is, the similarity of syntactic structure:

> The aria sinking,
> All else continuing, the stars shining,
> The winds blowing, the notes of the bird continuous
> echoing,
> With angry moans the fierce old mother incessantly
> moaning,
> On the sands of Paumanok's shore gray and rustling,
> The yellow half-moon enlarged, sagging down,
> drooping, the face of the sea almost touching,
> The boy ecstatic, with his bare feet the waves, with his
> hair the atmosphere dallying. ("Out of the Cradle
> Endlessly Rocking," 130–136)

Every item in nature joins in a kind of symphony of erotic desire, surrounding the boy (the speaker's earlier self) with its erotic force to transform him from a boy to an "outsetting bard." In this poem, as in the later "Scented Herbage of My Breast," the essential principle of similitude that binds all of nature and the poet together is the principle of death, made explicit by the sea near the poem's end. The poem suggests that it was the boy's witnessing the loss of the he-bird's mate that made possible his first awareness of this underlying principle of similitude and thus transformed him into a poet, just as it transformed the bird into an operatic singer. In the face of death, bird equals boy equals bard.

This use of syntactic parallelism suggests a unity of form and content that draws the text and the reader's thought-processes together.

Just as Whitman's symbolism denies the hierarchical duality of "seen" form and "unseen" significance, of vehicle and tenor, his verse form rejects the invidious dualism of meter and argument—the significance or inner truth housed in mere meters. For Whitman, the inner and the outer coincide, and his argument is no more an "argument" than his meter is a "metre"—a merely formal, quantitative measurement or, at least, a quantifying qualitative feature of verse.

Whitman's faith in a basic identity shapes every feature of his poetry. This belief yields, for example, an ethic of sympathy, and such a "natural" morality licenses the psychology of identification and projection, justifying the patternless patterns of his poems. The poet is able to move in and out of other lives, for all people feel and think alike, share the same desires, and make the same connections, because we are all constructed alike. (Blasing, 135, 130)

The controlling and ever-present principle of similitude may be thought of as an analogue in poetic technique and thinking to the mind-set which would seem appropriate to democracy. Everyone has a right to a say in government because everyone is fundamentally equal. This is a liberal humanist model of democracy as well. The majority should not make rules that harm minorities, since members of the former should recognize their fundamental likeness to members of the latter. Hence, in "I Sing the Body Electric" and section 7 generally, Whitman can speak on behalf of African-American slaves and can emphasize their humanity: "In this head the all-baffling brain, / In it and below it the makings of heroes" (102–103).

The assertion that there is a fundamental likeness within all beings, behind or beneath the appearance of difference, leads toward an undoing of boundaries and distinctions. Hierarchical differences such as class, gender, or race come to be understood as social contrivances based on mere surface differences. Hence, in Whitman's catalogs of people engaged in their occupations and characteristic activities, "The prostitute draggles her shawl . . . / The crowd laugh at her blackguard oaths . . ." can be followed by "The President holding a cabinet council" ("Song of Myself," 305–306, 308). Likewise, the boundary that is most significant within a discussion of poetic form, that between poetry and prose, is for Whitman false and undemocratic and must be torn down:

In my opinion the time has arrived to essentially break down the barriers of form between prose and poetry. I say the latter is henceforth to win and maintain its character regardless of rhyme, and the measurement-rules of iambic,

spondee, dactyl, &c., and that even if rhyme and those mea-
surements continue to furnish the medium for inferior writers and themes, (especially for persiflage and the comic . . .)
the truest and greatest *Poetry*, (while subtly and necessarily
always rhythmic, and distinguishable easily enough,) can
never again, in the English language, be express'd in the
arbitrary and rhyming metre, any more than the greatest
eloquence, or the truest power and passion. (quoted in
Blasing, 138)

Traditional meters are "arbitrary," according to Whitman, perhaps because they do not proceed "naturally" out of the same
thought-processes that create the thematic content and the images and rhetorical tropes. Clearly, the argument goes, the abandonment of traditional meter is a way of trying to achieve greater
coherency or unity in the relation between form and meaning.
Whitman thus would push poetry, in effect, in the direction of
prose, which is distinguished first of all from poetry by the fact
that one hardly pays attention to the form of prose—the focus is
entirely on content. The sympathetic reading of Whitman's form
need not question the assumption that traditional meters are "arbitrary" and free verse "natural," at least in part because almost
everyone who writes about poetry today assumes a rhetorical
model of poetry in which words, images, statements, tropes,
sound-effects, and form all contribute to the expression of content. This is true in spite of the critics' and Whitman's denial of
any division between form and content. Only by accepting the
idea that sound and form might function as something completely other than signs representing an idea or as supports for
other elements which are signs—only if we could recognize an
inherent meaninglessness at the core of poetic form—could we
begin to think of poetry as having any function other than the
rhetorical expression of an idea. And as long as we do not take
that step, then our very understanding of what poetry is will
push us in the direction in which Whitman already went: the direction of prose. Since our focus in reading prose is on what the
utterance means and not how it sounds or how it induces our
bodies to respond rhythmically, the rhetorical model of poetry

will always allow poetry to be outdone by prose. Clearly, the sympathetic reading of Whitman's form is already leading us into trouble.

Another widespread assumption among sympathetic Whitman readers is that Whitman's free verse represents a rejection of the "shackles" of traditional verse. It is here that we can see most clearly the connection between Whitman's poetic form and the prevalence of the erotic body in his content: the rebellion against "strict" meters is also against the Victorian middle-class repression of sexuality which was a feature of polite speech and therefore could be associated with traditional metrical verse. Thus the rhetoric and imagery in "Calamus," his most concentratedly homoerotic group of poems, emphasize a complex of associated ideas including a refusal to conform to standards imposed from outside (i.e., codes of polite silence), the organic origin of authentic speech in nature, confession, and the homoerotic body:

> In paths untrodden,
> In the growth by margins of pond-waters,
> Escaped from the life that exhibits itself,
> From all the standards hitherto publish'd, from the
>   pleasures, profits, conformities,
> Which too long I was offering to feed my soul,
> Clear to me now standards not yet publish'd, clear to
>   me that my soul,
> That the soul of the man I speak for rejoices in comrades,
> Here by myself away from the clank of the world,
> Tallying and talk'd to here by tongues aromatic [i.e., by
>   leaves of the calamus plant],
>   .   .   .   .
> I proceed for all who are or have been young men,
> To tell the secret of my nights and days,
> To celebrate the need of comrades. ("In Paths
>   Untrodden," 1–9, 16–18)

Whitman's verse is "rough" and comes from "Nature without check with original energy" ("Song of Myself," 13). It poses as the body bursting forth through the bonds of traditional, polite poetry and its attendant meter: "Unscrew the locks from the doors! / Unscrew the doors themselves from their jambs!" ("Song of Myself," 501–502).

But it is also precisely here that we see the inherent problem or contradiction in the sympathetic reading of Whitman's free verse. The reading is overdetermined; free verse means too many things, and these things begin to contradict each other. If Whitman's free verse is supposed to bring out the inherent similitude of all things, then it must show a continuity between the present and the past—which would argue for traditionality in form. If traditions are to be broken to make room for the new and the free, then the universe is not all the same but rather dual: there is a contrast between the standards imposed from outside and the authentic voice of nature with its "original energy."

What presents itself as a freeing of the body, moreover, is in another sense a suppression of the body—that is, a suppression of rhythm that can be heard and felt and its replacement with a great deal of talk about the freeing of the body. The place of the body has shifted from the physical experience of rhythm to the realm of discourse. If the unity of the world is to be felt everywhere in its material, bodily presence, then it would make better sense to make it felt precisely where it is most convincingly felt, in rhythm. Instead, we have words and images which provoke us not to *feel* our bodily presence but to *infer* the bodily presence of that which is suggested by the images. We have only images of what is made absent by the very presence of those words, in contrast to the words of traditionally metered poetry which actually conform to an audible rhythm and therefore function, on at least one level, as something other and more immediate than signification or representation. Whitman gives us not the body but a simulacrum of the body.

The Contexts of Whitman's Form

Whitman's shift toward the simulacrum of the body makes sense within the social context of the nineteenth century, which brought us the advent of psychoanalysis and other "discursive formations" such as criminal justice and sexology. The Victorian

Age was full of paradoxical symmetries. It was particularly un-seemly for middle-class people to speak openly about sex, yet there were more prostitutes in London than ever before. Psycho-analysis seemed to correct this imbalance by allowing the silent body recognition in speech. But as Michel Foucault suggests, the result was not the liberation of the body—far from it. People were endlessly talking about sex but in such a way as to prevent all that speech from ever allowing the actual pleasure of the body. Sex was taken away from the body and put into speech. Indeed, in early psychoanalytic practice the patient was rou-tinely asked to stop having sex as long as he or she was in analy-sis. Meanwhile, in poetry, the heavy-handed metrical rhythms of such Victorian standards as Longfellow's *Song of Hiawatha*, while clearly making some auditory appeal to the listener's body, also dramatize the suppression of the body in content. Others, like Tennyson's *In Memoriam*, simply leave the body out. In such po-etry, rhythm made its appeal to the body unconsciously, while the surface images and statements repressed that appeal. By con-trast, in Whitman's poetry, as in psychoanalysis, the body is loudly proclaimed in the overt content, while it is actually sup-pressed from any direct experience through rhythm.

Whitman's formal innovation can also be seen in the con-text of the shared poetic tradition. Whereas seventeenth- and eighteenth-century thinkers accepted the inherent arbitrariness and conventionality of signs (Locke, 268; Burke, 163–177), this assumption seems to have become more troublesome in the nine-teenth century, perhaps because religious faith was on the wane and therefore there was the danger that God might not manifest an immediate presence to insure the continued possibility of meaning despite the arbitrariness of signs. Thus Baudelaire's poem "Correspondances" in *Les Fleurs du mal*, which later be-came the keynote of symbolism, was almost exactly contempo-rary with Whitman's early work and was equally concerned with the discovery of similitudes that would inform the universe and save its connection with the divine by virtue of that similitude. Everything is like everything else, and everything is a manifesta-tion of a unitary principle, which is God (see de Man). This is, in effect, a version of the ancient doctrine of signatures, which made repeated appearances in late antiquity, medieval and Renaissance poetry, and seventeenth- and eighteenth-century mysticisms such as that of Swedenborg before arriving on Baudelaire's pages.

But it is also noteworthy that neither Baudelaire nor the symbolists, except Rimbaud (if he can be included in that group), rejected traditional French meter. Rather, Baudelaire seems to have exploited the idea of an all-encompassing physical rhythm which is revealed differently but analogously in the world of each individual sense. In Baudelaire, the rhythm reassures us that we are more like the speaker than unlike him, and, like him, we must celebrate the evils of a fallen world—enabling the speaker to call us *"mon semblable, mon frère."* In Baudelaire, the identity between reader and speaker and among all things, outside of and prior to the words and images, begins with the rhythmic body.

It is possible to argue, nevertheless, that such a contrast between Whitman and Baudelaire is unfair and that Whitman's poetry is *not* without rhythm, it simply follows a different rhythmic principle. Whereas traditional European meters are based on repeated configurations of sound qualities (such as syllables, stress, or quantity), Whitman's meter is based on repeated structures of syntax.

This argument sometimes cites the Bible as a model, an observation suggested by Gay Wilson Allen (*American Prosody*, 217–243) and easily supported by Whitman's general prophetic tone. This hypothesis also seems appealing because it places Whitman in a tradition which includes the religious and eccentric poem "Jubilate Agno" by the mid-eighteenth-century English poet Christopher Smart, whose form clearly imitates the New Testament beatitudes, as well as some "prophetic" writings of the late-eighteenth-century English poet William Blake, such as *The Marriage of Heaven and Hell* (although most of his "prophetic" works are in traditional fourteeners).

Granted that the English Bible might well have been a model for Whitman, there are a number of problems with the notion that Whitman would therefore have developed a rhythmic device whose effectiveness could equal that of traditional meters. First of all, as Whitman could have known, the English Bible provides line-by-line prose translations from a verse original; he certainly knew that, as a translation, it could not give him the sounds of the original. And although today some scholars believe that Hebrew biblical poetry is not metrical in the usual sense, nineteenth-century biblical scholars tended to go on the opposite assumption (Kugel, 70–76). Second, the nonmetricality of biblical poetry in translation would have come to Whitman along with the immediate social context of Christian tradition and metaphysics. As such, unmetricality would fit in with the Christian teachings that recommend transcendance of the body and prefer the soul in contradistinction to the body. Thus Whitman claims "I am the poet of the Body and I am the poet of the Soul" ("Song of Myself," 422) within a form in which the body is effaced and whose model (if the Bible is the model) connotes anti-body metaphysics—at least as much as traditional meters, for Whitman, connoted Victorian values.

Finally, it must be owned that Whitman's poetry does not resemble the poetry of the Bible very closely, if at all: it does not follow the binary/ternary pattern of "balance" as a rule. In some ways Whitman's verse may rather resemble literal prose translations from ancient Greek and Latin poetry (Avi-ram, 137–147; Rukeyser, 109). But then, as Roman Jakobson has shown, most poetry evidences syntactic patternings which work in a way analogous to their sound patterns. To say that Whitman's poetry resembles *any* poetry translated from another language into line-by-line prose is to say that it is poetry without sound patterns, poetry which preserves the other common features of the tradition but not the one feature which perhaps sets all the others in motion to begin with, the palpable and audible rhythm. Indeed, if Whitman's poetry follows models of poetry in translation, then one can draw an analogy that supports my initial claim that Whitman's verse gives us not the body but a simulacrum of the body—that is, Whitman's verse is to the rhythmic body as prose translations are to their verse originals.

Perhaps the safest claim to be made about the possible traditional context in which to place Whitman's poetic form, however, is that Whitman's poetry resembles most closely the form of public oratory prevalent in his time (and still today, as in the speeches of Jesse Jackson). Here, syntactic repetition and certain local sound-patternings prevail without any sense of a consistent underlying musical beat (Hollis). It is worth noting that, especially among ancient Greek and Roman writers, oratory is one of the two modes of literary discourse consistently opposed to poetry, the other being history. Oratory has the purpose of persuasion and therefore must harness the power of the body's rhythms without giving way too much to their irrational power.

The Death of the Body in Whitman

The suppression of the body from Whitman's verse-form and its replacement by a simulacrum in content can be seen to register itself in a variety of expressions and images in Whitman's poems. For example, when Whitman says that he sings of himself, when he refers to his poems as "these songs," he can mean those words only figuratively. It is traditional to use words of singing to refer to poetry—in several languages, including Hebrew, there is only one word for both "song" and "poem"—but this is precisely because the poem in these cases is not simply a figurative song. Rather, there is both a known etiological or historical continuity—poems are songs in written form or spoken without melody but with rhythm—and an implied possibility of reversing the process by setting the poems to a music that preserves their existing musical structures. In Whitman, "song" is a somewhat dead metaphor because it is traditional and yet lacks the traditional base in something concrete about the poems' very sound.

The death of song is also the death of the body to which a song would make its rhythmic, nonlinguistic, nonsymbolic appeal. One can actually discover references to this death if one reads certain of Whitman's poems as allegories of their own loss of the original, rhythmic, bodily being. Take for example Whitman's fairly early and deeply moving poem, "Out of the Cradle Endlessly Rocking." The poem begins with a long sentence composed of many parallel subordinate clauses which are the basis of its verse-structure, a sentence which ends with its main clause, "I, chanter of pains and joys . . . A reminiscence sing."

The poem recounts how the speaker has become a poet. As a child, he would listen to the songs of two mockingbirds, mates, delighting in their togetherness. Whitman does not use the word *song* until near the end of the poem, but it is probably important that we know that this is the word conventionally used. The speaker would "translate" the birds' songs into words, which he then records as part of the poem. This phase of the poem and of the speaker's young life serves as a kind of apprenticeship. What is significant is that the speaker is already "translating": what we read and what was really heard are at one remove from the immediacy of sound.

Next we learn that the she-bird is gone, never to return. Again, the speaker-as-boy translates the he-bird's "notes." Allegorically, we can read the she-bird's loss as the loss of the original song, for which we have only the translation. The she-bird's disappearance is a way that the loss of song-rhythms can be bodied forth figuratively in the image-language of the poem. In the poem, all we have left of the she-bird is the he-bird's expression of his desire for his lost mate. Likewise, the speaker's translations of these songs are an expression of his own longing, his own "sweet hell within, / The unknown want." Now that I am the outsetting bard, says the speaker, "Never more the cries of unsatisfied love be absent from me." In other words, the poem's allegory works on the analogy: he-bird's song is to she-bird as speaker's "song" is to bird's song.

Part of what is so compelling about the translation of the he-bird's second song is the delay in his recognition of the loss. Most of it, until line 119, issues out of a denial of the loss, a denial rich in poignant irony. The he-bird's eventual coming to terms with reality is the first of the poem's three climactic moments and is paralleled with the poem's third climax, when the sea issues up its "word final, superior to all" and the word *death* is repeated as an incantation. The speaker becomes an "outsetting bard" at the earlier climactic moment, when he has received and translated the he-bird's song, including the latter's sober acceptance of his loss. But at this earlier point the speaker has songs within him without any "key." This "key" is a figure for the word *death*. Thus the speaker's own "song," just like the bird's actual song, is motivated by the transition from naïve denial to acceptance of the reality of death. But while this reality is clear in the case of the bird, what is its analogue for the speaker? It is the death of song itself—as a reality rather than as a figure of speech. The speaker recounts the translation of the bird's song so long as he can deny the impossibility of that translation ever actually being a song. The sea's "clew," its "key," completes the speaker's knowledge by translating his own experience into the appropriate word, "death." At this point the speaker has no further to go, the illusion is broken, and the poem must come to an end.

But before this end, the second climax represents the speaker's delirium between denial and conscious knowledge as an orgasmic moment that unites the speaker with the entirety of surrounding nature. But this orgasm is achieved at the expense of the reality of nature, since nature at this point, including the he-bird himself, is transformed into a tragic operatic scene played out for his own solipsistic delight:

> The love in the heart long pent, now loose, now at last
>   tumultuously bursting,
> The aria's meaning, the ears, the soul, swiftly
>   depositing,
> The strange tears down the cheeks coursing,
> The colloquy there, the trio, each uttering,
> The undertone, the savage old mother incessantly
>   crying,
> To the boy's soul's questions sullenly timing, some
>   drown'd secret hissing,
> To the outsetting bard. (137–143)

It is striking how in this passage the speaker's orgasm is achieved precisely at the moment that the bird becomes the tenor singing an aria and nature becomes artifice—in other words, at the moment when what we thought was nature is revealed to be a mere simulacrum, an operatic scene. The only figure that remains is the "savage old mother," a "discordant" element in the scene, clearly not part of what is on stage. The message that death is the real meaning of the scene appears at the very moment that the speaker takes delight in its drama.

The sea is not a figure for the death of song but the source of the conscious articulation of that death. The sea's word *death*, however "low and delicious," is, after all, a translation for what actually occurred—that is, it substitutes the thing itself for its appropriate word—and is here a translation of a translation, from the bird's song to the speaker's "song" and from this loss to the word itself. At the same time, the word brings to an end the search for the knowledge of its own secret and thus brings the poem as a whole to an end.

But why should the origin of this conscious knowledge be portrayed as a "savage old mother" or "some old crone rocking the cradle, swathed in sweet garments, bending aside"? The sea is an instance of the mythic type of the "death-mother," the obverse side of the mother as origin of life: "Naked came I out of my mother's womb and naked shall I return" (Job 1:21). The crone is specifically represented as rocking the cradle, a powerful image of how the physical sense of rhythm is learned, nurtured, and encouraged by the mother even before speech is acquired. Who would know better about the loss of song and the death of rhythm in its literal, physical sense than the very being who first brought rhythm forth into the world for the child? The mother recognizes death for what it is and gives it a name which itself is a death and brings about the death of the poem, that is, the poem's end.

Thus "Out of the Cradle Endlessly Rocking" works as an allegory for its own relation to traditional poetic rhythm. The effacement of audible, palpable, songlike and dancelike rhythms and their replacement by mere figures and images of the body on the thematic surface are themselves figured dually as translation and death. And for this same death-by-translation we can now give a new name, the word that comes up from the sea of theory: the simulacrum.

Allen Ginsberg, the Simulacrum, and the Search for the Real

Whitman's free verse offers later poets a dual legacy. On the one hand, his replacement of the body with its simulacrum, of the body-in-form with the body-in-content, is akin to many other areas of repression in modern life. On the other hand, Whitman's more overt claim to spontaneity and naturalness may seem appealing as a way out of that very repression. The fact that the one side of Whitman is inseparable from the other puts poets of our age, such as Allen Ginsberg, in a position of intense ambivalence toward him. Ginsberg's encounter with Whitman is especially important because it contextualizes the simulacrum in the larger social scene of consumer capitalism.

I have been using the word *simulacrum* throughout this essay with special reference to Jean Baudrillard's recent cultural criticism. For Baudrillard, the society described by Foucault as full of talk about sex without pleasure itself has grown into a nightmare of images that create reality. The United States, according to Baudrillard, is especially characterized by images or fetish-objects that purport to refer back to some original "real thing" but that actually are substitutes for reality—a reality that itself does not exist; actually, reality *is* these false images. For example, television networks claim that they show us what we want to see—programs are a reflection of our reality. But our opinions about what we want to see and even our habits and decisions are based on what we see on television. Likewise, in politics, democracy itself is reduced to a mere effect of a circle of market research and targeted advertising. Political representation is a simulacrum of an original political will that does not actually exist.

Another characteristic of the society of simulation, one that has particular bearing on the Whitman-Ginsberg relationship, is the loneliness and isolation that come with the simulacrum. Today, instead of leaving our homes to see real people perform for us, to hear them, feel them, dance with them, we stay home and watch images of people doing these things on television. We eat a simulacrum of restaurant food defrosted in the microwave. Our automotive-age cities are vast networks of highways, malls, and suburban "neighborhoods." We have gone out of our way to avoid having more than the minimal contact with each other—as real people—or with nature as a daily presence. When we occasionally feel the need for such things, we can visit a national park (or watch one on a television documentary) or a reconstructed historic village such as Williamsburg. We are perishing of utter loneliness and desolation in the midst of our affluence.

This is the very America to which Ginsberg and so many other American writers have reacted. And, understandably, one of the poetic models to whom Ginsberg turned was Whitman. Foremost among the attractions Whitman's free verse offers, presumably, is a sense of authenticity created by the appearance of spontaneity. Along with spontaneity, of course, come the equality, democracy, and sexual freedom which are suggested by the baring of the essential person in spontaneous verse within the sympathetic reading of Whitman's free verse.

But what Whitman actually offers is the appearance of spontaneity, a simulacrum of the body. There is no evidence that Ginsberg consciously thought of Whitman in these critical terms— quite the contrary (see Ginsberg's rambling "Allen Ginsberg on Walt Whitman"). But he need not have done so in order to be confronted with the loss of palpable musical rhythms as the cost of spontaneity, rhetorical directness, and a populism of style, especially since Ginsberg's first book of poems, *The Gates of Wrath*, rhymed after the model of William Blake, Ginsberg's first inspiration. In "A Supermarket in California," Ginsberg figures his own impossible search for an authenticity that would include the body, appropriately, as an encounter with Whitman in a modern supermarket, an encounter whose playful tone sustains a tension between satirical irony and earnest tragedy.

The speaker, thinking of Walt Whitman and suffering from a headache of self-consciousness, resorts to the relief popular in simulacrum-age America, going shopping. He shops "for images," betraying his awareness of the priority of simulacra: even the fruits (in both senses?) as well as the shoppers are mere images of something purportedly real.

> I saw you, Walt Whitman, childless, lonely old grubber, poking among the meats in the refrigerator and eyeing the grocery boys.
> I heard you asking questions of each: Who killed the pork chops? What price bananas? Are you my Angel? (23)

The figure of Whitman is simultaneously the redeemer from simulacra and the very prophet of simulacra. He is characteristically childless and lonely even though, figuratively and poetically, Ginsberg is demonstrating his lineage from Whitman in this very poem. The grocery boys are only too much like the meats which Whitman pokes; neither is more real or less a mere commodity than the other. The same logic holds for the juxtaposition of killed pork chops, priced bananas, and angels.

Shopping is an erotic flirtation both with the imaginary "real" to be found somehow waiting underneath the fruits and meats and with the "real" Whitman who also suffers from the isolation brought about by the reign of the simulacrum. In response to Whitman's assertion in "So Long!" that "this is no book, / Who touches this touches a man," Ginsberg's speaker responds, "I touch your book and dream of our odyssey in the supermarket and feel absurd." The speaker implicitly recognizes the problem inherent in Whitman's characteristic line: it can work both ways, to vivify the book or, more likely, to suggest that there can be no man to touch, only the simulacrum of the man to be found in the book. The very physicality that Whitman seems so strenuously to have championed is destroyed and replaced by a simulacrum, not in the wake of Whitman but already in Whitman's own verse. Whitman becomes the prophet of rebellion against supermarket culture and the prophet of that very supermarket.

Ginsberg's poem attains an unexpected redemption, not so much by the invocation of Whitman as by the invocation of a whole tradition of poetry suggested by allusions, of which the one to "So Long!" is the first. The second occurs in the next long line:

Will we walk all night through solitary streets? The trees add shade to shade, lights out in the houses, we'll both be lonely. (23)

In the context of this melancholic poem, it is hard to escape the echo in "shade to shade" of Keats's "Ode on Melancholy": "For shade to shade will come too drowsily, / And drown the wakeful anguish of the soul" (247).

These lines warn the melancholic of the consequences of the suicide he is contemplating. "Shade" in the first instance is meant in the classical sense—the disembodied spirit of the dead, which in Latin poetry is also sometimes called simulacrum. Keats warns that suicide will put to sleep the anguished rhythms of alternating joy and melancholy, figured in the next stanza by natural images such as rain and flowers in spring (as part of the rhythm of the seasons) and waves of sea and sand. All of these images in turn may be seen as dream-images representing the slow but inevitable beat of Keats's verse itself. Do not commit suicide or you will bring this poem to an end too soon and banish its rhythms to forgetfulness: "No, no, go not to Lethe."

The danger here is that Whitman's image in Ginsberg's poem will only add "shade to shade" in the solitary streets, for the body's rhythm has already been foreclosed from poetry by Whitman's very effort to find vitality in a departure from poetic tradition. The allusion in a very Whitmanian way also preserves a sense of the tradition underlying the poetry, a faint memory of the rhythmic body that might have been there. Yet there is a difference: by using Keats's very words we have not only an allusion but a material echo. There is some possibility of a recollection of that body, both poetically through echo and physically through actual sexual contact with someone who is neither Whitman nor the speaker. This is only a faint possibility, but it is there.

An even bolder allusion supports this one and closes Ginsberg's poem:

Ah, dear father, graybeard, lonely old courage-teacher, what America did you have when Charon quit poling his

ferry and you got out on a smoking bank and stood watching the boat disappear on the black waters of Lethe? (24)

Here, Whitman's cheerful transcendental vision in "Crossing
Brooklyn Ferry" is recalled through the more traditional, classical image from which it is drawn. But at the same time, the image
seals the fate of Whitman's body and allows his ghost to rest on
the far side of the river of forgetfulness. Although the poem itself
does not resuscitate the rhythms that Whitman had lost, it enacts
the work of mourning for Whitman's gesture of renunciation.
There is room to dream of a freedom to remain on this side of
Lethe and to begin anew the rhythms of reality that the shades
have abandoned. Ginsberg is an Orpheus returned from the
dead who has not yet begun to sing anew the old strains that had
charmed the very trees.

Of course, this moment hardly signals a breaking point for
Ginsberg, nor for his generation. On the contrary, much of his
poetry and of American poetry since the fifties has continued
to represent the disembodiment of the Whitmanian free-verse
simulacrum. But Ginsberg's many later poems that are in meters
or close to meters, his performances of Blake's and his own verse
chanted to musical sounds, and his recent collaboration with
composer Philip Glass to form a musical *Gesamtkunstwerk* suggest an opposite tendency as well. Ginsberg's deep understanding of the dual bequest of both spontaneity and simulation and his
consequent ambivalence find a particularly poignant expression
in this early work, and a like ambivalence continues to charac-
terize the present scene in American poetry. It cannot do otherwise for, in poetry as in life, we are now surrounded by the very
simulacra toward which Whitman was both a rebel in opposition
and a cheerful prophet and contributor.

It doesn't take a lot of looking at David Hockney's paintings to realize
they're not about homosexuality.
—Michael Goldfarb

Fetishizing America

David Hockney and Thom Gunn

ROBERT K. MARTIN

Ten years separate the first visits the British artists David
Hockney and Thom Gunn made to America. Though their class
backgrounds and education are different, a look at their American work, particularly in the first years of their American experience, may illustrate certain shared ways of imagining America,
ways that reflect the complex relationships between projection
and reflection. While there is not space to go into the question
here, some of what can be observed in their poetry and paintings
may be of use in understanding the presentation of America in
many other works, including films such as Wenders's *American
Friend* or *Alice in the Cities* or Fassbinder's *American Soldier*. The

perspective of the outsider allows for a disengagement composed of simultaneous attraction and critical distance. The objects of everyday life, seen by the stranger's eyes, are decontextualized and hence re-created as pure objects.

In this regard Hockney and Gunn may be seen to play an important role in the mid-century reaction against modernism. Both were, at least in part, the product of modernist training and assumptions, but both attempt to modify those conventions and work toward the reestablishment of the figurative, the ethical, and the domestic. The two men incorporate the familiar images of popular culture into their works, showing the ways in which such figures or icons create social meaning. Both also make use of a constructed vision of America as part of an implicit critique of their European and British heritage and as a model for a socially situated sexuality.

Although Whitman had written a century earlier, the example of his use of native material may well lie behind these later examples, for he did much to create a certain American *imaginaire*, one which joins space, democracy, and the appeal of the youthful male body. However much his poems are set in Manhattan and celebrate an urban vision of multiplicity and continually renewed erotic opportunity, he was even more a poet of the as yet unstructured space of what he liked to call the "inland sea." Whitman's "promise to California" assured his future western readers that he would bring them "robust American love," the only love appropriate to this new, yet to be invented space. To this world would come the "tan-faced children," "the youthful sinewy races" whose bodies would quite literally represent a political and erotic future. A hundred years later that dream had been rendered somewhat banal, but it kept much of its fascination for a European visitor as well as for the thousands of gay male viewers who continue to locate their fantasies in a southern California choreographed by William Higgins.

Gunn's first American trip in 1954 was marked by the impact of what he has called "the American myth of the motorcyclist" as well as by the sense of a "foreign and exotic landscape," composed of elements of nature such as the palm trees—

visible in Hockney's early work as well, especially the Pershing Square tribute to John Rechy—and cultural phenomena including broad streets with fast cars and the "dirty glamour of a leather bar" (*Occasions of Poetry*, 177). This landscape was recorded in several poems in his first volume following his stay in America. The tone is set by the opening poem of *The Sense of Movement*, "On the Move," first published in 1955, with its concluding dateline, California, as if the poem itself were a record of the discovery of this new landscape. The motorcycle boys are at once erotic, as the noise of the cycles "Bulges to thunder held by calf and thigh," and artificial, the product of an existentialist Will. Similarly, the hustler in "Market at Turk" is "buckle[d] in" by "hard discipline." Such erotic figures are part of Gunn's reaction in "Lines for a Book" against a soft, liberal tradition of "pale curators." Through them Gunn uses his American experience to challenge the cultural assumptions of his own youth. Part of their appeal is also their transgressive quality, since they are hardly a traditional subject for poetry.

Similarly transgressive is Gunn's "Elvis Presley" poem, at least in subject matter. As in the poems already mentioned, Gunn does not make use of the free verse that had by then become a modernist convention, particularly in America, but instead continues to work in rhyming iambic pentameter. Although there may be a number of reasons for this choice, one of them is certainly the value of constraint, for Gunn's poems of the 1950s are preeminently poems of choice and limitation. In this he sees himself as like Elvis: "Our idiosyncrasy and our likeness." What Gunn admires in Presley is not his content, merely "hackneyed words in hackneyed songs," but his ability to aestheticize, to turn "revolt into a style." Popular culture, like bar life and the creation of an erotic self, is part of a project of cultural transformation. A poem such as "Elvis" would be echoed a few years later by Hockney in his Cliff Richard paintings and even later by a number of Warhol portraits; what is central to these projects is an attempt to break down hierarchical barriers between "high" and "low" art as well as a move to reintegrate representation without simple reproduction.

Although the leather boys are Gunn's most important recurring erotic image, they are by no means the only one he employs. In the poem "From the Wave" (1967), he makes use of the figure of the surfer, a crucial part of the mythology of California, especially for gay men. Here, as with Hockney, the interest appears to lie more in the encounter of human body and water. We never actually see the surfers, although they seem to prevail over nature as "they slice the face / In timed procession." In fact, their success lies in their ability to "imitate" the wave, to take on the rhythms of nature, act in harmony with it, as they "wait until / The right waves gather." In this they represent a considerable change against the earlier heroes of defiance and defeat. The poem's revision of Auden's 1935 "Look, stranger, at this island now," with its lines, "And the shingle scrambles after the suck- / ing surf," serves as a sign of Gunn's distance from his youthful models and his move toward the greater prosodic freedom hinted at in the "bare foot." The self-control, even self-punishment of the stricter forms, gives way to a more relaxed expression.

In an earlier poem, "Flying above California" (1961), Gunn had already begun to develop his metrical resources. The poem's half-rhyming syllabic couplets provide an appropriate form for this exploration of an embodied landscape. The "lean upland / sinewed and tawny in the sun" is simultaneously the state and the male body that represents it. California is "Mediterranean and Northern," offering a sensuality without softness. The poem concludes in praise of the "cold hard light," the absence of shadow and, by implication, of a past "that reveals merely what is." The scene is thus praised as if it were a photographic record in full sunlight, offering a "limiting candor," a blank truth that must be at once enough and not enough. As with Gunn's "toughs" who are all pose and no content, so his flat landscape is the richness of the meagre. It not only must be enough, it is valued as an escape from a tradition of deception.

That flattening light is also dominant in David Hockney's California paintings of only a few years later. Like Gunn, Hockney began his career in England, but, also like the poet, he may be said to have found his real subject in America and in his role as the painter of southern California's blank facades. His

world is as empty and melancholy as that of one of his American
mentors, Edward Hopper. Long before he had actually traveled
to the United States, Hockney had immersed himself in several
aspects of American culture. Among the most important for his
early years was his wide reading of Walt Whitman, which he un-
dertook in the summer of 1960, the hundredth anniversary of the
publication of Whitman's "Calamus" sequence. The most explicit
record of this interest can be found in Hockney's 1961 etching
Myself and My Heroes, which celebrates both Whitman and
Gandhi. The etching was the result of a decision made during his
student years to create out of his political and social convictions.
Whitman and Gandhi were figures of peace, of course, but they
also represented two more specific interests of Hockney's, homosexuality and vegetarianism. Hockney's emphasis on the "Calamus" poems was not simply occasioned by their anniversary but
rather by his search for a way to give expression to his own sexuality and its place in a social order.

During the early years of the 1960s Hockney made a number of
works that celebrate Whitman and his poetry and that proclaim
his sexuality as an important part of his nature as a poet, at a
time when this view was hardly ever acknowledged. The oil
painting *Adhesiveness* (1960) celebrates both Whitman's personal
experience of his sexuality, in his relationship with Peter Doyle,
and Whitman's ascription of a larger meaning to that sexuality, in
his adaptation of the phrenological term *adhesiveness* for male
love. Hockney's use in such a painting of the naïve style he had
derived largely from Dubuffet (see Webb, 38) indicates that, although very early on in his career he wanted to reinsert the human in the modernist tradition, he was not seeking to return to a
form of portraiture. Hockney records the figures in all his works
of his period as representations of a meaning situated historically. Whitman is present in the painting as someone who has
been able to make his sexuality part of his art. Hockney is thus
recording Whitman's meaning for him and not Whitman himself.
At the same time, the excerpts from Whitman, like most of the
textual fragments present in the paintings of this period, indicate
a reaction against the pure modernist notion of refusal of the verbal. Although the texts may recall Victorian painting, with its

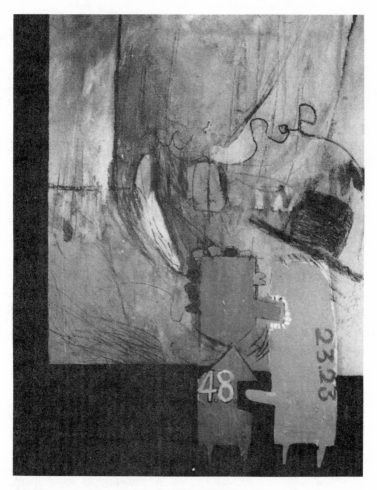

Adhesiveness, 1960, copyright David Hockney.

moral and narrative inscriptions, they actually function in a very
different way. For one thing, their form makes them look like
graffiti rather than a serious literary reference. Presented only as
fragments, these words are not part of an attempt to re-create the
poem or allusions to a once unshattered past (as in Eliot's *Waste
Land* fragments), they are objects that stand for the poem and
capture a part of it. Hockney's citations serve to locate his work
not in some timeless realm of art but in a specific historical context that includes both oppression and resistance.

The numerical code by which D.H. becomes 4.8 and W.W.

23.23 serves to indicate the artist's indebtedness to the poet. It is derived from Whitman's notations in which he recorded his love in a somewhat concealed form in his diaries (at the same time that he changed the pronouns to protect himself against discovery). Hockney's public works make the kind of proclamation that was, at least sometimes, impossible for Whitman. They also acknowledge an artistic indebtedness as one of the possible forms of love. (This idea is by no means restricted to shared sexuality for Hockney. He depicts himself nude with Picasso in *Artist and Model*, a 1974 etching.) But in the 1960 painting it was important for Hockney to record Whitman's need to censor himself at the same time that he could explicitly sexualize the relationship. It is not merely that Hockney shares an intellectual perception of sexuality with Whitman but that he feels himself loved by and loving Whitman.

We Two Boys Together Clinging (1961) makes even greater use of the text, in this case from Whitman's twenty-sixth "Calamus" poem of the same name. The figures resemble those in *Adhesiveness*, although now without any identification. The text slopes around the back of the right-hand figure, thus impelling him toward the other, to whom he is joined not only by an embracing arm but also by a series of lines linking the two bodies. This central panel is framed by two hearts, one on the right and one on the left, one red and the other blue, while the central figures are in shades of purple, joining the two. On the left the word "boy" appears, both in a formal printed version and as an element of graffiti, where it is followed immediately by "man." On the right-hand side of the canvas Hockney has quoted lines 5 and 6 of the poem, "Power enjoying, elbows stretching, fingers clutching, / Arm'd and fearless, eating, drinking, sleeping, loving," while the figure on the left speaks the word "never," from the poem's second line, "One the other never leaving." Even in these early paintings, along with their celebration of a free sexuality there is a strong appeal to the domestic and lasting in male love.

The apparent signature of the painting, the 4.2 or D.B. at the bottom left, is a reference to Hockney's pop star Cliff Richard, whom he represented as *Doll Boy* in another painting from this period. Hockney's decision to record his attraction for the singer

We Two Boys Together Clinging, 1961, Arts Council Collection, South Bank Centre, London, copyright David Hockney.

was, he has explained, a response to the female pinups the straight students hung in their cubicles. The term "doll" was based on Richard's song "Living Doll," but Hockney made Richard into his "doll," expressing his infatuation with the singer as an act of public avowal and at the same time arranging the images so they show the pressures of conventionality that will work against the love. The singer's head is bowed, presumably by the same pressures that write "Queen" on his clothing (apparently a dress). The graffiti in the lower right-hand corner spell out two messages, "Valentine" and "Your love means more to me," both somewhat ironic in their relationship to the necessary heterosexuality of mass culture. Packaging is similarly suggested in *The Most Beautiful Boy in the World*, where Hockney also plays with his numerical code by introducing the "other code" of 69. Here the naked male body is visible beneath the transparent dress that is the signifier of desirability.

In such works Hockney was looking for ways to situate his sense of himself; his inability to do so seems reflected in the

cramped and tortured quality of many of these images. Although
in at least one work he tried to find a symbolic place in Berlin, the
possibility of reviving the "Berlin meant boys" world of the 1920s
in the 1960s was small. Hockney came to locate his symbolic
"great good place" in California, and he made that identification,
beginning what Henry Geldzahler has called his "love-affair with
America," even before he had ever gone there. Like his model
Whitman, Hockney celebrated a generic American young man,
Whitman's "tan-faced prairie boy," a figure seemingly without
history or guile, meant to evoke a type rather than to establish an
identity. On such figures the American gay imagination of the
1950s and 1960s was nurtured.

The first of the California paintings is *Domestic Scene, Los
Angeles* of 1963. The source of this was a gay magazine, *Physique
Pictorial* (Webb, 55), the same source Hockney had used for his
required academic nude at the RCA, thus making a witty comment on the relationship of the academic nude to homosexual
iconography. In Hockney's painting of an imaginary Los Angeles, his sense of humor is obvious. The apron, used presumably as a cache-sexe in the magazine, is here an absurd element
of the domestic. The white socks take on a fetishistic quality, as
does the water of the shower. Hockney was fascinated by American showers and by the movement of water. Although this painting gave him the chance to portray the male nude, it also provided the opportunity to explore the conventions of the static
portrayal of movement. The two characters do not relate to each
other; as is usual in Hockney paintings, they each inhabit a private world, even in the most intimate moments.

One of the hallmarks of Hockney's work is the simultaneous yearning for communion and its impossibility. *Man Taking a
Shower in Beverly Hills* (1964) represents a single individual and is
rendered with far greater realism and observed detail. The body
is sculpted, bent forward in a way that emphasizes the muscles
as well as the inviting ass. The absence of facial detail and the
care with which the tiles are done indicate that once again this is
not to be seen as a portrait but rather as the depiction of a characteristic activity. This is a picture of someone taking a shower,

which is to say of the relationship between the body and water. The artist's role as voyeur is emphasized by the open curtain and the distant living room, while the absence of perspective signals the painting's lack of "realism." The male body and the flowing water have been fetishistically invested with all the power of Hockney's American dream.

As Hockney came to know California better, his fascination shifted from the English lower-middle-class vision of the shower to a concern with the swimming pool. Hockney's use of this motif is far removed from any "swimming hole" tradition of American painting or English homosexual literature. There are no frolicking youths like those Whitman celebrated and taught E. M. Forster to admire in *A Room with a View*. Hockney's pools are most often empty, signs of the vacancy of California life. *Sunbather* (1966) shows the development of Hockney's imagery. The bottom two-thirds of the canvas is based on a photograph of water, using curving lines as a signifier of movement rather than its depiction. The upper third of the painting is based on an image from a magazine and has the bland anonymity of such an illustration. There is no eye contact between the model and the viewer or artist, so the figure's loneliness stands out starkly. Although we presume that the sunbather has been or will go swimming, there is no sign that he actually has, indeed no sign of movement, no trace of water. The quality of the painting derives in part from Hockney's use of acrylics. The thick, clotted, expressionist surfaces of his early work are gone, apparently forever. The thin smooth surface of the paint means that we see only the image and not the hand of the artist. These works are as impersonal as photographs; their physical presence is another element in their construction of a world of surfaces. Although in such a painting there is only a hint of irony, with the full satiric flourish to develop later, we must remember Hockney's 1961–1963 series of illustrations to *The Rake's Progress*, an indication of his moral side. For the time being that sense of emptiness is overcome by a sense of personal happiness, due largely to the painter's relationship with Peter Schlesinger.

Peter Getting Out of Nick's Pool (1966) is an important landmark in Hockney's work, partly because of its role as a tribute to his love for Schlesinger. The three horizontal planes of the picture are intersected by Peter's body, with its strongly implied vertical movement. Although Peter is thus given a central place, he is reflected in neither the water nor the window. His body is enticing, especially the ass just removed from the water, but he looks offstage, as it were, not toward the artist or viewer. The ripples in the water give no sign of his having been there, and the chairs on the terrace hardly seem welcoming. The scene seems as empty as a midwestern landscape. Once again the work was composed of several elements. The glass windows, with their lines indicating reflected sunlight, are derived from commercial illustration, while the figure of Peter is based on a photo of Peter pulling himself up on the hood of a car. The flat, almost photographic quality of the image is deliberate; the square format of the painting suggests its origin in the snapshot. In such images we are reminded of Gunn's lines about the California light and its "limiting candor." If Hockney had begun by celebrating an American freedom from history, he is now moving toward an almost Jamesian melancholy about the thinness of social texture. As each house has its private pool, where, one must wonder, is the agora?

In the late 1960s, experiencing personal happiness with Peter Schlesinger, Hockney no longer created works that dealt with homosexuality or California from a distance. Since the body is that of the beloved, there is a warmth in the way it is observed and recorded. A greater familiarity with the reality of California, now observed on an intimate daily basis, gives rise to a greater sense of emptiness. In the *Splash* paintings of 1966–1967, the human body is evident only as a kind of ghostly presence. In the first of them the strong mock-photo quality creates something of the effect of the postcard. Although the splash refers to a human presence, the body itself is nowhere to be seen. The strong diagonal line created by the diving board leads our eye only to the blank reflection of the window and does not manage to overcome the dominant horizontals. The low flat building is as empty as any of Hopper's. In revisions of the scene, as in *The Bigger Splash* of 1967, the mountains in the background are removed, bringing the neutral sky down almost to the level of the water. The palm trees, almost absurdly elongated, seem as unpromising as the tree in *Waiting for Godot*. The empty chair in front of the house serves as a sign of absence, located at a great distance from the pool edge and dwarfed by the house itself. These are scenes not merely of a swimmer who has gone underwater but of a culture that has vanished. They are ghostly landscapes, their evocative quality deriving precisely from their lacks.

In the following year the human figure returns in two double portraits, a form that Hockney explored in a number of works, reflecting his interest in human relationships. *American Collectors* is more obviously satirical, as its title suggests. The primitive figures, sculptural in their mass, have blank looks that never meet, thus providing no center to the work. Confined in its little pot, the scrawny tree on the right, which also marks off the right-hand wall of the house, mocks nature, while the massive stones seem absurdly inappropriate in this suburban setting, where everything natural has been manipulated and controlled. The totem pole on the right seems to cast an angry glance at the scene, suggesting its own Americanness and the disappropriation of Native American culture that can now only be echoed in bourgeois works of art.

In contrast to the sharpness of this reflection on art collecting in California, the portrait *Christopher Isherwood and Don Bachardy* is warm and friendly, even if it acknowledges the ultimate impossibility of joining two personalities. Isherwood was an important figure for Hockney (and for Gunn as well) as one of the very first of the British exiles in California. Isherwood's domestic harmony is suggested by the way he looks at Bachardy, although Bachardy does not return the look. The painting is balanced by the ways the piles of books echo the figures behind them, suggesting once again separateness as well as a shared life of common interests. The fruit and the corn cob in the center are a kind of visual pun for the thematics of the painting: they suggest the fruitfulness of the relationship (even if that fruitfulness is artistic rather than physical) as well as the sexual nature of the bond. The louvered windows return us to the interior scene as well as to the inner life.

The breakup of Hockney's relationship with Schlesinger is recorded in two paintings from 1971. In one of them, *Sur la terrasse*,

Peter is seen from the rear, standing on the terrace, held in by the barrier of the railing, which casts long shadows across the balcony. The viewer is located within the room from which Peter apparently wants to escape. In the other painting, *Pool and Steps, Le Nid du Duc*, done in the south of France, Peter is completely absent, represented only by his sandals and towel. The swimming pool is empty, and the steps lead, apparently, nowhere. The depth of feeling in this painting may be related to Hockney's development here of a new technique in which he mixed acrylic with water and detergent, which was then stained into the weave of the canvas. The result has some of the fragility of watercolor without the flatness of conventional acrylics. In these paintings, which look back on California from other sunny, watery spots, Hockney continues his method of allowing objects to speak for the lives they are associated with. Although the road there began with a perception of Whitman as a guide to a paradise of young men and a way out of the macho styles of expressionism, the infatuation with California has led to a deeper encounter with human feeling and produced at least a partial recognition of the need for a more complex understanding of suffering and loss that may seem difficult in the bright light and timelessness of California. Led there by a fantasy that Whitman helped to create in his fetishized American boys, Hockney moved beyond celebration to the recording of passion, time, and loss. Portraying not himself but the objects of his experience, Hockney gives a visible form to feeling, even as the American dream vanishes into air—or should we say water?

III

Beyond the Borders

"Still on My Lips"

Walt Whitman in Britain

GREGORY WOODS

In the last years of Whitman's life, the most enthusiastic readers of his poetry were not Americans but were English men. And they read it not primarily for the innovation of his poetic line but for his exuberant homoeroticism. These English gentlemen were his fans because they were the first generation of homosexuals—who still tended to call themselves Uranians—and because, all soundly educated in the classics, they saw in his poems a vigorous reflowering of Greek love in representations of modern life. They shuddered, and not with horror, at the thought of how manhood might blossom, unrestrained. Only theoretically committed—if at all—to egalitarian principles, many of them envisaged thrilling forays across the boundaries between the classes.

Whitman thus sent shock waves through the furtive gentility of Britain's Uranian community. He transformed their nostalgia for pastoral Greece into yearning for a utopian New World of open frontiers and open-neck shirts. His influence in Britain up to the present day has continued to be most evident in the poetry of men who seek ways of expressing homoerotic themes: in short, in poetry by gay men.

Oscar Wilde said that there was "something so Greek and sane" about Whitman's poems (see Ellmann, 159–160). He did not mean the form of the verse, of which he did not approve. (Not that Wilde was English; in many ways, no one was more Irish. He was, however, a central member of an English literary elite.) Wilde had been familiar with Whitman's work ever since his enlightened mother had read *Leaves of Grass* to him when he was thirteen. We do not know to what extent she expurgated the text. But the "Greek" poetry that Wilde himself eventually came to write—the sentimental "Charmides," for instance—is insipid stuff; nothing could show less of the American poet's influence.

An even greater devotee was John Addington Symonds, but his enthusiasm did not make his verse any more receptive to the American's revolutionary poetic ideas. In "The Song of Love and Death" (1875), Symonds addresses Whitman as follows:

> Thou dost establish—and our hearts receive—
> New laws of Love to link and intertwine
> Majestic peoples; Love to weld and weave
> Comrade to comrade, man to bearded man,
> Whereby indissoluble hosts shall cleave
> Unto the primal truths republican. (Reade, 5)

This impresses me now, if at all, purely in the strength of its sincerity. While it is clear that Symonds was taking no lessons from the master in poetic technique, that is not what had struck him most about Whitman's project. The crux of the matter was those "New laws of Love."

Symonds was (and is) all too easy a target for mockery. Algernon Swinburne called him and his followers "Calamites," a wonderful sneer, neatly combining "calamities" with "catamites" in its reference to Whitman's holy writ "Calamus." But no matter what the waspish Swinburne may have thought, Symonds did have a serious project in mind and a determination to carry it out, even if he did not have the policy for doing so. What interested him were Greek love and the possibility of its survival in modern society. He thought Whitman's social thinking was the key to the matter, but he wanted reassurance that he was not reading *Leaves of Grass* at cross-purposes.

In a letter of August 1890, Symonds took the bull by the horns and asked the question he had been dying to ask for years: "In your conception of Comradeship, do you contemplate the possible intrusion of those semi-sexual emotions and actions which no doubt do occur between men?" (Kaplan, 46). This is hesitantly put, but does—just—get to the point. Whitman was or affected to be shocked. In his reply he referred to "such gratuitous and quite at the time entirely undream'd & unreck'd possibility of morbid inferences—wh' are disavow'd by me & seem damnable." A couple of paragraphs later, presumably apropos of the same topic, he made the famous claim: "Tho' always unmarried I have had six children—two are dead—One living southern grandchild, fine boy, who writes to me occasionally" (Kaplan, 47).

Edward Carpenter told Symonds he should never have addressed the issue to Whitman point-blank. He said Whitman's denial was a lie, clearly intended to shake the obstinate Symonds off, once and for all. Oscar Wilde came home from America and told the poet George Ives that Whitman made no secret of his homosexuality. "The kiss of Walt Whitman," he said, "is still on my lips" (Ellmann, 164). I daresay one must choose between the evidence of the two men who met Whitman face to face and that which he put in writing for a correspondent on the other side of the Atlantic.

In his book of the following year, *A Problem in Modern Ethics* (1891), Symonds did his duty by Whitman, saying of him: "At the outset it must be definitely stated that he has nothing to do with anomalous, abnormal, vicious, or diseased forms of the emotion which males entertain for males." But Symonds could still not resist putting as positive a gloss on this as he could:

"Whitman never suggests that comradeship may occasion the development of physical desires. But then he does not in set terms condemn these desires, or warn his disciples against them" (Reade, 275). This is a compromise of sorts. It allowed Symonds to go on to quote the famous footnote from *Democratic Vistas* (1871), which so many homosexual apologists would eventually turn to. The note in question speaks of "threads of manly friendship" running through the warp of American life, "unprecedentedly emotional, muscular, heroic, and refined," and ends as follows: "I say democracy infers such loving comradeship, as its most inevitable twin or counterpart, without which it will be incomplete, in vain, and incapable of perpetuating itself" (*Prose Works*, 415).

Thereafter, Symonds could quote Whitman's "I Dream'd in a Dream," "To the East and to the West," and "For You O Democracy" in order to establish that Whitman's poetry calls to mind the story of the Theban Band at the battle of Chaeronea—which is Symonds's supreme example of the intensity, purity, and masculinity of male homosexual love.

Gerard Manley Hopkins, too, was strongly attracted to the content of Whitman's verse, but he dared not submit to the implications of that attraction. Writing to Robert Bridges on October 18, 1882, he said: "I may as well say what I should not otherwise have said, that I always knew in my heart Walt Whitman's mind to be more like my own than any other man's living. As he is a very great scoundrel this is not a pleasant confession. And this also makes me the more desirous to read him and the more determined that I will not" (see Dellamora, 44–45, 49, 87–89). To identify with so complete a scoundrel cannot have been easy. But to repudiate the idea completely would have been a far greater denial, for Hopkins's poetry reveals how intimately his love of men and boys was connected with his love of Christ.

Edward Carpenter was mainly responsible for introducing Whitman to England. Carpenter first encountered Whitman in 1868 or 1869 in William Rossetti's selection from *Leaves of Grass*. He went on to try in his life-style and his writing alike to show that Whitman's democratic ideals could operate to beneficial effect even in the Britain of Empire and Victoria. In his opinion, there already existed in the hearts of the British the conditions under which a saner, more egalitarian society could thrive. Men loved men, in Britain as elsewhere, but this love had not yet been properly recognized as a creative force. Like Symonds, Carpenter mentions Whitman and the Theban Band in the same breath in the poem "Into the Regions of the Sun." Like Wilde, he saw in Whitman a trace of the Greek—but enlightened by American constitutional democracy.

In *Homogenic Love* (1894, the year before Wilde's trial), Carpenter quotes the famous *Democratic Vistas* footnote on the relationship between democracy and comradeship. Of Whitman himself, Carpenter writes: "Like all great artists he could but give form and light to that which already existed dim and inchoate in the heart of the people" (Reade, 345). What Carpenter means by this is "homogenic love," and this passage moves straight from the mention of the poet to the following detailed remarks on the presence of the "intermediate sex" in everyday life in Britain:

> To those who have dived at all below the surface in this direction it will be familiar enough that the homogenic passion ramifies widely through all modern society, and that among the masses of the people as among the classes, below the stolid surface and reserve of British manners, letters pass and enduring attachments are formed, differing in no very obvious respect from those correspondences which persons of opposite sexes knit with each other under similar circumstances; but hitherto while this passion has occasionally come into public notice through the police reports, etc., in its grosser and cruder forms, its more sane and spiritual manifestations—though really a moving force in the body politic—have remained unrecognized. (Reade, 345)

Like Symonds before him, Carpenter was at pains to point out that Whitman was a *healthy* lover of men. Whitman was living proof, if anybody was, that the state of being homosexual was not necessarily neurotic, not necessarily a "condition." Carpenter's book *Ioläus* (1902), an "Anthology of Friendship," includes Whitman's poems "Recorders Ages Hence," "When I Heard at the Close of the Day," and "I Hear It Was Charged against Me."

It also requotes the *Democratic Vistas* footnote. *Days with Walt Whitman* (1906) records visits to the master in 1877 and 1884.

However, it is in his own poetry that Carpenter's admiration for Whitman really catches fire. His huge book *Towards Democracy* was closely modeled on *Leaves of Grass*, not only in style (which eventually becomes labored and forced in Carpenter's thoroughly English cadences) but also in content and in the manner of its appearance in successively enlarged editions. He ended up writing a book that was politically magnificent if not aesthetically brilliant. Insofar as he believed that without new attitudes toward sex—to contraception and homosexuality in particular—the redistribution of capital could have only superficial effects on the structure of society, Carpenter's thinking was decades in advance of that of most other British socialists.

Carpenter also realized that there was more than aesthetics to Whitman's poetic line. The escape from metrics was a crucial sign that the poetry was no mere academic exercise and that the poet was not going to be hidebound by the obsolete rules of a narrow, literate class. Even if in the execution Carpenter's imitations of Whitman occasionally looked more like parodies, it is significant that he, unlike Symonds, felt able to take this radical step in his writing. It was a signal of the more important breaks with convention that he was eager to make in his personal life. (Why, after all, should a socialist be writing with the good-mannered measure of Lord Tennyson?)

Emile Delavenay has made out a convincing case for the influence of Carpenter on D. H. Lawrence. Lawrence's reasons for abandoning meter were, like Carpenter's, class-based. But the real fluency of Lawrence's free verse stems from readings of the American master, not the more stilted British student. In *The Dyer's Hand* (1963), W. H. Auden claims Lawrence is the only English poet on whom Whitman has had a beneficial influence.

Lawrence had an early poetic grounding in three deviant voices: Verlaine, Baudelaire, and Whitman. He admired Whitman's "adhesiveness" but not his attempts to "contain multitudes." Lawrence's own megalomania was to be of a different, altogether less egalitarian brand. In his famous essay on Whitman in *Studies in Classic American Literature* (1924), Lawrence speaks of "this awful Whitman." But he goes on to pay an incomparable tribute: "Whitman, the great poet, has meant so much to me. Whitman, the one man breaking a way ahead. Whitman, the one pioneer. And only Whitman. No English pioneers, no French. No European pioneer-poets" (162).

In a poem like "Future Relationships," Lawrence can be seen starting near Whitman but veering away toward power relations of his own devising:

> The world is moving, moving still, towards further
>   democracy
> But not a democracy of idea or ideal, nor of property,
>   nor even of the emotion of brotherhood.
> But a democracy of men, a democracy of touch.
>   (*Complete Poems*, 611)

If one examines further this notion of touch, one finds that Lawrence means a physical contact which may be quasisexual but is more likely to be combative than loving. Men start out as equals, but Lawrence's "democracy of touch" sorts them into ranks. When Whitman speaks of democracy, he means his own society, the nation he lives in and loves. Lawrence, the self-exiled wanderer, on the other hand, is free to dismiss political idealism and to devise his own hierarchical system of *Blutbruderschaft* within a social vacuum.

It was not only to poetry that Whitman's influence reached. The English novel, too, is much enriched by it. Whether we think of it as homosexuality or as male bonding, Lawrence's version of the new relation between men—even when it turns fascist in books like *Kangaroo*—clearly owes much to what Whitman outlined as the political powers of the solidarity of comradeship. While *The Prussian Officer* is Germanic in both subject and spirit, it is difficult to imagine Lawrence's feeling able to write *Women in Love* without having read Whitman.

In the "Terminal Note" (1960) to *Maurice* (1971), E. M. Forster acknowledges that it was a visit to "the Whitmannic poet" Edward Carpenter—and, more specifically, an encounter between George Merrill's hand and Forster's bottom—that led to the writing of the novel. These flirtatious maneuvers seem to have been something of a habit with Carpenter and Merrill. In his famous autobiography, *The World, The Flesh and Myself,* Michael Davidson boasts that he was once "pinched on the bum by England's Walt Whitman" (66).

As Forster tells it, this account of lumbar inspiration is faintly ridiculous; but it is seriously meant. The point is the contact, the moment of connection. Forster had not felt it on his previous visit to the "shrine" that Carpenter's home was to him. It took a minor physical act to complete the major psychological circuit and cause a (literally) fundamental shock to Forster's system. "Only connect," he used to insist. It was a policy that partly came to him, via Carpenter, from Whitman, and its proof came in that touch of a hand, which seemed to plug him into Whitman's power source. Although it heralded the end of his career as a novelist, it gave him the strength to be, for once and for better or worse, a novelist who was homosexual. (Remember, too, that the very title of *A Passage to India* is not only Forster's but Whitman's as well.)

Forster's inability to find a satisfactory way of concluding *Maurice* stems from the difficulty he had in imagining Whitman's optimism and openness about comradeship transferred to a class-ridden European society presided over, in matters of homosexuality, by the Labouchère Amendment. Maurice's relationship with Alec Scudder, to some extent like Constance Chatterley's with Mellors, is a developed version of what so many Uranian poets yearned for and saw expressed in the "classlessness" (itself debatable) of Whitman's poetry. Forster's implausible happy ending to *Maurice,* satisfying in full measure the homosexual English gentleman's yearning for intercourse with working-class boys, is an unhappy translation of Whitman's democratic utopianism into a European setting.

Perhaps as important as those who allowed themselves to follow Whitman's poetically and sexually liberating influence are those who (like Hopkins) strove not to. For instance, it was important to W. H. Auden not to be seen to like Whitman. After an early enthusiasm for Eliot, Auden's poetic anti-modernism became radical: even Whitman was too new. All of Auden's texts depended on structural rigor, which obviated spontaneity. His notorious revisions, retitlings, and disowning of popular lines, stanzas, or even whole poems all militated against the idea of an oeuvre that depended on the original idea from which it sprang. He also detested sentimentality, Whitman's no less than anyone else's.

However, if we go back to Auden's early work, we cannot avoid evidence of a respectful reading of Whitman. *The Orators* (1932) seems to be particularly fruitful ground in this respect. For all its references to hermetic British structures, institutions, and traditions, *The Orators* includes moments that are recognizably Whitmanesque. I am thinking of book 1, part 3 ("Statement"), and the more obviously parodic section of book 2 called "Of the Enemy." In the former, when Auden compiles a list of the old boys of an English public school, he is seeking comic effects quite unlike anything of Whitman's. It is, above all, sheer proliferation that Auden is most concerned to express. For this, Whitman is the most suitable model. Throughout his career Auden's omnivorous interests demanded poetic techniques capable of bearing massive weights of eclectic information and an abstruse vocabulary. This early dalliance with Whitman seems to have been an experiment in inclusiveness.

There are similar accumulations of detail in parts of *The Dog Beneath the Skin*, such as "You with shooting-sticks," "So, under the local images," and "The Summer holds," all probably dating from 1934. Too much information is marshaled across the heavily printed page in these poems for Whitman's influence to go unremarked. Again, it is the technique—or part of it—rather than the message that Auden has adopted. He seems at pains to sound as little like Whitman as he can. To put it simply, I doubt that a line as long as the following, about the great English country houses, could have been written in England without Whitman as model: "Some have been turned into prep-schools where the diet is in the hands of an experienced matron" (*English Poems*, 212). However, no one could mistake his voice for the American's—that is, perhaps, one of the jokes implicit in its tone. Auden is at this stage preposterously English. By the time he moved to the United States he had partially dropped this aspect of his voice, but he had also dropped the Whitmanesque measure.

Other writers working from the 1930s onward found their sexuality given some degree of representation in Whitman. For instance, the bisexual surrealist David Gascoyne often adopted a lanky, relaxed vers libre in his early verse that looked like Whitman's, even if its content would have baffled and annoyed him.

In more recent years there has been a long-running debate in the United Kingdom about the validity of two distinct poetic tendencies, mainly centered on the question of which—if either—is the more representative of contemporary British verse as a whole. Academic anthologies have been followed by counter-anthologies. Letters have been written to the press.

The controversy arose, in part, from the way in which in the 1950s the so-called Movement was invented and then taken to represent the best young British poets. This group was formulated in two anthologies, Robert Conquest's *New Lines* and G. S. Frazer's *Poetry Now* (both 1956), and was principally represented by such writers as Kingsley Amis, Donald Davie, Thom Gunn, and Philip Larkin. Although its birth was presided over by T. S. Eliot from behind his desk at Faber and Faber, the Movement was antimodernist in spirit and technique. With Eliot's help, it consolidated its position of assumed preeminence and remained there until the present. (Hence the disproportionate amount of attention paid to Philip Larkin in Britain since his death; hence, too, the poet laureateship of the unsuited Ted Hughes.) A similarly narrow version of British poetry was purveyed in the more recent *Penguin Book of Contemporary British Poetry*, edited by Blake Morrison and Andrew Motion (1982).

Antipathy to this line resulted in a counter-movement of loyalty to modernism and, necessarily therefore, to American poetry, to the likes of Pound, Eliot, and Williams, and to Whitman himself. (Essentially, this is a debate about influences.) When these poets looked back, they did so not to Thomas Hardy but beyond: to William Blake and thence to the Bible, one of Whitman's sources.

That this second or alternative strand of British poetry was rich and flourishing in 1969 is evidenced in that year's *Children of Albion* anthology, edited by Michael Horovitz and dedicated to Allen Ginsberg. For most of the 1970s the Poetry Society supported this transatlantic tendency and published these poets in its own house journal, *Poetry Review*, edited by Eric Mottram. But by the end of the decade the Arts Council of Great Britain, apparently fearing American cultural imperialism and preferring insular security, stepped in to wrest back control of the Poetry Society, leaving it in the hands of the conservatives who were poised to prevail.

Many of *Albion*'s children were first introduced to Whitman by reading and hearing Ginsberg. Indeed, in the afterword to his anthology Horovitz admits that the influence of William Blake, too, came back to England by this long route, via Ginsberg. (Such indirection is not rare and may be a distinct advantage. Some contemporary gay writers have arrived at Whitman by the European path that leads through Federico García Lorca, others, if fewer, via Pier Paolo Pasolini.)

Some poets clearly straddle the divide. Thom Gunn, for instance, does so chronologically. Indeed, in midcareer Gunn offered the interesting prospect of a Movement poet in revolt against Movement poets. He escaped the Movement by emigrating to California, by starting to write syllabics, and by coming out. James Kirkup, too, strayed further from meter and rhyme the longer he stayed out of Britain, and the development of his voice as an out gay poet coincided with his increasing confidence in free verse.

Lee Harwood, one of the poets included in *Children of Albion*, much later allowed his poems to be reprinted in such gay anthologies as Stephen Coote's *The Penguin Book of Homosexual Verse* (1983), Martin Humphries's *Not Love Alone* (1985), and Peter Daniels's *Take Any Train* (1990). Harwood takes his American influence most directly from the New York school and from John Ashbery in particular. But, as poems like "Just Friends" (in *All the Wrong Notes* [1981] and reprinted in Humphries's anthology) demonstrate, he has assimilated important lessons from Whitman.

"Just Friends" is structured as a simple catalog of twelve events of tableaux, each involving at least two men; a thirteenth image of a man alone; and the closing line, "At this moment I feel close to tears." Each item is both one sentence and one line in length, and each line flexibly accommodates the full extent of the individual thought. The poem has no argument beyond its thirteen presentations. As in Whitman, each of the catalog's parts is of equal significance; none takes meaningful precedence. All contribute to a sequence of evidence, a manifestation, from which no explicit conclusion is drawn. Relationships are presented as facts, emotional realities, as solid as anything one might chance to observe. They no more require justification than items on a shopping list. Naming them is sufficient.

Edwin Morgan also appeared in both Horovitz's and Coote's anthologies but in the latter only as the translator of an epigram by Philip of Thessalonica. In the former, the poem "The Death of Marilyn Monroe" seems particularly to show a knowledge of Ginsberg and, through him, of Whitman. Of course, the choice of topic is itself a sign that Morgan's poetic gaze was, at least in part, fixed on the opposite side of the Atlantic. Morgan did not come out publicly until 1990, at the age of seventy, by which time many readers had come to see him as the unofficial poet laureate of Scotland. He then contributed to Daniels's *Take Any Train*.

In Britain, as in the United States, far more has been learned from Walt Whitman than merely the way of writing poems—although that would in itself be no small thing. Throughout the "century of homosexuality"—from the invention of the word in 1869 to the Stonewall riots in 1969—and for the two decades since, gay writers have sought, in their poetry as in their daily lives, new ways of fitting in and refraining from fitting in with the heterosexual majority and ways of expressing their new lives. One of the great triumphs of Whitman's career—barely visible at all, it seems, to straight critics—has been the way in which his work has continued to offer itself as a viable model to gay writers and readers throughout this century. It would have delighted him to know that a hundred years after his death I am able to say: he is still on our lips.

Walt Whitman in Ontario

MICHAEL LYNCH

It is a little known fact that Walt Whitman appeared in a glory in the sky of southern Ontario—much like Woody Allen's mother in *New York Stories*—on August 28, 1919. But we'll get to that later.

Firm dividing lines between Whitman as poet and Whitman as cultural icon cannot be drawn. He made sure of that from the 1850s on, when he not only invented "Walt Whitman" but promulgated him with an energy that would put Norman Mailer or Andy Warhol to shame. Advertisements for himself: the original self-image-maker. This was not, however, a single image. Whitman is less a cultural icon than a node of possibilities for proliferating cultural icons.

The possibilities were so diverse and productive that they did not end with Whitman's death. They multiplied. He used to be on mass-produced cigar boxes, but these days we see him in the American film industry, where in the last two years he turns up in *Dead Poets Society, Bull Durham,* and the English-Canadian production, *Beautiful Dreamers.* In the first he's the unthreatening, desexualized rhymster of "O Captain! My Captain!" In the second his lines are an erotic toy for heterosexual foreplay. In the third he's a genial old chap whose visit to London, Ontario, shakes up the local Anglicans, socialites, and medical establishment—and along the way he reeroticizes the heterosexual marriage of Jessie and Richard Bucke.

In 1980, a hundred years after Whitman's visit to the Buckes, Alan Miller, Bert Hansen, and I organized a conference to explore the proliferations and reticulations of Whitman in Ontario. The conference brought together contemporary scholarship on an unexpected mix of characters: socialists, mystics, reformers, writers, and medical progressives, from 1880 to 1919.

I published the following narrative—or hooked rug of anecdotes—for a popular readership on the occasion of the conference.[1] Many of the presenters at the conference went on to publish their work, and others (such as Ramsay Cook and S. E. D. Shortt) have subsequently sophisticated our grasp of the mix of reform and religion in this network of Whitmanians. But the project implicit in my little rug has not been taken up: sexuality and gender analysis have been crowded out by a disembodied history of ideas. Much like the three films I mentioned above, recent studies heterosexualize or desexualize the Whitman presence. Pity. The Whitman-Bucke and Whitman-Traubel passions could, if attended to, tell us much about male-male intimacy in two overlapping generations of progressives. Socialist thinking and, yes, table-tapping mysticism could also benefit from such reexamination.

In the summer of 1880 Walt Whitman came to Canada for four months, his first and only visit to a country he had often referred to in his poetry. He liked to call it "Kanada" and, in his enthusiastic continentalism, to consider it as a future part of the United States of America.

From London, Ontario, where he spent most of his visit,

Whitman managed a short trip to Sarnia and a long one down the Saint Lawrence to the Thousand Islands, Montreal, and Quebec, then up the Saguenay to Chicoutimi and Ha!Ha! Bay. He basked in the long sunsets near London, tasted the wines of Niagara, and found the Thousand Islands an adequate vacation spot for all of North America.

On September 28 Whitman was in "Niagara Falls America" where as a true tourist to the Falls, he wrote postcards to friends in many places—including one to Edward Carpenter in Brighton. Whitman's former lover Peter Doyle, whom he had seen only infrequently since leaving Washington seven years earlier, came up from Washington to meet him in Niagara Falls and accompany him back East. But before making that trip, Walt and Pete spent a short time together in the nation's honeymoon capital. As Whitman later wrote, "We stopped a day & a night at Niagara & had a first rate time."

In Toronto, Whitman found horse chestnut trees everywhere. He noted the elegant residences along Sherbourne and Jarvis streets, the busy shopping along King Street (which he compared to Broadway), and the slight haze over the sunlit blue Ontario waters.

Wherever he went, he also admired the men. There were the "sundown groups of sweating, tan-faced men" leaving the hayfields near London. On Lake Saint Clair the oarsmen attracted him, especially one crew of four "stript to their rowing shirts" that swept by him in their handsome shell. (He seems even to have met Ned Hanlan, the world champion rower.) In eastern Quebec, Whitman's eye was turned by the "priests in their black gowns everywhere"—often, as he said, "groups of handsome young fellows."

In Toronto, he climbed to the top of the omnibus to ride with the driver, as he had done regularly thirty years before in Manhattan. Twice he took down the name and address of men who especially fascinated him.

Whitman's host during this visit was one of Canada's most colorful, brilliant eccentrics, an alienist named Dr. Richard Maurice Bucke. Bucke grew up on a pioneer homestead near London and at the age of twenty was lost in a snowstorm for one week while exploring the Sierra Nevadas in California. He lost all of one foot and part of the other from frostbite and crude amputation. After graduating in medicine at McGill, he set up practice in Sarnia, where he married. One year later, in 1866, he read a book that was to lead to trouble in his marriage. The book? Whitman's *Poems*. Immediately he was taken by Whitman, but it was eleven years before they met.

This first meeting was brief. Whitman, then fifty-eight, spoke no more than a hundred words. But shortly afterward, Bucke, who was forty, experienced a state of mental exaltation which he could only describe by comparing it to slight intoxication from champagne—or to falling in love. The exaltation lasted for six weeks and changed his whole life. For the next fifteen years he often visited Whitman with, as he said, "the same purpose—to hold that hand, to look at that face and to listen to that noble and musical voice." He was in love with Whitman as he was in love with eternity, and the visits became for him a symbol and proof of the afterlife, when he would again meet Whitman in bliss.

The same year of his first meeting with Whitman, Bucke was appointed superintendent of the Mental Hospital in London, where he worked until his sudden death from a fall on a piece of ice twenty-five years later. At this asylum, one of the largest on the continent, he instigated some drastic reforms in the care of the insane, such as abolishing restraint and seclusion. These progressive moves were highly influential in the Ontario asylum system. More controversial, both then and now, were his attempts to curb masturbation (thought sometimes to be a cause of insanity, sometimes a symptom) by inserting wire through the penises of fifteen male patients. Likewise controversial were his far more extensive gynecological operations on female patients— just over two hundred of them.

By the time Bucke invited his idol Walt Whitman to visit him at the asylum, he had undertaken to write the first biography of Whitman. He had also published a book which related Darwinism and mysticism, *Man's Moral Nature*, and dedicated it to Whitman. The year before he died, Bucke would publish his mystical master- work, *Cosmic Consciousness*; it may seem odd to anyone but Bucke that during the same year he published an article, "How Shall We

Dispose of Our Sewage?" Like Whitman and a number of other nineteenth-century figures, Bucke took both the sublime and the mundane as subjects of his enthusiasm.

Bucke's love for Whitman was powerful. While he never seems to have understood it in relation to the notions about homosexuality that were being developed at the time, it is hard not to see such a relation in retrospect. When in 1888 Bucke thought that Whitman, an invalid in New Jersey, needed a new nurse, he sent down a young man who had been working for him at the asylum. "His name is Edward Wilkins," he wrote to Whitman, "I know you would like him. He is a real good, nice-looking young fellow. I have known him some years—he is as good as he looks." Whitman did like "Ed," so much that when someone referred to him as Whitman's nurse, Whitman corrected the reference to read "Whitman's Canadian friend and nurse."

By the time of Whitman's death in 1892, Bucke was important enough to be named an honorary pallbearer and one of the three literary executors. He took the latter seriously and edited three volumes of Whitman's writings for publication—including the letters Whitman had written over many years to Peter Doyle. Bucke got these from Doyle, wrote an introduction that glossed over the homosexual basis for the friendship, and yet published both the letters and introduction under the title *Calamus*, the name of the plant which Whitman had used to symbolize male-male sexual love in his 1860 *Leaves of Grass*. Bucke had to struggle to find a publisher for these letters, and he was encouraged by the homosexual writer Edward Carpenter.

Just what Bucke understood about Whitman's—and his own— sexuality is as yet unclear. It seems hard to believe that a psychiatrist of his stature, after the writings of Moll, Krafft-Ebing, Symonds, and Ellis, could not see what was there. And yet his idolization of Whitman into a modern divinity—Bucke was one of a number of Whitmanites who considered Whitman a modern Jesus or Muhammad and was included in the dismissive label they all received: Whitman's "hot little prophets"—and need to avoid facing too clearly his own response to Whitman may have led to his failure to see.

The trouble in Dr. Bucke's marriage came during Whitman's

visit to the asylum when Jessie Bucke felt slighted because of the amount and kind of attention her husband was bestowing on the man he so loved. She was also alarmed by something—we do not know what—her friends had told her about the poet. When Dr. Bucke invited Whitman to return for a second visit, she objected to the point of threatening to move back to her family in Sarnia. Dr. Bucke acquiesced and retracted his invitation. "But Jessie," he wrote her, "never allow yourself to imagine for a moment that you or any of you can shake my affection for Walt Whitman. If all the world stood on one side, and Walt Whitman and general contempt on the other, and I had to choose which I would take, I do not think I should hesitate (I hope I should not) to choose Walt Whitman."

Bucke's relationship with Whitman demonstrates the paradox that surrounds most of the "hot little prophets"—Whitman was, to them, both a god in the flesh and a fleshly scandal. His celebration of male-male comradeship and intimacy allowed them to engage their own homosexual emotions as if with the blessing of his celebrations of passionate comradeship, yet they were ever uncomfortable with the implications of the calamus root.

One of these prophets was Horace Traubel, who, as a young man, visited the invalid Whitman daily during the last years of the poet's life and kept an elaborate record of everything the man said and did—from the books he read to his days of constipation. After Bucke's death in 1902, an even decade after Whitman's, Traubel was the sole leading prophet, the surrogate for Whitman himself to the growing number of Whitmanites in North America and England. A vigorous socialist and newspaper editor, Horace Traubel came to Ontario in 1919 and moved another generation of Whitmanites much as the original had moved Dr. Bucke.

In February 1919, eight adults and one boy gathered together in the house at 10 Euclid Avenue, Toronto, for a seance. Someone had covered the overhead lamp with a shade so that it shed a pink light that to the group symbolized Mother Love, but mixed with "Lover's Love, Fraternal Love, and Universal Love." One of the group, Flora MacDonald Denison, thought later that of the hundreds of psychical circles she had known, in none was "the dominant note of Love" so pronounced as it was that evening on Euclid Avenue.

Instead of a Ouija board, the group used a heavy plate of glass to communicate with the intelligences of the "twentieth plane." Louis Benjamin, the father of the little boy, was in the center of the room. He was the director of the Psychical Research Society, and his book, *Twentieth Plane*, was the subject of a major controversy in the Toronto newspapers. But none of those present felt it was controversial at all.

Dr. A. D. Watson, in whose house they were meeting, began by communing with his Spirit Mother and arranging through her a conversation with Whitman, who of course had been dead for twenty-seven years. Then Whitman appeared, took the board, and held it for an hour and a half during which the group felt that "we had moved into the Holy of Holies of our beings."

Among the words of Whitman which Denison was allowed to repeat in public was a message about Horace Traubel—now, in 1919, a prematurely old man of sixty-one. "On my lips I feel the imprint of his kiss," Whitman said. "He is a noble man. Write him large in the literature of your sphere." With these words Denison saw a vision of Traubel as a young man of thirty years before, ministering to the dying Whitman. "How young Horace looked," she said.

She had met Traubel three years earlier in Toronto, through Henry Scholey Saunders. Saunders was a cellist who had taught at the conservatory and played with the Toronto symphony, a son of the man who had invented the early-ripening Marquis wheat that revolutionized prairie farming and an eminent Whitmaniac; his father had been a friend of Dr. Bucke's. When Whitman was in London, Henry, a boy of sixteen, had met the poet when his father entertained him and Bucke at a Sunday supper. He never forgot this meeting, and for the rest of his life his prime passion was Whitman—in collecting and publishing.

Among his publications was the first translation into English of the first major public debate about Whitman's sexuality. It took place in the *Mercure de France* in 1913, and Saunders published the entire debate—for private distribution only.

When Saunders introduced Denison to Traubel, she was so impressed she gave him, for Mrs. Traubel, a rose-point handkerchief made by a Blood Nun in Belgium. She met him twice again before persuading him to come in August 1919 to the summer resort which she owned at Bon Echo, north of Peterborough. She ran it primarily for Whitman disciples, both American and Canadian, and was eager for him to be present at the centennial convention of the Whitman Club of Bon Echo. (Whitman was born in 1819.) They were going to rename the large rock that jutted out into Lake Mazinaw in the poet's honor.

Far from being just a kooky psychic researcher, Denison was Ontario's most radical feminist leader. A seamstress, single mother, businesswoman, journalist, and tireless campaigner for women's rights, Denison was very much in the world even while she was listening to voices from the twentieth plane. Many of her ideas about feminism were derived from those of the American radical feminist and lesbian Charlotte Perkins Gilman, who was one of the regular guests at Bon Echo. And Gilman had derived a considerable amount of her social thought from reading Walt Whitman.

On August 4, about four o'clock, an auto drove into Bon Echo and was greeted by a "Welcome Home" sign over the door, the Union Jack on one side and Old Glory on the other. In the car sat Horace Traubel and three others. Horace was almost a skeleton now, but his "exquisitely modeled death-like face, the shaggy bundles of snow-white hair, and the wondrous blue eyes" struck everyone gathered to welcome him. The young men tenderly assisted him from the auto. "Flora," he said, "I told you I'd be here."

Traubel enjoyed the convention, laughing with and entertaining the company during the next two weeks. Letters arrived for him every day, all of which he fussed over; those from J. W. Wallace, one of Whitman's most devoted English disciples, he kissed and cried over. Traubel loved the young men there, and after one of them, a young Russian they called Dave Cummings, left Bon Echo, he frequently burst out crying at the mention of his name.

By August 25, the day of the convention, Traubel was getting weaker. But on the big day he insisted on walking down the steps to the dock where he climbed into a rowboat. His and the other boats were rowed down the lake alongside the big rock, through the narrows and around to its massive head. There Traubel and Denison placed their hands on the rock and re-named it, quietly uttering its new cognomen: Old Walt. Traubel and his wife burst into sobs while the rest of the crowd remained silent, awestruck.

By the end of the month Traubel was sicker yet. He was given a bed in the tower room of the hotel, where he could look out over the great grayish red gibraltar they had rechristened, could see Old Walt in the famous Bon Echo sunsets. On the 28th Deni-son heard him tapping his cane and rushed up to the room.

"Look, look, Flora, quick, he is going."

"What, where, Horace? I do not see anyone."

"Why just over the rock Walt appeared, head and shoulders and a hat on, in a golden glory—brilliant and splendid. He reas-sured me—beckoned to me, and spoke to me. I heard his voice, but did not understand all he said, only, 'Come on.'"

Traubel was uplifted by this vision. On September 3 he asked for his "toys," Whitman's watch and purse and letters. On Sep-tember 6 one of the men present saw Walt on the opposite side of Traubel's bed and then felt Walt, passing through the bed, touch his hand. "The contrast was like an electric shock." Traubel, too, remarked on Walt's visible presence.

The next day Traubel died. Or, as Denison put it, he "joined Walt Whitman."

Denison had been visited at her Whitmanite retreat by the greatest of the "hot little prophets"—and he had died on her. With difficulty she found a coffin barely in time to catch the night train to Montreal. The weather was hot and there had not been time for proper embalming, so by the time they got to New York the body, badly shaken in the baggage car and beginning to smell, had to be re-embalmed. It took some effort to find a suit-able church for the funeral since Traubel was a socialist and not a Christian. When they found one (one that had departed from al-most "all semblance of orthodoxy") and the funeral was about to begin, the organ loft caught fire and the service was confusedly moved elsewhere. "He burned the church down before he'd be taken into it," one wit remarked. "The church," replied another, "burned down before it would have him in it."

At the service, Dave Cummings, the young Russian, nearly collapsed with intense emotion over the casket. Traubel's dear Toronto friend Mildred Bain, who wrote a book about him and may have had a son by him, said that "comradeship was his religion." He told her that the next issue of his newspaper was to be about Peter Doyle. "There are some things about Pete that I've not yet said." But his death came before he got to say them.

Back at Bon Echo, alone in the cottage one night in December 1919, Denison listened to the lake freeze over and re-read Whitman's poems to herself, aloud. It was twenty below out and the lake was snapping and cracking, but her dog and cat were cozy in down cushions. Before turning into bed, she read Nietzsche's ideas of a superman, thinking of Whitman, thinking of Traubel.

She might also have thought of Dr. Bucke, who had also appeared and spoken to the Euclid Avenue gathering ten months earlier. Seventeen years after his own death, Bucke had recalled Whitman in these words: "He must have had the silver soul of the silent lover of his fellows. I mean silent, for strength, when vast, is always still; and he who, as Walt did, could be a democratic man, loving the truck-driver, the ferry-boat attendant, the newsboy, and receive them in his simple house as he often did— that man, I say, is one of the gods."

Visits and visions—to most, the admixture of mysticism and politics in Whitman's Ontario disciples may seem odd. But for someone like Bucke there was no conflict between the impulses that led to reforms in the care of the insane and those that responded to cosmic consciousness. Weren't both impulses, after all, to be found in his master, Walt Whitman?

NOTE

1. My original article, "The Lover of His Fellows and the Hot Little Prophets: Walt Whitman in Ontario," appeared in *Body Politic*. Its anecdotes are drawn from Whitman (*Diary in Canada*), Lozynsky, Gorham, Traubel, the journal *The Sunset of Bon Echo*, particularly 1:5 (1919) and

1:6 (April–May 1920), and various private publications by Henry S. Saunders.

Subsequent sources include Cook, Weir, Mitchinson and McGinnis, and Shortt.

For incisive comments on the role of Whitman in *Dead Poets Society* see Robert Martin's review of *Manhood and the American Renaissance.* For comments on *Beautiful Dreamers* see my op-ed, "Putting Whitman Back in the Closet," in the *Globe and Mail*, April 17, 1990.

After the seas are all cross'd . . .

.　　.　　.　　.

Finally shall come the poet worthy that name
—Walt Whitman

Atlantic Poets

"Discovery" as Metaphor and Ideology

MARIA IRENA RAMALHO

DE SOUSA SANTOS

This essay, part of my work-in-progress on the ideology of modernist poetics, deals with the influence on Crane and Pessoa of Whitman's use of "discovery" as metaphor. My aim is to inquire into the relationship between the imaginations and ideals of these poets and the ideology of western centrality and supremacy.

While Whitman and Crane need no introduction here, the work of Portugal's greatest modernist poet, Fernando Pessoa

(1888–1935), has come to us thanks mainly to Edwin Honig, whose translations (with Susan Brown) were published in 1986. I shall be referring here to *Mensagem* (1934), the only book of Pessoa's poetry published during his lifetime. In an earlier paper, "An Imperialism of Poets" (1987), I examined the striking similarities of conception and inspiration in Crane's *The Bridge* (1930) and Pessoa's *Mensagem*. Whitman, I found, is an obvious poetic link between these two modernists; though they had almost certainly never even heard of each other, both were avid readers and admirers of Whitman's work. My main argument here is that all three poets share a view of the West as the gravitational center of the world.

The Atlantic Ocean and the Idea of the West

Pessoa's many scattered notes on Portugal or, in his own words, "The National Problem [or Empire]" include a projected chapter in *Sobre Portugal* on what he calls "Atlantism." He associates this concept with the idea of empire and imperialism, as well as with the myths of Sebastianism and the Fifth Empire, and sketches his vision of a universalizing national utopia.[1] The concept, however, is barely defined in these fragmentary notes or even considered in any detail. Nevertheless, the associations woven around Pessoa's Atlantism point to a reassessment of western values, a reassertion of the civilizing mission of the West, and a redefinition of Portugal's role in that mission. For reasons relating in a complex and ambiguous way to its discoveries and to the past glories and ensuing decadence of its old sea empire, Pessoa presents Portugal here as the nation whose manifest destiny, as it were, is to lead the westernizing mission of civilization in the twentieth century.

For Pessoa, the Atlantic Ocean seems to play a decisive role in determining the nations which, under Portugal's leadership, will shape the future. Hence his focus on the Iberian Peninsula, Ireland, and the Americas. Pessoa significantly excludes powerful and influential centers such as Rome, London, and Paris, as well as Christianity, democratic and plebeian French liberalism (his own expression), and the Portuguese colonies. Major countries are dismissed, while lesser countries are expected to contribute to the desired future. At the same time, a number of values, though never fully discussed, are posited as essential: the Atlantic concept of life and the Atlantism of race (both linked, according to Pessoa, to "Walt Whitman's high Atlantic spirit"), the imaginative re-creation of the discoveries, spiritual imperialism, the myths of Sebastianism and the Fifth Empire, artistic absorption, mysticism, paganism, aristocratism, and, finally, the Portuguese modernist movements in poetry, which Pessoa himself had termed "sensationism" and "intersectionism." Furthermore, in other related prose fragments, he indicates that by bringing together politics and power, geography and hegemony, influence and prophecy, elitist expansion and cultural dominion, race and nation, religion and myth, art and poetry, his intention is to define the terms of a discussion of what he calls "cultural imperialism" or "an imperialism of poets."

In my essay "An Imperialism of Poets," I examined this concept in the context of Pessoa's modernist poetics through a comparative study of *Mensagem* and *The Bridge*. Both Pessoa and Crane, I argued, claim for poetry and art the power to realize the western ideal of universal harmony and understanding, the putative but unachieved aim of so many wars, political revolutions, and civilizing missions. I would now like to propose an understanding of this poetic ideal not only as a Whitmanian romantic inheritance but also as part of the advancement of capitalism and the world economic order at the turn of the century—part, therefore, of the ideology of imperialism that had for decades been evolving in the West, particularly in England. Or, to put it another way, both Pessoa's "Atlantic soul" ("Atlantan soul" in the Honig/Brown translation) and Crane's "Atlantis" are Whitmanian metaphors for poetry; but while they draw inspiration for their poetical utopias from the great sea voyages of discovery, which they regard as basically creative gestures, both poets are nonetheless situated in the important historical and ideological moment—termed "the age of Empire" by Eric Hobsbawm—that at midcentury was to engender "Atlanticism."

Atlanticism refers to the idea that the Atlantic nations (or some of them, at least) must combine their efforts to maintain the economic and political balance of the world under certain terms. Essentially, those terms involve the creation of an Atlantic community in order to preserve white European supremacy in a world increasingly upset by decolonization and the emergence of "menacing" nations in Asia and Africa. What is interesting is that, whether in the poetic or the political imagination, the Atlantic Ocean functions rhetorically as a symbol of the West, one that encompasses the image of world harmony and wholeness first inspired by the discoveries and the ideology of western expansion and mission. Hence, a homology can be established between the political concepts and concerns of the day and the metaphors of Crane and Pessoa. And if, as I contend, "Atlantis" and the "Atlantic soul" are primarily their metaphors for poetry, then, in light of the major theories and practices of literary modernism, they must also be metaphors for Poetry—that idealizing abstract concept which, suspending history and canceling difference, may easily become responsible for cultural domination.

The notion of imperialism as we understand it today—that is to say, the division of the world into strong and weak, rich and poor, developed and developing countries, as well as the political and economic dependence of nations placed in the subservient position within those dichotomies—began to take shape primarily in England in the 1870s. However, the notion did not at first necessarily have the pejorative connotations it does today: "In 1874 plenty of politicians were proud to call themselves imperialists but in the course of our century they have virtually disappeared from sight" (Hobsbawm, 60). A political and economic phenomenon related to the development of modern capitalism, imperialism is rooted in the fifteenth- and sixteenth-century European discoveries and the ensuing "civilizing" and Christianizing missions which unquestionably took the racial and cultural superiority of the West for granted. The literature of colonialism has undoubtedly helped shape the western understanding of imperialism in terms of the inevitable power relation between "advanced" and "backward" countries, currently commonly referred to as core and periphery. From the standpoint of the core, that relation is of course seen as the most advantageous for all

concerned. It is my contention that as of the late 1850s, Whitman's poetry played a crucial role in the articulation of the modern rhetoric of this ideology. That such an ideology has moreover contributed greatly to the poetics of modernism is in my
opinion demonstrated in Crane's and Pessoa's use of Whitman's
rhetoric.

Whitman's Atlantic Spirit and the Idea of an Atlantic Community

My purpose here is not to belittle Whitman's brave vision of
world democracy, his generous belief in the possibility of universal love and understanding or his exalted chants of human equality and solidarity. In its daring imaginings of a global social
utopia, *Leaves of Grass* remains a deeply inspiring if not a revolutionary book. My argument, however, is that the democratic
ideal of the bard of America amounts to what Emerson in "The
American Scholar" called "the conversion of the world"—a
phrase that itself also rings of the discoveries and of the civilizing
mission of the West. Oliver Wendell Holmes justifiably termed
Emerson's essay America's "intellectual Declaration of Independence" (Rusk, 263). But perhaps we should briefly ponder the
notion, firmly implanted in the best minds of an expanding
United States in the middle of the nineteenth century, whereby
independence stands in opposition to dependence. Accordingly,
it is the prerogative of independent peoples not only to be free of
influence or domination but to influence and dominate others.
Independence, then, is centrality and point of view. It is to be
right at the center or rather to be right *and* at the center, to have
the privilege of overview that alone grants the powers of persuasion and, ultimately, dominion in any exchange.

Such is the stance of the subject in Whitman's "Salut au
Monde!"—a vision which appears as early as the second edition
of *Leaves of Grass* under the title "Poem of Salutation" (1856). According to some critics, the poet's concern here is to balance the
extreme self-centeredness and the exacerbated nationalism expressed in the first edition, particularly in the preface. If this is

indeed the case, perhaps we should compare the poet's worthy intention with the poem's ultimate message. "Salut au Monde!" comprises thirteen sections of amazed contemplation of the inhabited world's immense variety translated into the perfection of the terrestrial sphere or, as the poet himself says, into "a great round wonder rolling through space." The opening lines establish the setting and tone of the poem, with Walt Whitman re-created as a persona by an ecstatic lyric "I." The effect is that of an unfolding of subjectivity—curiously anticipating Pessoa's heteronymous splittings—that ends up totally encompassing its object: "O take my hand Walt Whitman!" the poem begins, and then, four lines later, "What widens *within* you Walt Whitman?" I emphasize "within," a crucial word that Whitman repeats four times in the second section:

> Within me latitude widens, longitude lengthens,
> Asia, Africa, Europe, are to the east—America is
>   provided for in the west,
> Banding the bulge of the earth winds the hot equator,
> Curiously north and south turn the axis-ends,
> Within me is the longest day, the sun wheels in slanting
>   rings, it does not set for months,
> Stretch'd in due time within me the midnight sun just
>   rises above the horizon and sinks again,
> Within me zones, seas, cataracts, forests, volcanoes,
>   groups,
> Malaysia, Polynesia, and the great West Indian islands.
>   (14–21)

The anaphoric orgies of hearing and sight that follow ("I see," "I hear"), reaching their climax in the solidary assertion of identity in section 8 ("I am," "I belong"), are entirely performed in the poet's imagination—the axis of his vision, Emerson would say, perfectly coinciding with the axis of things. The poet's mind is thus the center and measure of all reality, so that his ample and generous salutation is actually his and America's sympathetic projection onto all other lands, nations, and peoples. "Health to you! good will to you all, from me and America sent!" (194). The suspicion that this salutation to the world may only be the obverse of Emerson's "conversion of the world" is heightened in the last two sections of the poem, where the poet expresses the hope that the assumed inferiority of certain peoples will "in due time" be overcome. But the world must first have been "penetrated" (the phallic metaphor is Whitman's) by the "divine rapport" of America's all-encompassing, indeed, all-generating spermatic imagination embodied in the bard (Aspiz, 379–395). The process described here in terms of the compassionate creation of time and space is what Pessoa calls, quite approvingly, the "essence of imperialism": "to convert the others into our own substance; to convert the others into our own selves" (*Sobre Portugal*, 237). Hence, as the poet imagines the other's desire or lack of desire, point of view translates into total identity.

It must be possible, Wallace Stevens's poetry cries out wistfully, to discover and not to impose. The history of western discoveries tells us otherwise. Still, the Atlantic poets often use the concept of discovery to signify the very freedom of poetic creativity. In Whitman's "Passage to India," for instance, the voyage of discovery is the aptest metaphor for the reinvention of the subject's daring imagining. The centrality of the subjective imagination in this poem is characteristic of the romantic tradition to which the poets examined here are heirs. "Song of Myself" is perhaps exemplary in this regard but, given the national and universalizing meanings he attaches to "Walt Whitman, the Bard of America," the identification of poetry and the poet's mind in Whitman's work as a whole yields an astonishing "supreme fiction," "the fiction of an absolute" that is nothing less than "the great idea of America."[2] In other words, America is the poet's message. In "Passage to India" Whitman reimagines Columbus's dream as that of the world accomplished, but such accomplishment is clearly the constitution of "these United States" in the New World: "(Ah Genoese thy dream! thy dream! / Centuries after thou art laid in thy grave, / The shore thou foundest verifies thy dream.)" (65–67). The poem's song of a network of relations and connections, of a welding of lands and marrying of peoples, clearly points to a utopian achievement of universal harmony that is best represented in Whitman by the American nation itself: "Lands found and nations born, thou born America, / For purpose vast, man's long probation fill'd / Thou rondure of the world at last accomplish'd" (78–80). So, after the seas have all been crossed comes the poet that is truly "worthy [of] that name," for "resuming all," the poet of American democracy is perfectly identical with the whole world.

The stance of authorial self-projection and creative absorption of the other is the kind of "spiritual imperialism" Pessoa has in mind when he refers in his notes on Atlantism to the concept of an "Atlantic expansion . . . already present by nocturnal intuition in Walt Whitman's high Atlantic spirit" (*Sobre Portugal*, 224). It is a poetic stance that claims an extraordinarily ambitious role for language and poetry, as when Crane says of "Atlantis" (the poem), "it IS the real Atlantis" (*Letters*, 268). This is a "discovery" that Crane could have made only by impersonating, as he does in *The Bridge*, a Whitmanian Columbus from "Passage to India." It is comparable to a new traversing of the Atlantic, effectively substituting the poem—which Crane perceives as a "*conquest* of space and knowledge" (*Letters*, 241, emphasis added)—for the vision of the western empire as the last imaginable utopia. For his part, having depicted the Portuguese discoveries as a voyage across the Atlantic "to create a major civilization," Pessoa also thinks of Whitman and of his "passage to more than India." He propounds another crossing, that of "an Atlantic soul and spirit . . . in quest of the ultimate civilization." To better understand this emphasis on the Atlantic Ocean as a source of inspiration and to problematize the enunciation of an imperial vision of poetry, let us consider the ferment of political, economic, and cultural ideas in the western world at the end of the nineteenth century and, especially, during the first decades of the twentieth.

The turn of the century brought on both sides of the Atlantic a renewed interest in the myth of Atlantis. This revival coincided with a period of profound crisis in the West: Europe was shaken by struggles and self-doubts that culminated in World War I and are best summarized in Oswald Spengler's *The Decline of the West*. Western thinkers were concentrating on finding new forms of inspiration and power capable of recuperating the identity of the West as a center. The myth of Atlantis serves to demonstrate that the cultural affinities of both North Atlantic continents derive from a common source, the "intermediate" ancient island, the perfect imperial society swallowed by the ocean. As Lewis Spence put it in *Atlantis in America*—a book avidly read by Crane—only a "bridging" of the Atlantic would bring Europe and America together again as the accomplished West.[3] The return to the myth, then, momentarily allows the re-creation of the center of a utopian ideal of universal harmony and wholeness, constantly shattered by the facts of modern history.

At the same time more pragmatic intellectuals on both sides of the ocean were also engaging in debates about the possibilities of transatlantic exchange aimed at western renewal and progress. This is the subject of Waldo Frank's foreword to the American edition of *Our America* (1919), a book intended to reveal America to European visitors as much as to the American people themselves. Crane's development as a poet was powerfully influenced not only by Spence's writings on the myth of Atlantis but also by Frank's vision of America as the last hope for the West. Pessoa, too, I suspect, would have liked Frank's notion, formulated in *The Rediscovery of America* (1929), that the fifteenth-century explorers had merely discovered the ocean, "the sense of the whole" remaining in abeyance forever to lure the modern western explorer onward. Furthermore, Pessoa's invocation of an "Atlantic soul" anticipated the concept of Atlanticism developed after midcentury.[4]

Ultimately, then, the very idea of discovery presupposes a center that is absoluely not available for discovery, a center that is always there so to speak. There is no discovery before the discoverer arrives, for the discoverer, setting out from the center, paradoxically brings along discovery itself. Pessoa sums it up when he says that the Portuguese discovered the "idea of discovery" (*Sobre Portugal*, 223). We need only think of the course of political and economic world history from the fifteenth century onward. The expansionist wars that broke out at the close of the nineteenth century—the Spanish-American War of 1898 and the South African War of 1899–1902—are only a continuation of that trajectory. As to World War I, there is no question in our minds today about which world was at stake.

The totalizing vocation of the West, redefined by the modern idea of empire and of which the discoveries remain the aptest image,[5] nourished the imaginations of Crane and Pessoa and determined their use of the discovery image as well as what the image itself projects of the self-appointed centrality of the western world and of its lust for wholeness and a controllable identity.

We know that Crane conceived of *The Bridge* as a synthesis of America. But the peculiar nature of this synthesis, which may well yield less of a synchronic summing up than a diachronic comprehensiveness, comes directly from Whitman's trope of extension, as Lee Edelman has shown in his fine study of Crane's catachrestic style. From the opening lines of the preface in the first edition of *Leaves of Grass*, there is the identification of poet, poem, nation, and the nation's vocation to become the whole world, such that when the poet proclaims "I sing myself," he is already voicing his vision of America as a totality, a vision coterminous with that of empire. The contiguity increases and the vision strengthens throughout the poems in which Whitman develops what Pessoa termed the "Atlantic spirit": the poems of crossing, passage, discovery, and salutation of the world at last accomplished. This vision is explicitly reclaimed by Crane in "Cape Hatteras," where the phrase "Afoot again" deliberately echoes Whitman's "I am afoot with my vision," the bard's claim for absolute inspiration in "Song of Myself." Crane's vision begins, therefore, as it must, where he understands Whitman's to end: in America, the West realized as the discovering, originating center, a symbol of creativity itself—of poetry. Such, to my mind, is the "myth of America" elaborated in *The Bridge*. Crane's self-ascribed task there is to develop or discover, as he says, the spiritual illuminations and the "new hierarchy of faith" (*Complete Poems*, 219) that he feels sure is the renewed promise of America.

Pessoa's Fifth Empire

As a bilingual poet educated in a British school in South Africa until the age of seventeen, Pessoa is heir to not one but two empires. And, as outlined earlier, Pessoa's conception of his poem also owes a great deal to Whitman's influence, particularly in regard to the use of discovery as a metaphor.[6] I would furthermore argue that in *Mensagem* the poet returns aura, glory, and beauty to the idea of the West while bewailing the loss of one of its major symbols, Portugal's old sea empire. Indeed, such loss seems to be the very condition of the re-creation he is engaged in. The poem, together with the prose notes discussed earlier, actually makes quite clear the thrust of Pessoa's reasoning and imagining. In his view, the course of world events during the first decades of the twentieth century puts the supremacy of the West severely in doubt, its major powers having obviously failed to fulfill the promise of its centrality.

In 1917, precisely when World War I was being waged, Pessoa's futurist heteronym Alvaro de Campos launched a vicious, albeit hilarious, attack on the "mandarins of Europe" in his outrageous (and outraged) "Ultimatum." His fierce denunciation is aimed as much at the lingering imperial powers of decadent Europe as at the preposterous pretensions of "bastard" America. It is, in fact, an indictment of western civilization's failure to hold itself together. It should be remembered that Campos's "Ultimatum" came in belated response to the humiliation inflicted on the Portuguese nation by the British ultimatum of 1890, which forced the Portuguese troops to withdraw from the Southern African region known as the Pink Map. The reaction of the Portuguese was passionately patriotic ("A Portuguesa," later to be adopted as the national anthem, dates from that time) and eventually led to the fall of the monarchy in 1910. By 1917, however, there were reasons, at least from Pessoa's vantage point, to doubt the greater capacity of republican rule to defend Portuguese interests in Europe and elsewhere. The ironies of Pessoa's parodic "Ultimatum" are thus endless. On the one hand, there is the bitter memory of Portuguese dependency and powerlessness vis-à-vis the expansionist ambitions of the British empire, the centuries-old Portuguese-British alliance adding a touch of perversity to the bitterness. On the other hand, signs of the decadence of the western empire are steadily gathering; the "superiority" of western values and traditions is gradually found to have no un-

challengeable "center" after all and gives way to national political and economic interests as well as to a series of national
struggles for the international right to exploit. In 1917, during
the most important of these struggles, the Portuguese were du-
tifully fighting alongside their British allies, ostensibly in Portugal's own imperial interest; but Pessoa may have uncannily
foreseen the reason Portugal still held its colonies at the end of
World War I—the *real* imperial powers could not agree on how to
share them to their best advantage (Hobsbawm, 18).

Curiously enough, Pessoa was perhaps among the first to
point out that, for contemporary Portugal, the colonies are a lia-
bility rather than an asset. His belief that for Portugal there is still
a worthwhile future is anchored in his firm rejection of a Portuguese overseas empire defined in terms of material possessions.
Such an empire, we recall, is the Portuguese national "problem."
That Portugal never managed to take full advantage of its empire, the subject of many jokes among the Portuguese, may be
part of the "problem" as Pessoa saw it. But his denunciation of
the Portuguese empire—which he referred to in *Obra em Prosa* as
having been "forced upon us" by "our discoveries"—is surely
more complex than that. Considering Pessoa's elitism and aristocratism, it is unlikely that the general idea of the strong prevailing over the weak troubled him; he felt, rather, that Portugal's
capacity to rule and dominate, in light of all its weaknesses and
failures, had never before been correctly understood. The idea of
a centripetal imperialist center is, therefore, far from put into
question. From his difficult stance as a self-consciously ambitious
western poet in an increasingly dependent nation, Pessoa is determined to reinvent, in "spiritual terms," Portugal's independence and hence its capacity to influence and dominate. The poetical reenactment of the Portuguese voyages of discovery as the
foundational events of the western empire is Pessoa's task in
Mensagem, his vision and his aim, what he calls the "Spiritual
Empire."

In Pessoa's distinction between material and spiritual imperialism there is, for obvious reasons, a kind of indirect correlation
and exchange: the more powerful and influential the nation, the
less its spiritual potential. Or, in his own almost esoteric terms,

"only a small nation could usefully fulfill the Spiritual Empire" (*Sobre Portugal,* 225). Hence his desire to value Portugal's power-lessness in the world system by defining the Portuguese empire in terms of spiritual imperialism in order to reassess the role of modern Portugal in the world. In his vision, the language and poetry of Portugal have a universal mission to fulfill. The same paradoxical indirect correlation between power and potential is at work here also. Since Portuguese poetry has thus far accomplished so little, Pessoa argues outrageously, it is now possible in Portugal "to do everything as it should be done" (239). Everything? or Poetry, with a capital P? The fact remains that when Pessoa sets out to imagine the future of Portugal, it is poetry as sheer creativity and possibility that engages him. "Let us fulfill Apollo spiritually," he urges (226). But the totalizing idea of empire, no matter how spiritual, is still his sole inspiration. As he himself insisted, "imperialism is always imperialism" (232).

The prophecies of the redemptive mythic return of Sebastian, the king who remains the very emblem of the utter failure of Portuguese imperialism, combined with the nationalized version of the myth of the Fifth Empire, the ultimate universal utopia, help Pessoa to shape his imagining. Consistently taking the discoveries as his major structuring metaphor, Pessoa realizes his project in *Mensagem,* a poem conceived on the one hand as the Fifth Empire itself, on the other as the finest heterocosm of modernist poetry.[7]

In *Mensagem,* Pessoa, too, takes Whitman's hand, breathes his "high Atlantic spirit," and, following him faithfully on the bard's daring passage to "more than India" (or, to use Pessoa's formulation, "the spiritual Indies"), reinvents himself as the poet truly "worthy [of] that name." We have already seen in his notes that Pessoa relates spiritual imperialism and Whitman's Atlantism to sensationism and intersectionism, that is to say, to poetic modernism. When he speaks of Atlantism he is, therefore, also speaking of poetry. Thus, in "The Last Ship," the poetic subject is identified by the Whitmanian "Atlantic soul":

> Ah, quanto mais ao povo a alma falta,
> Mais a minha alma atlântica se exalta

E entorna,
E en mim, num mar que nao tem tempo ou spaço,
Vejo entre a cerraçao teu vulto baço
Que torna.

Ah, the more a people's soul has faltered
The more my own Atlantan soul exalting
Pours forth,
And in me, a timeless, boundless sea,
I spy through fog your dim shape
Turning back. (*Poems*, 174)

The people's faltering soul is the soul that has failed the people. It is, in other words, the failure of the Portuguese empire in Sebastian's defeat and disappearance in Alcázarquiver in 1578. Again, the indirect correlation is at work here, for the poet's Atlantic soul pours forth as if it were a consequence of the decadence of the material empire, thus engendering, as the Portuguese rhyme emphasizes, the spiritual empire symbolized by the prophesied return of King Sebastian. Moreover, it seems that the absence of empire—represented by Sebastian's disappearance—had to be imagined before the empire could be reimagined in the fiction of Sebastian's return. The question of the "undiscovered island" in the second stanza problematizes the very idea of discovery and of an empire grounded in discovering and imposing, even as the metaphor of the Portuguese discoveries grants the poem—this particular lyric and *Mensagem* as a whole—its own grounding. The crossing of the seas, the discoveries, and the rondure of the earth paradoxically symbolize the decadence of the Portuguese empire, which the poem also bewails, and the renewed "spiritual" voyage to the ultimate western empire—the Fifth—which is Portugal's fulfillment in Sebastian's return. Since Pessoa, by making the year of his birth coincide with the date of the prophesied return of the Desired One, had already "demonstrated" that he himself *is* King Sebastian returned, the conclusion that *Mensagem* is the Fifth Empire becomes unavoidable. Thus is the fiction of an absolute fulfilled by the poet truly worthy of the name. I know of no more daring metaphor for poetry than that of an ahistorical, self-contained, all-encompassing totality.

NOTES

1. King Sebastian (1557–1578)—the "Desired One"—of Portugal was defeated by the Moslems and disappeared in North Africa in 1578. In the absence of a legitimate Portuguese monarch, the country fell under Spanish rule for sixty years. Sebastianism is a messianic myth wherein the king returns one day to save Portugal from oppression and decadence and to herald a new age. The famous writer, preacher, and missionary António Vieira (1608–1697) dubbed this new age the "Fifth Empire."

2. "By Blue Ontario's Shore" is a celebration of the "great idea"; *Democratic Vistas* is its critique. Responding to Tate's reservations about his use of Whitman in *The Bridge* shortly after the book came out, Crane argued in Whitman's defense that *Democratic Vistas* strongly qualifies his glorification of America, thus highlighting his "positive and universal tendencies" (*Letters*, 353–354).

3. The bridge metaphor appeared before in Spence (see, for example, page 132). For recent perspectives on the myth of Atlantis and its influence, see Ramage.

4. See Hahn and Pfaltzgraff, Kleiman, and Ballard (a precursory study which may have interested Crane and Pessoa).

5. When modern voyagers cross the boundaries of the earthly globe, the destination is still the center and the metaphor is still very powerful: "This is a new ocean," exclaimed John F. Kennedy at the beginning of the Apollo project, "and the U.S. must sail upon it" (Mailer, 9).

6. Brown lists all the major studies to date bearing on the subject. For Whitman in Pessoa's *Mensagem*, see Santos, "An Imperialism of Poets."

7. I develop this idea in "A Hora do Poeta."

Pessoa and Whitman

Brothers in the Universe

SUSAN MARGARET BROWN

I still remember vividly the shock of recognition back in 1977 as I began reading the poetry of Fernando Pessoa for the first time. The presence of Whitman in poem after poem of Portugal's major modern poet was overwhelming. At times it seemed to hover, oblique and hard to nail down in its evocation of Whitman—a tonal quality, a certain rhythm, an ever-so-slight gesture on the part of the speaker. At other times the presence was blatant, outdoing Whitman himself in sheer visceral energy, in the wild barbaric yawping. More curious still was the way this Whitmanian presence seemed to pervade the entire corpus of two of Pessoa's three fictional poets or, as he alternately called them, his "fictions of the interlude," his "drama in characters," his heteronyms. How was it possible, I wondered, for Fernando Pessoa, creator of manifold identities and exemplary poet of the self as other, to have felt an affinity with the solitary singer of "one's-self," that "chanter of personality" who had made it his lifelong endeavor "to put a *Person*, a human being . . . freely, fully and truly on record" ("A Backward Glance," 573–574)? Furthermore, how was it possible for Pessoa to have imbibed Whitman so deeply that two poets in his heteronymic coterie, Alberto Caeiro and Alvaro de Campos, actually sounded like transfigurations of Whitman?

Eduardo Lourenço, one of Pessoa's finest critics and the only one to study seriously the impact of Whitman upon Pessoa, schematized the question of influence (to use the traditional term) in a way that enabled me to examine these questions in depth. In Lourenço's opinion, it was through Whitman, singer of concrete reality, that Pessoa became the supreme poet of Absence. In "Walt Whitman e Pessoa" ("Walt Whitman and Pessoa"), Lourenço claims unequivocally that Pessoa's encounter with Whitman provoked the creation of the heteronyms. Two fictional poets with two separate interpretations of Whitman's paradisiacal vision emerged as a result of that imaginary meeting between Pessoa and Whitman: Caeiro is "Whitman without flesh" and Campos is an "anti-Whitman." Caeiro, whose link to Whitman is less visible, sustains a more profound relationship with Whitman, for it is Caeiro who appropriates both Whitman's sensorial world and his clarity of vision. The central importance of Caeiro, however, does not lie in his contact with concrete reality (as it does in Whitman) but rather in the philosophical affirmation of the existence of that reality.

In an essay in *Pessoa Revisitado* entitled "A Curiosa Singularidade De 'Mestre Caeiro'" ("The Curious Singularity of 'Master Caeiro'") Lourenço looks more closely at the crucial importance of Alberto Caeiro by addressing the question of his genesis, since it was in relation to the creation of Caeiro that the other two heteronyms were established. Lourenço asserts that Pessoa "stripped Whitman of all his passion for real things, keeping only the nostalgia for the health of the American bard, a health which Pessoa himself didn't possess" (47). In this way Whitman gave Pessoa access to the dream of reality (as embodied in the heteronym of Caeiro) rather than concrete reality. Caeiro represents the imaginary Whitman or, better, the idea of Whitman. Lourenço then proceeds in another essay included in the same book, entitled "O Mistério-Caeiro na Luz de Campos e Vice-Versa" ("The Caeiro Mystery in the Light of Campos and Vice-Versa"), to emphasize the inextricable link between Caeiro and Campos. His claim is that Campos, who emerges directly from Caeiro—the "transformed echo" of Whitman's vision of concrete reality—could appear only after Pessoa had "proven to himself" that he had an incomparable master somewhere beyond the reach of his own consciousness. Thus Campos emerges as the shadow of the master Caeiro and retrospectively illuminates him.

Lourenço's insights are exceptionally valuable in delineating the Pessoa-Whitman connection. He correctly identifies Whitman as the catalyzing force which opened Pessoa's inner self to an amazonic estuary of two powerful currents and which generated the impulse toward the invention of the two interrelated personae, Caeiro and Campos. Since he is primarily a historian of ideas, however, Lourenço's notions are largely psychological. In many respects his views recall Harold Bloom's formulations of influence as the misreadings or misprisions of the belated poet on a precursor. Lourenço writes of the deliberate concealment of Whitman's impact on Caeiro, for example, pointing out Pessoa's many attempts at masking and mystification in an effort to avoid identification with Whitman, and he repeatedly insists that in trying to overcome or conquer the mother text, *Leaves of Grass*, Pessoa "strangled" the master. Still, Lourenço's instigating work has provided invaluable guidelines for any further inquiry, in strictly literary terms, into the intertextual presence of Whitman. In the remainder of this essay it is my purpose to elaborate and translate Lourenço's intuitions of a psychological order into a language and structure that reveal the aesthetic nature of Whitman's impact.

Turning first to Alberto Caeiro: What does it mean to say that he is a Whitman without flesh, an imaginary Whitman, the idea of Whitman? And what does it mean to say that Pessoa gained access through Whitman to the dream of reality as embodied in the poetic figure of Caeiro?

To begin with, an interesting analogy can be drawn between the way Whitman addresses Emerson as "Master" in his unauthorized publication of Emerson's letter of encouragement of July 21, 1855, and the way Pessoa speaks of his master Caeiro.[1] In the same way that Whitman was "simmering" until Emerson brought him "to a boil," Pessoa's eruption into the heteronymic world was catalyzed by the transformed echo of Whitman as embodied in Alberto Caeiro. More specifically, it was the Whitmanian expression of the Emersonian gnosis lying at the heart of Caeiro's persona that engendered the forty-nine poems of the innocent shepherd poet, the poetic sequence entitled *O Guardador de Rebanhos* (*The Keeper of Sheep*). Thus, just as Emerson's orphic poet of nature turned out to be Walt Whitman, Pessoa's turned out to be Alberto Caeiro.

To better grasp this we need to remember that the revolutionary poetics of Caeiro's *The Keeper of Sheep* firmly plants the heteronymic "drama in characters" in the intermediate landscape of the dream. Caeiro bridges the abyss of consciousness by postulating a third reality where, in dreamlike transparency, an absolute conjunction exists between the language of the inward eye and the language of the outer world. Through the power of his dream vision of the paganized child Jesus in poem 8, Caeiro liberates the personal ego, compelling it outward, beyond the "absurdity of the Christian dualism."[2] Constructing a "metaphysics" (poem 5) similar to Emerson's freedom to imagine "the pure idea in your mind" and defining himself in terms similar to Emerson's "transparent eyeball," Caeiro fuses inner and outer into a single reality so that he becomes one with all he sees: "Porque eu sou do tamanho do que vejo / E não do tamanho da minha altura" ("Because I am the size of what I see / And not the measure of my height") (*Keeper of Sheep*, 14).

Vision and desire are thus merged in the poetic eye that is Caeiro. Embodying the new insight of one's godliness as a poet, Caeiro is made to symbolize orphic seeing. Caeiro's emphasis upon sight must be understood in this sense: He is the radiant image of poetic light standing in the abyss of consciousness after having learned the gnostic truth of the Christ-like Whitman on the knoll speaking to poets to come in section 46 of "Song of Myself." We therefore need to understand Caeiro as the image-voice of what it means to "habit yourself to the dazzle of the light and of every moment of your life."

All that Caeiro will say in his forty-nine poems derives from this new poetic power of sight—a power so intensely human it is divine, so intensely private it is totally impersonal. Furthermore, this power originates in Caeiro's dream vision of the new child Jesus, *o menino Jesus*, in poem 8. It is imperative to remember that the whole sequence derives its meaning from this central poem, as Caeiro makes clear in the middle of the poem. Recalling Whitman's "my words itch at your ears until you understand them," the words of the child Jesus tickle at Caeiro's ears:

> He taught me everything.
> He taught me to look at things.
> He points out everything there is inside flowers.
> He shows me how funny rocks are
> When people take them in hand
> And look slowly at them.
>
> .   .   .   .
>
> The Eternal Child is with me always.
> My glance takes the direction of his pointing finger.
> My hearing, happily alert to every sound,
> Is his playful tickling in my ears. (*Keeper of Sheep*, 16–18)

The "Eternal Child" Jesus is really, upon closer examination, a disguised Whitman. This scene represents Caeiro's communion with the American poet who in the poem appears transfigured as *"o deus que faltava"* ("the God that was missing"). Once we perceive the transformational process at work here we begin to see how the whole of poem 8 alludes to section 5 of "Song of Myself" and we are better able to understand how Caeiro, in his quest for poetic identity, desires the experience of his own eternity just as Whitman had desired it in section 5. It is this quest, in fact, that alone explains the purpose of Caeiro's pastoral attachment to the child Jesus.

In his role as poet of the new sensibility—"*o Descobridor da Natureza*" ("Discoverer of Nature"), "*o Argonauta das sensações verdadeiras*" ("Argonaut of true sensations")—Caeiro brings "a new Universe into the Universe" ("*Trago ao Universo um novo Universo / Porque trago ao Universo ele-próprio*") by revealing the world of original Adamic sight, just as Whitman had done before him. He does this by making his own image a mirror image of the gnostic truth learned in the dream: the truth of oneself as a creative force, as an ongoing shimmer of volatile light, partaking of both the human and the divine. Transformed by the vision of a paganized Jesus and/or a divinized Whitman in poem 8, Caeiro goes on to define himself in poem 30 as the singer of nature and in poem 46 as "*um animal humano que a Natureza produziu*" ("a human animal Nature produced"). In so doing, Caeiro revives Whitman's famous lines—"I harbor for good or bad, I permit to speak at every hazard, / Nature without check with original energy" ("Song of Myself," 12–13)—as well as the meaning of the orphic poet as Emerson had described him in his essay "Nature."

The whole thrust of the forty-nine poems is to effect a decomposition of the real in order to raise a new cosmos of the self in which paganism serves as a religion of the (self-creative) imagination—a religion which is a "*teoria científica para durar o universo*" ("scientific theory capable of making the universe last") (*Obra em Prosa*, 545). Caeiro, essence of the new religion, acts as the stabilizing force in the heteronymic cosmos. He is the disciplined intelligence in the anarchy of feeling, the dream of Being's fullness in its confrontation with the void, the acceptance of the chaos without the need for illusions. His aim is to bring proof of the deeper intuitive self: the poetic knowledge which sees the timeless moment. Making it his duty to feel all things distinctly and intensely yet with the serenity of the meditative eye alone, he eliminates the confusion of the senses and softens the shock of abysmal consciousness.

With Caeiro's appearance, then, Pessoa assumed his new role as conscious ironist involved in a fictional self-making. Establishing Caeiro as the image-voice for the Emersonian knowledge that "we are nothing but the light is all" ("Selections," 386–387), Pessoa grounded his lyrical narration of mind in the paradoxical image of a self-presencing absence. And if we do not refer the various heteronymic voices back to the lost ideal that Master Caeiro embodies, we will fail to see how heteronymic consciousness is fundamentally rooted in absence, in Caeiro's image-voice of Whitman's "Me myself," the "lull" and "hum" of his "valvèd voice" in section 5 of "Song of Myself." Furthermore, we will fail to see that Caeiro and Campos are involved in a continuing dialectic just as Whitman's yawp and his lull play against one another.

To understand how central Alberto Caeiro's role is as master and how overwhelming his effect on the persona of Alvaro de Campos is, one has only to look at Campos's essay entitled "Notas para a Recordação do Meu Mestre Caeiro" ("Notes for the Memory of My Master Caeiro"). Take this passage, for example, where he poignantly underscores his nostalgia and affection for the master:

> Nobody remains inconsolable near the memory of Caeiro or his poems; and the very idea of nothing—the most terrifying of all ideas when it is thought of with feeling—has, in the work and memory of my dear master, something luminous and high about it, like the sun on the snow-capped and unreachable mountaintops. (*Obra em Prosa*, 107–110, my translation)

An even better illustration of Campos's intimate link to Caeiro occurs in his poem "Mestre, Meu Querido Mestre" ("Master, My Dear Master"). The poem begins with the following invocation:

> Master, my dear Master!
> Heart of my body, intellectual and whole!
> Life-root of my inspiration!
> Master, what became of you in this form of life?
> (*Poems*, 92)

The key here is in the second line—"*Coração do meu corpo*" ("Heart of my body")—for it becomes clear, particularly once we recognize how Whitman's presence in both heteronyms functions, that Caeiro represents the lost soul of Campos; he is the pagan poet inside Campos that Pessoa refers to in his surprisingly revealing statement that "Alvaro de Campos is excellently defined as a Walt Whitman with a Greek poet inside."[3] As we have seen, Caeiro enacts the moment of vision, something beyond the human, and he therefore does not embody subjectivity as Campos does. On this point Pessoa serves as his own best critic when he writes that the great originality of Caeiro is his

> almost inconceivable objectiveness [objectivity]. He sees things with the eyes only, not with the mind. He does not let any thoughts arise when he looks at a flower. . . . A state of mind may be conceived resembling this. But it cannot be conceived in a poet. . . . The stupendous fact about Caeiro is that out of this sentiment, or rather, absence of sentiment, he makes poetry. (*Páginas Íntimas*, 335–343)[4]

Arising directly, then, out of the "Me myself" that is Caeiro, Alvaro de Campos proceeds as the darker side of the pastoral poet, the human subjective response to that transcendental voice.

If Whitman emerges in Caeiro as an almost imperceptible presence, in Campos he explodes in a torrent of language. Opening the floodgates of the soul, Whitman's language inundates the poems with Campos's insatiable desire to be Other; it fertilizes and shapes his persona as sensationist poet by providing the means, both structural and semantic, for expressing identity as a hesitation between Being and Non-Being, between the *cío* (sexual itch) and *cansaço* (exhaustion) of imagination. It is, in fact, precisely this continually frustrated desire to be Other that characterizes the essential configuration of Campos as an anti-Whitman. And nowhere is this trait of Campos more visible than in his long ode to Whitman entitled "Saudação a Walt Whitman" ("Salutation to Walt Whitman") (see *Poems*, 72–78).

Campos's direct invocation of Whitman in "Salutation to Walt Whitman" follows a pattern similar to the one established in the aforementioned poem to Master Caeiro, "Master, My Dear Master." After a catalog of epithets in praise of Whitman's erotic "adhesiveness"—an expanded descriptive system of Whitman as the "*souteneur de todo o Universo*" ("*souteneur* of the whole Universe")—Campos writes of Whitman in terms similar to Caeiro:

Though in facing the Universe yours was the attitude of
  a woman,
And every blade of grass, every stone, every man was a
  Universe for you. (*Poems*, 73)

Following four pages of identification with his *"velho Walt, meu grande camerada"* ("Walt, dearest old man, my great comrade") in an attempt to belong to his *"orgia báquica de sensações-em-liberdade"* ("bacchic orgy of freed sensations"), Campos, the *"franzino e civilizado"* ("slight and civilized"), ends his salutation in the anguished tone of failed identity, again in terms that recall his lamentation for the lost Caeiro:

Now that I'm almost dead and see everything so clearly,
I bow to you, Great Liberator.

Surely my personality had some purpose.
Surely it meant something, since it expressed itself,
Yet looking back today, only one thing troubles me—
Not to have had your self-transcending calm,
Your liberation like star-clustered Infinite Night.

Maybe I had no mission at all on earth. (*Poems*, 78)

This poem, like "Master, My Dear Master," is a reminiscence song, recounting Campos's moment of poetic awakening to his more-than-human mission. That mission involves becoming, like Whitman, a cosmos of self-contradicting and unlimited sensations. This is made excruciatingly clear in the following long passage:

Open all the doors!
Because I have to go in!
My password? Walt Whitman!
But I don't give any password . . .
I go in without explaining . . .

  .   .   .   .

Let no son of a bitch get in my way!
My path goes through Infinity before reaching its end!
It's not up to you whether I reach this end or not,

It's up to me, up to God—up to what I mean by the
   word *Infinite* . . .
Onward!
I spur ahead!
I feel the spurs, I am the very horse I mount,
Because I, since I want to be consubstantial with God,
Can be everything, or I can be nothing, or anything,
Just as I please . . . It's nobody's business . . .
Raging madness! Wanting to yelp, jump,
Scream, bray, do handsprings and somersaults, my
   body yelling,
Cramponner at the car wheels and to go under,
Get inside the whirling whiplash that's about to strike,
Be the bitch to all dogs and they not enough for me,
Be the steering wheel of all machines and their speed
   too slow for me,
Be the one who's crushed, abandoned, pulled apart, or
   done for,
Come dance this fury with me, Walt, you there in that
   other world,
Swing this hoedown with me knocking at the stars,
Fall exhausted to the ground with me,
Beat the walls with me like mad,
Break down, tear yourself apart with me,
Through everything, in everything, around everything,
   without anything,
In an abstract body rage that stirs up maelstroms in the
   soul . . . (*Poems*, 74–75)

To be cosmic lover of the universe is what constitutes Campos's
(ideal) poetic ambition. Translating the meaning of Caeiro's new
poetics as obliquely outlined in his forty-nine poems, Campos
reads an echo of Whitman's call to traveling souls as expounded
in "Song of the Open Road" and resung in Caeiro's poems. But
unlike Caeiro, Campos is incapable of carrying the universe
in his arms. The reverse image of Caeiro, he is the one who
thinks, becomes momentarily moved, and then falls back to exacerbated consciousness. Campos's awakening to the open road

of the soul is thus a burden as much as a liberation, as he makes known to Master Caeiro: *"Libertaste-me, mas o destino humano é ser escravo"* ("You freed me but the fate of man is to be enslaved") (*Poems*, 93).

The identity of Campos depends—as it did for Caeiro—upon the energy and vitality of imagination to transform and internalize the elements of the world: to see one's countenance in outerness and inscribe oneself as a projection of otherness. But unlike Caeiro, a steady self-reflecting eye at the center of the universe, Campos loses himself in his immediate vision. His response to the Whitman in Caeiro is feverish, unbalanced and hallucinatory. He is the abstract mechanical man, the engineer-poet involved in the *"mágoa quotidiana das matemáticas de ser"* ("the daily pain inflicted by the mathematics of Being") (*Poems*, 92). His contact is ultimately with the artificial stimuli of modern life, forcing the rhythm of his imaginational experience to follow a distinct pattern based on mechanical processes: Slowly shifting into first gear, the mind accelerates rapidly until it reaches an explosive climax which, in turn, produces an abrupt decline. Virtually all the poems end in the exhaustion and breakdown of imagination precisely because Campos is incapable of sustaining the sympathetic feel, the Whitmanian merge. In identifying with Whitman, then, Campos emerges as the *"raiva abstrato do corpo"* ("abstract body rage") described above. And his plight, in the end, resides in his inability to carry through, as Whitman had, in identifying with otherness, in containing the many by becoming one with all he sees.

Whitman was Pessoa's liberator, and his value as a liberating force needs to be seen partially in terms of form: namely, the personal epic. Commenting on Whitman's redefinition of the epic and outlining its characteristic features, James E. Miller writes that it is

a long poem whose narrative is of an interior rather than exterior action, with emphasis on successive mental or emotional states; on a subject or theme not special or superior but common and vital; related not in a literary, measured, and elevated style but in a personal, free, and familiar style; focusing not on a heroic or semidivine individual but on the poet himself as representative figure, comprehending and illuminating the age; and whose awareness, insight, being—rather than heroic actions—involve, however obliquely, the fate of the society, the nation, the human race. Such, sketched forth in rather simple terms, was Whitman's redefinition of the epic. (*American Quest*, 36)

Pessoa's heteronymic experiment as a whole needs to be viewed in a way similar to this portrayal of Whitman's poem; it too needs to be understood in terms of that Adamic drive which Whitman represented so thoroughly. I would even go so far as to suggest that Whitman's cosmic persona functioned for Pessoa as the ideal representation of the romantic construct of Self that Pessoa describes so magnificently:

> That individual grandiose person the romantics gave shape to I have often tried living in dreams, and just as often have found myself laughing aloud at my idea of living it. Mortal man, in the end, exists in his own dreams, which are those of all men, and Romanticism is nothing if not the turning inside out of the daily power we exert over ourselves. Almost all men dream deep down in their hearts of their magnificent dominion over an empire, the subjugation of all men, the submission of all women, the adoration of all people, and in the noblest terms. . . . Few men are so habituated to dreaming as I am, and therefore sufficiently lucid to laugh at the aesthetic possibility of dreaming oneself in such a way.
>
> The greatest charge one can level against Romanticism has not yet been made: namely, that it represents the inner truth of human nature. Its exaggerations, its ridiculous aspects, its various powers to compel and seduce stem from the fact that it is an external figuration of what is most intimate in the soul, yet concretely visible, even possible if being possible only depended on something other than Fate. (*Poems*, 195–196)

It is that "external figuration of what is most intimate in the soul" which Pessoa turns inside out in order to give shape to his own version of the cosmic persona, the self-propagating heteronymic persona of various voices, various selves. Molding two poetic figures out of the Whitmanian persona, Pessoa takes the Adamic mode to its furthest limits. Whereas Whitman had centered his persona squarely within the world of reality, Pessoa uses the Whitman paradigm as a way of decentering subjectivity and, recalling the "King of Gaps," he sets up a world of interbeings "Between our silence and our speech, between / Us and the consciousness of us." [5]

Unlike Whitman's world of various voices, the world of personae has no overriding narrational speaker to hold them together as a unity. Where Whitman would include and fuse, Pessoa separates and discriminates. Where Whitman would personalize, Pessoa depersonalizes. The form and the technique are thus entirely opposed. The crux of the opposition lies in the two antithetical treatments of consciousness. For Whitman it binds the me to the "Me myself"; for Pessoa, it throws open the abyss between the two. Yet both poets have one interest in common: the preoccupation with identity as infinite dialectical Being, "Both in and out of the game and watching and wondering at it" ("Song of Myself," 79).[6] Out of this mutual interest both are compelled to follow the Adamic impulse, to create an original world which is nothing if not self-infused, word-rooted, and process-oriented. But what emerges from the core of these worlds is distinctly different. Out of *Leaves of Grass* arises the simulation of a real "Walt Whitman, liberal and lusty as Nature" ("To a Common Prostitute," 1).[7] What emerges from a reading of the heteronyms is the abstract idea of the Self: metaphorical images which expose the inner motion of mind and imagination at odds with one another.

In the course of time traveled from the poetry of Whitman to the poetry of Pessoa (approximately 1855 to 1914), the genre—Whitman's epic of the integral and cosmic Self—would necessarily change. Nobody was more aware of the necessity to "make it new" than Pessoa. His development of the personae is the manifest result of his creative need to renew Whitman through inversion, thus keeping alive both the Whitmanian language and the Adamic impulse while integrating both into the broader mythic mode of the heteronymic scheme.

NOTES

1. There are numerous references by Pessoa—sometimes in the guise of one of his other heteronyms—to Caeiro's role as master. One of the most important references occurs in Pessoa's letter to his friend Adolfo Casais Monteiro, explaining the genesis of the heteronyms. In this letter he describes how Alberto Caeiro appeared spontaneously as a voice on March 8, 1914, and he goes on to say, "Forgive the absurdity of the sentence: 'In me there appeared my master.'" Other extremely important sources for understanding the role of Caeiro as master are the prose notes and the poem of Alvaro de Campos entitled "Mestre, Meu Querido Mestre" ("Master, My Dear Master"). I will discuss the poem later in the essay.

2. In the years before the heteronymic outburst, Pessoa sought a philosophical system beyond systems, an organizational principle not reductionist in nature, a metaphysics capable of speaking of humanity's consciousness of reality without anthropomorphizing or personalizing nature. In his essay of 1908 on the absurdity of Christian dualism he argues that any concept which affirms two realities, both of the flesh and of the spirit, is impossible. Reality cannot be both eternal time and real, spatial time; it must be one or the other or something else. He concludes by stating that while humans see a duality, the duality is transitory; the only reality is spiritual. And it is the voicing of that spiritual reality—in my mind—which Alberto Caeiro unleashes in *The Keeper of Sheep*.

3. This reference to Whitman appears in an English preface, written by Alvaro de Campos for a never-realized project, an anthology of sensationist poets (see Pessoa, *Páginas Íntimas*, 140–142). Sensationism was the term Pessoa used to describe Portugal's specific brand of modernism in poetry, and the term is intimately connected with Pessoa's theories on the Greek sensibility and the new Portuguese paganism. The three practitioners of this new paganism, according to Pessoa, are Al-

berto Caeiro, Alvaro de Campos, and Walt Whitman. For more in this connection, see *Obra em Prosa*, 240–246.

4. This is taken from an essay written in English, supposedly as an introduction to Alberto Caeiro's poems. It is an extremely important essay for what it says about Pessoa's understanding of the similarities and differences between Caeiro and Whitman.

5. The "King of Gaps" is in Pessoa's collection of English poems, *The Mad Fiddler*. The first stanza of that poem is as follows:

> There lived, I know not when, never perhaps—
> But the fact is he lived—an unknown king
> Whose kingdom was the strange Kingdom of Gaps.
> He was lord of what is twixt thing and thing,
> Of interbeings, of that part of us
> That lies between our waking and our sleep,
> Between our silence and our speech, between
> Us and the consciousness of us; and thus
> A strange mute kingdom did that weird king keep
> Sequestered from our thought of time and scene.

6. This line is underlined in Pessoa's copy of the *Poems of Walt Whitman*. For a complete list of all the lines Pessoa underlined, bracketed, and/or commented upon in both the aforementioned edition of Whitman and in his copy of *Leaves of Grass*, see Brown.

7. The first three lines of this poem were bracketed by Pessoa in his copy of *Leaves of Grass*.

IV

The Poets Respond

Whitman's "Live Oak with Moss"

ALAN HELMS

Almost forty years ago, while working on Whitman's manuscripts for the third edition of *Leaves of Grass*, Fredson Bowers discovered that twelve of the poems had originally formed a sequence entitled "Live Oak with Moss," which tells the story of Whitman's unhappy love affair with a man. Bowers immediately published his extraordinary findings (in *Studies in Bibliography* and then in *Whitman's Manuscripts: Leaves of Grass (1860)*, yet since that time "Live Oak" has been virtually ignored. No one has discussed it at length, and the few who have remarked on it merely point out that it gave rise to the "Calamus" sequence and leave it at that.

We know, however, that Whitman valued the poems of "Live Oak" enough to include all of them among the forty-five poems of "Calamus" (published in the third *Leaves* in 1860), although he first reordered them in such a way that he obliterated the narrative they contain. He was obviously sensitive not so much about the separate poems but about the sequence itself: he never published it, never so far as we know even mentioned it, and in his fourth edition of the *Leaves*, two of the three poems dropped from "Calamus" were crucial "Live Oak" poems (5 and 8). Perhaps he felt the sequence revealed too much, for it gives us the only sustained treatment of homosexual love in all of his poetry. True, Whitman had written of men loving men before "Live Oak" but only fleetingly or in ways so opaquely figurative that most readers still aren't sure what's going on. Only in "Live Oak" do we get a clear story of a love affair with a man, along with a story of a coming out that affects Whitman's other poetry in this period and even changes the course of his life. In understanding what it meant to Whitman to love a man and to come out as America's first self-identified "homosexual," in seeing how that affects the best poetry of his third edition, and in making sense of his subsequent career, we might at last begin where Whitman himself began.

By Bowers's calculations, Whitman copied the twelve poems into a little notebook sometime in the spring of 1859, apparently transcribing them from originals composed a short time before but now lost. Bowers says the fact that the poems "had a special significance for Whitman seems clear from the form he gave them in the little notebook" (*Whitman's Manuscripts*, lxvii), and this significance is confirmed by a note in Whitman's hand found on the back of a separate manuscript of the title poem:

> A Cluster of Poems, Sonnets expressing the thoughts,
>   pictures, aspirations &c
> Fit to be perused during the days of the approach of
>   Death.
> (that I have prepared myself for that purpose.—
> (Remember now—
> Remember then (lxvii)

The injunction to "Remember now—Remember then" strongly suggests that "Live Oak" is autobiographical, for we rarely remind ourselves to remember anything but our actual experience.

(In *Calamus Lovers*, Charley Shively has identified the lover of this period as Fred Vaughan, a young man who lived with Whitman in the late 1850s.) Whatever Whitman's original plan for the poems (personal memento? publication? circulation among special friends in the manner of Shakespeare's sonnets?), he soon dispersed them among the "Calamus" cluster which he began assembling in the summer of 1859 from poems mostly composed after "Live Oak." In order, the twelve poems of "Live Oak" became "Calamus" 14, 20, 11, 23, 8, 32, 10, 9, 34, 43, 36, and 42—a rearrangement so complete that no one suspected the existence of the sequence until Bowers discovered Whitman's little notebook almost a century later. ("There is something *furtive* in my nature," Whitman told Edward Carpenter, "like an old hen" [Carpenter, *Days with Walt Whitman*, 42–43].)

A reader unfamiliar with the sequence should turn to it now, at the end of this essay. As with the other poems I quote, I give the "Live Oak" poems in their first published form—that is, as they appeared in the third *Leaves of Grass* in 1860 in the form Whitman approved for publication. I've simply removed them from "Calamus" and restored them to Whitman's original order.

The love narrative of "Live Oak" tells a fairly simple story of infatuation, abandonment, and accommodation. In the beginning, Whitman is so ecstatically in love that an image of his formerly independent self (the live oak) now bemuses him. His lover joins him, and soon thereafter Whitman renounces his poetry on the lover's behalf. The lover then abandons Whitman, and from that point on Whitman struggles with his loss. That much is clear, but the accompanying narrative of Whitman's coming out and its consequences is harder to discern.

Whitman starts off his sequence in a high-pitched, rhapsodic key that recalls how agitated he could become when he was in love, as in the following entry from his journal for July 1870: "Depress the adhesive nature / It is in excess—making life a torment / Ah this diseased, feverish disproportionate adhesiveness / Remember Fred Vaughan" (*Notebooks*, 888–890). Whitman is certainly "feverish" in poem 1 and as "out" as he could possibly be in proclaiming his new love, but the poem is also musical, one of the "overtures" that mark key poems of this period and that serve to announce a theme while transporting us from our world into Whitman's. The theme is clear—consuming love of . . . a man? men? love? friendship? the reader/lover of the earlier poetry? It's hard to tell and hard to know whom Whitman is addressing, for he ends the poem exclaiming that his soul is "Wafted in all directions, O love, for friendship, for you." From the start, Whitman is having trouble imagining his reader.

Poem 2 gives the sequence part of its title: "I saw in Louisiana a live-oak growing." The live oak shows Whitman the gulf now separating his former self from the new self he's beginning to explore in these poems. He's mesmerized by the tree, as we all are by vivid reminders of former selves, but he ends the poem affirming his new self, saying that although the live oak thrives alone (creatively in "uttering joyous leaves" and sexually in that it "glistens"), "I know very well I could not." We learn why in poem 3, a great love poem and the most contented poem Whitman ever wrote. It has the best of his tenderness and his homespun grandeur, and it's prosodically masterful—the lines swelling, cresting, and subsiding like the ocean waves Whitman sought to re-create in language. In its mingling of excitement and serenity at the end, the poem recalls the aftermath of the visionary experience in "Song of Myself," but Whitman isn't describing a visionary experience here—just a deeply loving, deeply human one. Note how he places the beach at a safe distance from the capitol, site of the reigning ideology of love and sex that he transgresses in this poem. Note too the nice awareness by which this "crime against nature" is endorsed by nature's congratulations. Clearly, nature isn't bothered by anything these lovers are doing.

The world of the capitol is bound to be, however, and that must be why, after the joyful satisfactions of poem 3, Whitman is "yearning and thoughtful" in poem 4, pining for men "in other lands . . . far, far away." The poem makes sense in terms of the love narrative (since Whitman has a lover, he imagines the whole world full of lovers), but it's also a conventional homosexual fantasy in which the world is conceived as a hospitable place for same-sex lovers. Oddly, the poem reads as though the experience of the previous poem had never happened, for why would the satisfied lover of poem 3 suddenly be "alone" and yearning for "brethren and lovers" in places further and further beyond the boundaries of his own country?

Transgression, retreat; transgression, retreat: therein we have the choreography of "Live Oak" and "Calamus." Thus, after the transgression in poem 3 and the retreat in poem 4 in which Whitman passively yearns for remote men, he transgresses again in poem 5, this time confrontationally by telling the United States that "I can be your singer of songs no longer" for "One who loves me is jealous of me, and withdraws me from all but love." Whitman affirms his new identity here, but his willed conclusion ("It is to be enough for us that we are together") along with his inflated diction ("I sever from what I thought would suffice me") suggest that the capitol is finding ways to invade his new territory. The capitol in fact occupies most of the poem in the form of Whitman's list of things he's renouncing, while the "One who loves me" (the ostensible subject of the poem) hardly appears. A split between the two narratives becomes obvious, for Whitman's claim that he no longer cares about his "songs of the New World" is belied by the space he accords them, while what he presents as his voluntary renunciation of his poetry is no such thing because he cannot be both America's foremost poet and its first homosexual lover. Whitman *must* renounce his former poetry, and his confused view of the matter results in an ambivalent, bombastic poem in which he sounds more like a man addressing Congress than one celebrating his lover. A deep tension appears in Whitman between pride in his new self and a resistance to that self which absorbs him and provokes his blustering defiance.

The tension breaks out again in poem 7 when Whitman instructs "You bards of ages hence" to "Publish my name and hang up my picture as that of the tenderest lover" but then walks with his lover "apart from other men." Somewhere in the future it's fine for Whitman to be known as a man-lover; in the present, however, he and his lover had better become invisible. All lovers prefer privacy, but Whitman is learning that in a homophobic society, homosexual lovers require it. That's surely why he looks so yearningly at those men in poem 6 who hug and kiss "in the midst of the crowd." If they get to do that, why can't he? But he knows he can't—except of course in "parting," which by this point in Whitman's career has become the central act of his poetry—and so the more he exposes and expresses his love in "Live Oak," the more there's a contrary, self-protective impulse in him to hide it or somehow displace it, distance it or sequester it from public view.

In poem 8 Whitman has been abandoned, and it's here that the two narratives most forcefully coincide. Without the narrative of homophobic oppression I'm trying to expose, it's merely odd that a man who has boasted of so many like-minded lovers and friends would "harbor" his love "silent and endless," along with his "anguish and passion." And odder still that in being abandoned, he would of all feelings feel shame. Yet Whitman's sense of shame and isolation will be painfully familiar to most lesbians and gay men as a part of the process of coming out. "Is there even one other like me?" is a question that gay men and lesbians have asked themselves by the millions. At the heart of this poem, Whitman echoes Shakespeare's Sonnet 121 ("I am that I am") in which Shakespeare is "vile esteemed" by those who "count bad what I think good." But Shakespeare's self-definition is affirmative and defiant in the face of such judgment, whereas in Whitman the judgment combines with his pain at being abandoned in a way that defeats him: "(I am ashamed—but it is useless—I am what I am)." "It is useless" describes the related efforts to love a man and to write about that love, for everything in Whitman's culture tells him that both efforts are wrong. He thus enacts the centuries-old response to such cultural judgment—he stifles his cries, harbors his feelings "silent and endless" (he hides them and protects them, hides them *to* protect them), and he ends the poem "taciturn and deprest" in a mood reminiscent of a Poe nightmare. By shaming Whitman, by isolating him, and—most disastrous for a writer—by silencing him, homophobia wins the determining agon of "Live Oak." From here to the end, it controls the sequence.

Immediately after Whitman's abandonment, poem 9 gives us a compensation in the form of a wish fulfillment, a utopian solution to the twin pains of abandonment and social oppression: "I dreamed in a dream, I saw a city invincible to the attacks of the whole of the rest of the earth, / I dreamed that was the new City of Friends." The danger Whitman now perceives is clear from the fact that his imagined city is attacked by "the whole of the rest of the earth." How perfectly typical, then, for a man who feels so threatened, who locates the site of love far from the capitol, who daydreams of sympathetic men "far, far away," who walks with his lover "apart from other men," and who feels isolated and shamed in his loving to dream of a safe city of male lovers, a subversively different capitol where men can safely love men in public. As always in his poetry, Whitman is entranced by the visibility of men loving men: "It was seen every hour in the actions of the men of that city, / And in all their looks and words." The images of men publicly touching, kissing, embracing, and holding hands that run throughout the first three editions of *Leaves of Grass* comprise a set of personal icons for Whitman, for they represent not his satisfactions but his yearnings, as in this poem where the images occur in a dream within a dream. It's hard to imagine anything more remote from possibility or a maneuver more self-protective.

In the last three poems, the former lover returns or a new lover appears—it's not entirely clear, but it hardly matters as far as the love narrative is concerned since the prohibition against speaking of homosexual love has triumphed. In poem 10 Whitman expresses his love only in the silence of thought ("Little you know the subtle electric fire that for your sake is burning within me"), now boasting of what only two poems earlier had caused him great pain. In poem 11 he imagines his love as so "fierce and terrible" that "I dare not tell it in words—not even in these songs." In his earlier poetry Whitman has said that he won't speak because he chooses not to or that he can't speak because words fail him, but never has he said that he *dare* not speak—though he will say so in other poems written in this period. Little wonder then that in the final poem Whitman abandons his new self, exchanging the role of seeking lover for that of sought-for teacher.

What a sad journey the sequence takes us on, from the proud

lover in the beginning who boasts of loving men to the cautious teacher at the end who can only profit young men who've already learned the lesson of loving "silently." (What then is there for this teacher to teach?) The whole weight of his homophobic culture finally descends on Whitman, exacting silence and with it the end of the sequence. There is literally nowhere for Whitman the lover and writer to go from this point on.

"Live Oak" is a deeply troubled sequence, mostly about the confusion, pain, and fear that surround the fact of men loving men. It's tremulous with yearning, but Whitman's satisfactions are accomplished mostly in reminiscence, in boast, in dream or daydream, or somewhere in the future. It contains some excellent but also some terrible writing, including one of the most awkward inversions ever "penned," as Whitman might say: "All alone stood it." But then, improbable as it seems, Whitman is writing sonnets, and he naturally has Shakespeare in mind since Shakespeare provides him with sanction for writing about homosexual love. Shakespeare is an otherwise unfortunate influence, however, since the more Whitman transgresses, the more there's a compensatory, even propitiatory move in him toward conventionally approved forms of writing, and Shakespeare fuels that unfortunate tendency. A line like "What think you I take my pen in hand to record?" is as awful as it is because it's Whitman filtered through Shakespeare—the pose of poet in awkward pentameter, as if Whitman can't trust his new identity or even his prosody. In the next few years, the thy's and thou's Whitman banished from his early work begin to reappear, and before long this radically original poet becomes a largely conventional one, producing second-rate verse that wins him some of the popular audience he always longed for. The retreat from his sexuality that follows the third edition thus has its counterpart in a degeneration of Whitman's style.

Such problems of style in "Live Oak" also derive from Whitman's difficulty in finding a way to deal with his subject, a difficulty that shows in euphemisms like "manly love" and "robust love" and in frequent couplings of friend and lover; friendship and love; a friend, a lover; my dear friends, my lovers. Whitman is searching for a new vocabulary with which to speak of men loving men, but his paired words and phrases (the former disarming the latter) convey not new meanings so much as his discomfort in speaking of his love. He's extremely ambivalent about the act of writing poetry: in poem 2 he needs a lover to "utter leaves," but because he has a lover in poem 5, "I am indifferent to my own songs." He never fully imagines his lover, who fades in and out until finally disappearing toward the end, and he's having a hard time imagining his audience. Is he writing to himself as his private memo suggests, to the reader/lover of his earlier work, to "bards of ages hence," to the United States, or to some potential readership "eligible to burst forth" if only he can find the right attitude and tone? The odd omission here is the lover himself (think again of Shakespeare). Not once does Whitman speak to his lover about his desire; in fact, he's quite clear in saying at the end that "I dare not tell it in words—not even in these songs." In a sequence written about men loving men in general and one man in particular in which he initially boasts of singing songs of "manly love," to arrive at a prohibition so strong that he ends by not daring to speak at all is astounding—at least until we recall where and when Whitman wrote these poems.

Though "Live Oak with Moss" ends in silence, Whitman pressed on in exploring his homosexuality by assembling the much longer "Calamus" sequence. In working up "Calamus" he worked out some of the problems in the earlier sequence. For one, his readership comes into view; he's now writing for "them that love, as I myself am capable of loving." It's as if Whitman has rewritten the opening lines of "Song of Myself" to read "I celebrate my homosexuality, / And what I assume, you, dear common reader, shall *not* assume." Yet Whitman's clearer sense of audience brings with it a heightened awareness of further transgressing the boundaries of the culturally acceptable. After all, he knows that he will publish "Calamus," so the bolder he becomes, the more aware he is of the cultural prohibitions surrounding his project. "Calamus" is shot through with a sense of fear and impending danger, the need for caution and seclusion, and again the sense of a prohibition against speaking of desire

for men. Whitman's attention is so troubled by thoughts of what
he dare and dare not do that he sometimes seems oblivious to
what he's up against, as in "Calamus" 22:

> Passing stranger! you do not know how longingly I look
>   upon you,
> You must be he I was seeking, or she I was seeking, (It
>   comes to me, as of a dream,)
>
> .   .   .   .
>
> You give me the pleasure of your eyes, face, flesh, as we
>   pass—you take of my beard, breast, hands, in return,
> I am not to speak to you—I am to think of you when I
>   sit alone, or wake at night alone,
> I am to wait—I do not doubt I am to meet you again,
> I am to see to it that I do not lose you. ("To a Stranger,"
>   1–2, 7–10)

It's a bold imagination that in mid-nineteenth-century America
could replace a heterosexual model of love relationships based
on capitalist possession with this gliding exchange of erotic gifts
between strangers, but the poem ends in defeat for Whitman. "I
am not to speak to you—I am to think of you . . . I am to wait"—
these are the words of someone who's following orders. As he
often does in "Live Oak" and "Calamus," Whitman settles for an
empty boast, a kind of whistling in the homophobic dark.

"Calamus" is in fact framed by such incoherence. Whitman
begins the sequence declaring that he is "Resolved to sing no
songs to-day but those of manly attachment" and that he will
therefore "tell the secret of my nights and days." But by the penultimate poem, the songs are silent, the secret untold:

> Here my last words, and the most baffling,
> Here the frailest leaves of me, and yet my strongest-
>   lasting,
> Here I shade down and hide my thoughts—I do not
>   expose them,
> And yet they expose me more than all my other poems.

"Calamus" thus repeats the same movement I've outlined in
"Live Oak with Moss"—a frank, unashamed celebration of

same-sex love in the beginning, silence at the end. Insofar as "Calamus" is more ambitious than "Live Oak" and published besides, the tension between the need to speak and the prohibition against doing so becomes excruciating. It finally erupts in "As I Ebb'd with the Ocean of Life."

In his third edition, Whitman places "As I Ebb'd" first in a group of poems titled "Leaves of Grass," so we now find "Leaves of Grass" inside *Leaves of Grass*. Perhaps we're invited to take "As I Ebb'd" as a new "Song of Myself"; but if so, how different from the ebullient, self-confident speaker of five years before is this new speaker so full of self-disgust and shame. When the poem begins, Whitman is walking along the beach, one of those marginal settings that constitute for him the sites of love and knowledge. It's "late in the autumn day" and he's tormented by doubt and confusion:

> As the ocean so mysterious rolls toward me closer and
> closer,
> At once I find, the least thing that belongs to me, or that
> I see or touch, I know not;
> I, too, but signify, at the utmost, a little washed-up drift,
> A few sands and dead leaves to gather,
> Gather, and merge myself as part of the sands and drift.
>
> O baffled, balked,
> Bent to the very earth . . .
> Oppressed with myself that I have dared to open my
> mouth,
> Aware now, that, amid all the blab whose echoes recoil
> upon me, I have not once had the least idea who or
> what I am,
> But that before all my insolent poems the real ME still
> stands untouched, untold, altogether unreached,
> Withdrawn far, mocking me with mock-congratulatory
> signs and bows,
> With peals of distant ironical laughter at every word I
> have written or shall write,
> Striking me with insults till I fall helpless upon the sand.

The beach that Whitman made safe for his lover in "When I Heard at the Close of the Day" has been invaded by an embodiment of the oppression he struggled with in "Live Oak" and "Calamus." The "real ME" that in "Song of Myself" was imagined as compassionate and companionable has become humiliating and violent. This horribly changed "real ME" is in essence an outraged superego, an ideology on a rampage. Immense and terrifying, it reaches through all time and space, it leaves no room for Whitman, and at this moment it frankly wouldn't care if he died. Then nature attacks, as if in league with the phantom overhead:

> O I perceive I have not understood anything—not a
>   single object—and that no man ever can.
>
> I perceive Nature here, in sight of the sea, is taking
>   advantage of me, to dart upon me, and sting me,
> Because I was assuming so much,
> And because I have dared to open my mouth to sing
>   at all. (36–39)

Threatened with annihilation, Whitman pleads with nature, "Be not too rough with me." Then what little remains of the new self he exposed and expressed in "Live Oak" and "Calamus" is swallowed up:

> . . . I submit—I close with you . . .
> What is yours is mine, my father . . .
> I throw myself upon your breast, my father,
> I cling to you so that you cannot unloose me,
> I hold you so firm, till you answer me something.
> Kiss me, my father,
> Touch me with your lips, as I touch those I love,
> Breathe to me, while I hold you close, the secret of the
>   wondrous murmuring I envy,
> For I fear I shall become crazed, if I cannot emulate it,
>   and utter myself as well as it.

In the words "I submit" and the address to the father that follows, Whitman pays the price of having dared so much. The poet who previously had merged with and absorbed the people and things of his experience is now himself merged and absorbed. In *De Profundis*, Oscar Wilde, another nineteenth-century writer who offended his culture because of his sexual difference, says that "the moment of repentence is the moment of initiation," and so it is here. Initiated into the father's ideology, Whitman the lover, singing his unabashed songs of homosexual love, henceforth ceases to exist. His place is taken by Whitman the father, the "good gray poet" who writes publicly acceptable poems of American patriotism so dear to the father's heart, Whitman the male nurse who ministers to the Civil War soldiers he called "my boys" and "my sons," Whitman the "laughing philosopher" who wrote no more successful love poems except his great elegy for a father.

Some may think it simplistic to argue that homophobia is the sole or even the main reason why, after his third edition, Whitman never again wrote frankly about loving men. Granted, other influences played their part in the sea-change that took place in Whitman's life and work, foremost among them the continued failure of his book, his Civil War nursing, his advancing age and declining health, and his abrupt dismissal from his government job by Secretary of the Interior James Harlan. But it would be at least as simplistic to think that the operations of any ideology are ever less than complicated, covert, and pervasive, by which I mean to suggest that these additional influences contributed, each in its different way, to the pressures on Whitman whereby he henceforth remained silent on the subject of homosexual love. To take only one example, shortly after Whitman was fired, William D. O'Connor wrote a letter of protest to Secretary Harlan in which he mounted a new defense of Whitman's poetry, one that he would elaborate in *The Good Gray Poet* and that would become a dominant theme in future defenses of *Leaves of Grass*: "I think it imperative that the productions of an author of this kind, be largely tried by the standard of his actual life" (F. D. Miller, 93). In other words, in O'Connor's muddled view there couldn't possibly be anything offensive to public morality in the *Leaves* because Whitman lived a pure life. A man that pure couldn't write anything that wasn't free of taint and certainly couldn't be as vile as many said he was. Thus, in attempting to defend Whitman, O'Connor created yet one more reason why Whitman began a lifelong effort to mute and suppress the evidence of homosexuality in his work, for obviously the man O'Connor argued for couldn't possibly be a man-lover. At the very least, he could not be perceived as such.

Imagine if you will one last sequence, a frankly biographical one. Whitman copies "Live Oak with Moss" into his little notebook in the spring of 1859. That summer, he begins assembling the "Calamus" cluster from poems mostly written around the same time. In December he publishes "Out of the Cradle Endlessly Rocking" in which the boy on the beach at night is awakened to his vocation as poet by the bird's song of loss, whereupon the boy realizes that "Never again [shall] the cries of unsatisfied love be absent from me." Imagine that "Live Oak with Moss" contains those "cries of unsatisfied love" (their epigraph "We two together no more!") and shows Whitman exploring the world of homosexual love he'd longed for in his earlier poetry while learning the costs of expressing that love. Imagine that "Calamus" shows him continuing that exploration but with the growing sense that his project is doomed. Imagine finally that "As I Ebb'd" (completed last in this sequence and published in April 1860) conveys the outcome of his struggle between a deep need to express his love and a prohibition against doing so that was so powerful it finally defeated him.

"Remember now—Remember then." A tantalizing, poignant couplet. For if Whitman did in fact recall his suppressed sequence "during the days of the approach of Death," did he also remember enough to realize how much more than a lover he had lost?

"Live Oak with Moss"

1

Not heat flames up and consumes,
Not sea-waves hurry in and out,
Not the air, delicious and dry, the air of the ripe

summer, bears lightly along white down-balls of
    myriads of seeds, wafted, sailing gracefully, to drop
    where they may,
Not these—O none of these, more than the flames of
    me, consuming, burning for his love whom I love!
O none, more than I, hurrying in and out;
Does the tide hurry, seeking something, and never give
    up? O I the same;
O nor down-balls, nor perfumes, nor the high rain-
    emitting clouds, are borne through the open air,
Any more than my Soul is borne through the open air,
Wafted in all directions, O love, for friendship, for you.

2

I SAW in Louisiana a live-oak growing,
All alone stood it, and the moss hung down from the
    branches,
Without any companion it grew there, uttering joyous
    leaves of dark green,
And its look, rude, unbending, lusty, made me think of
    myself,
But I wondered how it could utter joyous leaves,
    standing alone there, without its friend, its lover
    near—for I knew I could not,
And I broke off a twig with a certain number of leaves
    upon it, and twined around it a little moss,
And brought it away—and I have placed it in sight in
    my room,
It is not needed to remind me as of my own dear
    friends,
(For I believe lately I think of little else than of them,)
Yet it remains to me a curious token—it makes me think
    of manly love;
For all that, and though the live-oak glistens there in
    Louisiana, solitary, in a wide flat space,
Uttering joyous leaves all its life, without a friend, a
    lover, near,
I know very well I could not.

3

WHEN I heard at the close of the day how my name had
  been received with plaudits in the capitol, still it was
  not a happy night for me that followed;
And else, when I caroused, or when my plans were
  accomplished, still I was not happy;
But the day when I rose at dawn from the bed of perfect
  health, refreshed, singing, inhaling the ripe breath of
  autumn,
When I saw the full moon in the west grow pale and
  disappear in the morning light,
When I wandered alone over the beach, and,
  undressing, bathed, laughing with the cool waters,
  and saw the sun rise,
And when I thought how my dear friend, my lover, was
  on his way coming, O then I was happy;
O then each breath tasted sweeter—and all that day my
  food nourished me more—And the beautiful day
  passed well,
And the next came with equal joy—And with the next,
  at evening, came my friend;
And that night, while all was still, I heard the waters roll
  slowly continually up the shores,
I heard the hissing rustle of the liquid and sands, as
  directed to me, whispering, to congratulate me,
For the one I love most lay sleeping by me under the
  same cover in the cool night,
In the stillness, in the autumn moonbeams, his face was
  inclined toward me,
And his arm lay lightly around my breast—And that
  night I was happy.

4

THIS moment as I sit alone, yearning and thoughtful, it
  seems to me there are other men in other lands,
  yearning and thoughtful;

It seems to me I can look over and behold them, in
   Germany, Italy, France, Spain—Or far, far away, in
   China, or in Russia or India—talking other dialects;
And it seems to me if I could know those men better, I
   should become attached to them, as I do to men in
   my own lands,
It seems to me they are as wise, beautiful, benevolent,
   as any in my own lands;
O I know we should be brethren and lovers,
I know I should be happy with them.

5

LONG I thought that knowledge alone would suffice
   me—O if I could but obtain knowledge!
Then my lands engrossed me—Lands of the prairies,
   Ohio's land, the southern savannas, engrossed me—
   For them I would live—I would be their orator;
Then I met the examples of old and new heroes—I
   heard of warriors, sailors, and all dauntless persons—
   And it seemed to me that I too had it in me to be as
   dauntless as any—and would be so;
And then, to enclose all, it came to me to strike up the
   songs of the New World—And then I believed my life
   must be spent in singing;
But now take notice, land of the prairies, land of the
   south savannas, Ohio's land,
Take notice, you Kanuck woods—and you Lake
   Huron—and all that with you roll toward Niagara—
   and you Niagara also,
And you, Californian mountains—That you each and all
   find somebody else to be your singer of songs,
For I can be your singer of songs no longer—One who
   loves me is jealous of me, and withdraws me from all
   but love,
With the rest I dispense—I sever from what I thought
   would suffice me, for it does not—it is now empty
   and tasteless to me,

I heed knowledge, and the grandeur of The States, and
the example of heroes, no more,
I am indifferent to my own songs—I will go with him I
love,
It is to be enough for us that we are together—We never
separate again.

6

WHAT think you I take my pen in hand to record?
The battle-ship, perfect-model'd, majestic, that I saw
pass the offing to-day under full sail?
The splendors of the past day? Or the splendor of the
night that envelops me?
Or the vaunted glory and growth of the great city
spread around me?—No;
But I record of two simple men I saw to-day, on the pier,
in the midst of the crowd, parting the parting of dear
friends,
The one to remain hung on the other's neck, and
passionately kissed him,
While the one to depart, tightly prest the one to remain
in his arms.

7

YOU bards of ages hence! when you refer to me, mind
not so much my poems,
Nor speak of me that I prophesied of The States, and led
them the way of their glories;
But come, I will take you down underneath this
impassive exterior—I will tell you what to say of me:
Publish my name and hang up my picture as that of the
tenderest lover,
The friend, the lover's portrait, of whom his friend, his
lover, was fondest,
Who was not proud of his songs, but of the measureless
ocean of love within him—and freely poured it forth,

Who often walked lonesome walks, thinking of his dear
  friends, his lovers,
Who pensive, away from one he loved, often lay
  sleepless and dissatisfied at night,
Who knew too well the sick, sick dread lest the one he
  loved might secretly be indifferent to him,
Whose happiest days were far away, through fields, in
  woods, on hills, he and another, wandering hand in
  hand, they twain, apart from other men,
Who oft as he sauntered the streets, curved with his
  arm the shoulder of his friend—while the arm of his
  friend rested upon him also.

8

Hours continuing long, sore and heavy-hearted,
Hours of the dusk, when I withdraw to a lonesome and
  unfrequented spot, seating myself, leaning my face in
  my hands;
Hours sleepless, deep in the night, when I go forth,
  speeding swiftly the country roads, or through the
  city streets, or pacing miles and miles, stifling
  plaintive cries;
Hours discouraged, distracted—for the one I cannot
  content myself without, soon I saw him content
  himself without me;
Hours when I am forgotten, (O weeks and months are
  passing, but I believe I am never to forget!)
Sullen and suffering hours! (I am ashamed—but it is
  useless—I am what I am;)
Hours of my torment—I wonder if other men ever have
  the like, out of the like feelings?
Is there even one other like me—distracted—his friend,
  his lover, lost to him?
Is he too as I am now? Does he still rise in the morning,
  dejected, thinking who is lost to him? and at night,
  awaking, think who is lost?

Does he too harbor his friendship silent and endless?
    harbor his anguish and passion?
Does some stray reminder, or the casual mention of a
    name, bring the fit back upon him, taciturn and
    deprest?
Does he see himself reflected in me? In these hours,
    does he see the face of his hours reflected?

9

I DREAMED in a dream, I saw a city invincible to the
    attacks of the whole of the rest of the earth,
I dreamed that was the new City of Friends,
Nothing was greater there than the quality of robust
    love—it led the rest,
It was seen every hour in the actions of the men of that
    city,
And in all their looks and words.

10

O YOU whom I often and silently come where you are,
    that I may be with you,
As I walk by your side, or sit near, or remain in the
    same room with you,
Little you know the subtle electric fire that for your sake
    is playing within me.

11

EARTH! my likeness!
Though you look so impassive, ample and spheric
    there,
I now suspect that is not all;
I now suspect there is something fierce in you, eligible
    to burst forth;
For an athlete is enamoured of me—and I of him,
But toward him there is something fierce and terrible in
    me, eligible to burst forth,
I dare not tell it in words—not even in these songs.

12

To the young man, many things to absorb, to engraft, to
   develop, I teach, to help him become élève of mine,
But if blood like mine circle not in his veins,
If he be not silently selected by lovers, and do not
   silently select lovers,
Of what use is it that he seek to become élève of mine?

Forays against the Republic

THOM GUNN

It is in discussing the structure of "Song of Myself" that we find some of the most marked disagreements among the critics. They all feel that the work holds together, but how? Edwin Haviland Miller summarizes nineteen detailed plans of the overall organization, and it is fascinating to see how little they agree. Robert Creeley would certainly not be surprised: he tells an anecdote about a teacher asking graduate students to produce thematic outlines of "Song of Myself," and no two of them were the same. Creeley therefore claims Whitman as his own precursor, composing "in a 'field' of activity" rather than according to logical narrative norms (195).

Whitman might well have understood, in old age having said of his entire collected poetry: "I consider (it) and its theory experimental—as, in the deepest sense, I consider our American republic itself to be, with its theory" (*Prose Works*, 713). Developing book and developing country, each creates itself as it goes along, realizing itself through its very continued activity, edition by edition.

The initiation and unstopped bubbling source appear to have been "Song of Myself," and a large part of the character of that experiment sprang from the concept of "myself," so different from the first person of Wordsworth's *Prelude*. Whitman's self is both exceptional and average, representative and individual, a rich young woman and Walt Whitman, one of the roughs and Jesus Christ. Each merges into the others like leaves of grass into a prairie or individuals into a visionary democracy. A democracy is supposed to be a society of free association, as opposed to one in which there is hierarchical subordination. Thus the poem proceeds in a loosely associationistic manner, its very structure promiscuous and democratic. Whitman transforms the early romantic practice of a rather mild associationism into an assured and extreme narrative disjunctiveness that is not equaled for some sixty years.

Written with an almost modernist trust in juxtaposition and improvisation and in the continuing heat of a revelatory experience from 1853, the rich and complex work still has an originality difficult to describe—and not only in its structure. First of all, its free verse, whatever its antecedents, is an invention of great flexibility. It ranges from the anaphoric patterns learned out of the Authorized Version of the Bible, through a serviceable prosiness, through a mid-Victorian anapestic jig, to the bold nonce rhythms of "How the flukes splash!" and of the following lines:

> Here and there with dimes on the eyes walking,
> To feed the greed of the belly the brains liberally
>   spooning,
> Tickets buying, taking, selling, but in to the feast never
>   once going (1070–1072)

Though these lines tend toward the trochaic, they do not stay quite long enough with it to make it a norm. Nor is their originality only rhythmical. The imagery has a kind of prelapsarian freshness, boldness, and directness, even while describing such obvious postlapsarians as the midcentury achievers.

The vigor of Whitman's observation matches the vigor of what he observes, as if he has only to name it to bring it to life. In "This Compost" he writes, "Out of its little hill faithfully rise the potato's dark green leaves" (28) (Lawrence sounds like this in "Trees in the Garden"). And in the course of another early poem, "To Think of Time," he describes a stagedriver's funeral and treats the cant phrases of the driver's daily life ("somebody loafing on you, you loafing on somebody, headway, man before and man behind") (50) as if they were *things*, as defined and physical as the apron, cape, gloves, and whip that they are mixed in with during his account. To these distinctions of overall structure, verse-line, imagery, and language may be added that of the rhetoric itself, the unique approach taken by his whole art of persuasion—so that summing it up in Alastair Fowler's phrase, "Victorian sententiousness," seems inadequate; much more useful is W. S. Di Piero's passing remark that it "is first of all revelatory, often interpretive, seldom explanatory."

The basic revelation seems to have had something to do with a sense of a democracy so generous that there is room in it for everyone and everything. One of the most moving parts of "Song of Myself" is the passage in which Whitman speaks for the inarticulate and the unheard, for the "deform'd, trivial, flat, foolish, despised, / Fog in the air, beetles rolling balls of dung" (514–515)—that is, for those who lack even self-definition and for the lowest of the low. Such a revelation is religious in ultimate purport, but his religious feelings are connected with all his other feelings, not only with the political but with the sexual too (which overlap, in their turn). In the words of 1855, later modified several times, he tells us of a hot night with God:

> As God comes a loving bedfellow and sleeps at my side
> all night and close on the peep of the day,
> And leaves for me baskets covered with white towels
> bulging the house with their plenty. ("Song of
> Myself" [1855]: 52–53)

The baskets contain rising dough, of course. Critics refer to the rising baskets variously as "pregnant," as "an allusion to communion baskets," as male naked bellies, as mother's breasts, and as male erections (see E. H. Miller, *Mosaic*). But the significance of bread is proverbial, and surely the emphasis here is both more obvious and more irrational than those readings. Lewis Hyde, with a better sense of proportion than the others, reads the second line most helpfully, stressing the *free gift* of what nourishes the soul as well as the body. The stylistic analogy to be made is with the imagery of the New Testament: "What man is there of you, to whom if his son ask bread, will he give him a stone?" (Matthew 7:9)—which is, as Di Piero would say, revelatory but not explanatory.

It is not enough, then, to call the tone of Whitman's best poetry—that is, "Song of Myself" and some other poems of the 1850s and a few later poems—sententious. It leans, rather, toward the dramatic (it is seldom far from the spoken voice) and does so most pointedly in "Song of Myself" at the transitions between section and section because there he is uncertain where his drifting consciousness has brought him. "I talk wildly, I have lost my wits," he exclaims, or "Somehow I have been stunn'd." He is often disoriented, not sure where or even who he is, speaking with surprise, bewilderment, or wonder. The transitions are, in fact, like those of dreams, and Robert Martin justifiably classes not only "The Sleepers" but "Song of Myself" among the "dream-vision poems" (*Homosexual Tradition*).

Such openness to the irrational associations of the unconscious seems to have freed Whitman's imagination into some of the most energetic writing of his early work. I am thinking less of the "ladled cups" of the waves in "Crossing Brooklyn Ferry" than of the later-omitted passages from "The Sleepers" which have properly become so famous in the last few decades. In the longer of these, the dreamer as young woman with and without her lover is abruptly replaced by a presumably male dreamer who finds himself in the street naked ("my clothes were stolen while I was abed"). In his nightmare he regresses to an infant of polymorphous appetite, an appetite both convivial and erotic in its fantasy, where clarity and sharpness of image only accentuate the sense of confusion.

> The cloth laps a first sweet eating and drinking,
> Laps life-swelling yolks . . . laps ear of rose-corn, milky
>   and just ripened:
> The white teeth stay, and the boss-tooth advances in
>   darkness,
> And liquor is spilled on lips and bosoms by touching
>   glasses, and the best liquor afterward.
>   ("The Sleepers" [1855], 67–70)

The cloth, I think, doubles for both the bedclothes and the table-napkin around the speaker's neck, and "laps" has perhaps a primary sense of "wraps around" but with several ancillary senses. Rimbaud would have been interested in this writing, in the way the imagination is freed from traditional restraints—almost but not quite into the meaningless.

But in emphasizing Whitman's experimental orginality I should point out that he could also make resourceful use of the rhetoric he found available. He concludes "Crossing Brooklyn Ferry" with a long series of apostrophes to a mainly inhuman world, of a tiresome sort with which readers had already been long familiar ("Roll on, thou deep and dark blue ocean—roll!"). Whitman gives the device a new function. By granting the river, clouds, and foundries permission, as it were, to be what they are, he is also granting himself permission to be what he is—a man, specifically in this poem, promiscuously attracted by other men and brimming with a mixture of guilt and joy about it.

At the basis of the basic revelation—that of an ideally generous democracy—is to be found what may be its source: that point, already alluded to, at which the public and political intersect with the private and sexual. His vision of democracy originates from what might be called a populist taste in men. Though he insists "I am the poet of the woman the same as the man" ("Song of Myself," 425), though he wants to write equally about both sexes from sheer fairness as well as from a sense of duty, though it was his acceptance of unabashed female sexuality that most shocked his contemporaries, it is clear ultimately that he loves humanity so much because he loves hunky workingmen. This is not to call him a hypocrite, for his sympathies do indeed extend to "the snag-tooth'd hostler with red hair," to dwarfs and to the deformed, but it is to point out what seems to have started off and continued to vivify those sympathies. Watching firemen march in a parade, Whitman notices "the play of masculine muscle through clean-setting trowsers and waist-straps," a line in "I Sing the Body Electric" which I have always found especially revealing (though it is probably as revealing of me that I should notice it). He likes a body that is at the same time "athletic" in development and "negligent" in attitudes, two favorite words. And they are words that carry a political charge for him as well, for he constantly refers to an athletic democracy and "negligence" in a context that includes the suggestion of generosity carried to the point of carelessness.

There is a contradiction, though, which he does not always acknowledge. However many partners he may find among the drivers, conductors, delivery boys, milkmen, sailors, and soldiers who carry out the business of the republic, loving them sexually was still an act subversive to the authority of that republic. The contradiction surfaces in one of the "Calamus" poems, like most of them rather thinly written, "We Two Boys Together Clinging." This is a nine-line poem about two lifelong lovers, outlaws, "Up and down the roads going" of the United States, of which the last line is "Fulfilling our foray." The foray is against the republic itself: an explicit conflict surfaces, here at least, between the populist athletic democracy and the specific athletic lovers.

We are sometimes tempted to see Whitman only as the ebullient celebrator of an idealized democracy, as if his whole career were of a piece with its initiation. But much of that lengthy experiment consisted of revision, changes of mind, and silences. It ended, it might be said, in prose. And further, if we read carefully enough, we may see that he had always been troubled by inconsistency and conflict, had endured nightmares, and had recurred often to the "terrible doubt of appearances."

What we primarily value about Whitman and will continue to value is the way he extends the defiant admiration of impulse, learned from the early romantics, and makes it his own. What poet is more generous? He looks to liberation not merely for the educated, for the noble loners, but for all of us. "Unscrew the locks from the doors! / Unscrew the doors themselves from their jambs!" ("Song of Myself," 501–502) is an extraordinary utterance for 1855, and it was still fresh enough in 1955 for Ginsberg to use it as an epigraph for *Howl and Other Poems*. What makes the documentary labors of recent critics such as Betsy Erkkila and M. Jimmie Killingsworth useful to us is that they detail the confusions out of which it arises and show how easily the great gesture dissipated into confusion again; they are helping to demonstrate the full complexity and richness and rareness of what seems, at first hearing, so simple.

A Postscript on Whitman

NED ROREM

"I pour the stuff to start sons and daughters," Whitman exclaimed ("A Woman Waits," 28). Those sons and daughters cover the earth, singing for better or worse through the impulse of their father.

More than anyone in history save Shakespeare, Whitman has appealed to song composers whatever their style or nationality, possibly because he spoke as much through his pen, contagiously craving immortality. "I spring from the pages into your arms," cries the dead author to his living reader.

The act of reading is no more passive than being a spectator at the theater, despite what sponsors of total-audience participation would today have us think. To read is to act. It takes two to make a poem; an attentive reader participates constantly. But with Whitman the participation becomes more than usually evident, more physical. The reason may lie in his emphasis on immediate sensation rather than on philosophic introspection. At least that explains his century-old appeal to musicians and his more recent revival within our collective poetic sensibility, specifically with Allen Ginsberg and the flower children of 1960s pop culture. That explains also why so many primarily vocal composers started early with Whitman, especially during the 1940s when it seemed urgent to be American at any price, and why so many of these songs sing embarrassingly now like the youthful indiscretions they are. During that same period, but for other reasons (reasons of gratitude), certain riper Europeans used Whitman and used him more touchingly than many Americans—Kurt Weill, for example, or Paul Hindemith, whose *When Lilacs Last in the Dooryard Bloomed* is surely his choral masterwork.[1]

My own choices of words have usually been somehow more practical. When planning to write a song I seek poems more for sound than meaning, more for shape than sentiment. Sometimes (this is a confession), the music being already within me, I'll take literally any verse at hand and force it into a preconceived melodic mold. When the outcome "works," it's precisely because I have not wallowed in the sense of the words so much as tried to objectify or illustrate them.

But Whitman has proved exceptional to this kind of choice. For if I love form for its own sake and challenge, I also love and need Whitman, whose style, in a sense, is lack of style: an unprecedented freedom that, with its built-in void of formal versified variety, offers unlimited potential for formal musical variety. Whitman is content. A poet's content is a musician's form; any other way a song is merely redundant and becomes, in the words of Paul Valéry, like a painting seen through a stained-glass window. Looking back, I find that the dozen Whitman poems I have musicalized over the years were selected less for intellectual motives than because they spoke to my condition at a certain time. I adopted them through that dangerous impulse called inspiration, not for their music but for their meaning.

The first was "Reconciliation," an appeal to my pacifism in time of war. A few years later "Sometimes with One I Love" so sharply described my frame of mind that the music served as a sort of superfluous necessity.[2] But once, when commissioned to provide accompaniments for recitations of Whitman, I failed; for if the human voice in song is the most satisfying of all instruments—indeed the instrument all others would emulate—the spoken voice is the least musical, and a sonic background to it simply interferes.

Another time, however, I was so overcome by the sensuality of "The Dalliance of the Eagles" that song was not enough. In *Eagles*, a tone poem for huge orchestra, I composed a purely instrumental tissue on Whitman's strophic format and followed (symbolically, if you will) his development of idea.[3] Listeners aware of the program are appropriately titillated by the sound picture of aerial carnality, though of course no nonvocal music really connotes an unvariable picture beyond what the composer tells you, in words, it's supposed to connote.

Contrary in resources if not intent were my 1957 settings of five Whitman poems for baritone and clavichord.[4] And in 1966 I turned to this catholic writer for help in still another domain. I was plotting a large-scale suite for voice and orchestra titled *Sun*,[5] and I proposed to use descriptions of that star by eight poets—from King Akhenaton in 1360 B.C. to the late Theodore Roethke. At a loss for a penultimate selection (I required something tranquil, almost motionless, before the final explosion), I turned to Whitman as naturally as some turn to the Bible and found, not to my surprise, in his *Specimen Days* a prose paragraph whose low key proved to be the high point of the cycle.

Much current enthusiasm for Whitman, indeed for any admired artist, centers less in quality per se than in how that quality applies to our times. We hear a good deal about protest and involvement, with implicit hints that a committed artist is a good artist—or vice versa. The premise is false, for talent is conspicuously rarer than integrity. Artists speaking politics succeed on the strength of their names; they are not speaking art. The prime movers of public thought have never been major artists, who, almost by definition, are not in positions of authority; when they are, their art atrophies. Romantic though it sounds, artists need time for the introspection of creation. That time cannot be spent in the obligatory extroversion of "committed" oratory. Anyone can be right; nor are artists necessarily invested with rightness. Their function is not to convert so much as to explain pleasurably—albeit with sometimes agonizing pleasure. At least that's how I understand my function.

Yet when I consider my musical use of Whitman I can, in a sense, see it as engaged. Still, the song "Reconciliation" is not the product of a pacifist but of a composer who happens to be a pacifist, just as "Sometimes with One I Love" is the product not of a lover but of a composer who once felt the experience. How easy to misread the intent of these songs because they have words! The misreading may declare them good when, in fact, they could be bad. Actually no nonvocal music can be proved to be political or committed and by extension neither can vocal music nor any other so-called representational art.

Having heart and head well placed, then, does not inherently produce art, though it's safe to assume that most artists are no fools. Genius-bigots like Wagner are really exceptional; artistic natures do tend to the compassionate left.

Thus it was not Whitman's good intentions that made him what he was but his expression of those intentions. And with mere contradictory words, what more can I say of Whitman's intentions that I hope I've not said better with music?

NOTES

1. Paul Hindemith, *When Lilacs Last in the Dooryard Bloomed: A Requiem for Those We Love*, Munich: Orfeo, C-112851, 1983.

2. Ned Rorem, *Five Poems of Walt Whitman*, 1957. Score available: New York and London: Boosey and Hawkes; *Rosalind Rees Sings Ned Rorem with the Composer at the Piano*, Saranac Lake, N.Y.: GGS 104, 1983.

3. Ned Rorem, *Eagles*, New York: New World, NW-353-2, n.d.

4. Ned Rorem, "War Scenes" and five songs by Ned Rorem, texts by Walt Whitman; "Four Dialogues," words by Frank O'Hara. Franklin Lakes, N.J.: Desto, DC 7101, n.d.

5. Ned Rorem, *Sun*, eight poems in one movement for voice and orchestra. 1966. Vocal score available: New York and London: Boosey and Hawkes.

Loving Walt Whitman

and the Problem of America

ALICIA OSTRIKER

"The poem of these States . . ."

It is a question of who is to be master. Who among the poets is to define the American character. Whitman the exuberant Emersonian contender, Longfellow the genteel Tennysonian whose *Hiawatha* appeared in the same year as the first edition of *Leaves of Grass*, or Poe, that obsessional Christopher Marlowe of the American Renaissance, decadent while yet in bud. I imagine this question must have troubled them all. Whitman at any rate reminds us constantly, in a dozen different ways, of his yearning to influence posterity. To touch it intimately. To *be* there. Exceed-

ing the vaulting ambition of Shakespeare's sonnets, his lines announce not merely the poet's intention to achieve poetic immortality but the intention to make his identity inescapable, his poem
ubiquitous. Look for me under your bootsoles. I sound my barbaric yawp over the roof of the world. I'll be good health to you
and filter and fiber your blood. Under, over, and inside. Can't
get away from the man. What he assumes, you shall assume.
Whitman's extraordinary verbal embrace is a far cry from the cool
confidence of Shakespeare's "My love shall in my verse ever live
young," closer to Keats's "This living hand," though on a larger
scale.[1] But who or what is signified by the "you" in Whitman?
Isn't that pronoun as mysterious and fluid as his "I"? To read
the poem of "these States," you the reader must be you the
American. He'll explain to you, brother, sister, what that means.
Using whatever material is on hand, he'll make the myth and en-
list you.

An oscillation between the self defined as individual and the
self defined as a portion of a collective is one part of the myth.
"One's-Self I sing, a simple separate person, / Yet utter the word
Democratic, the word En-Masse" ("One's-Self I Sing," 1–2). A
corollary is the ostentatious break with high culture. Whitman's
patriotism is such that he decides never in his poetry to allude to
foreign literatures or philosophies, deviating sharply here from
Emerson. Indeed, he avoids literary allusion altogether. "Make
no quotations and no reference to any other writer," he commands himself in a notebook. "Do not go into criticism or arguments at all." To his readers he announces, "No one will get at
my verses who insists on viewing them as a literary performance,
or attempt at such performance, or as aiming mainly toward art
or aestheticism" ("A Backward Glance," 574). So radical a stance
perplexes scholarship. How can we capture between journal
covers a major literary figure who pretends literature doesn't
exist? Or mocks our critical acumen ("Have you felt so proud to
get at the meaning of poems?" ["Song of Myself," 32]) and tries
to slip what he calls "the origin of all poems" past our guard, like
some engaging fast-talking salesperson at our door? When we literary and scholarly people have accomplished a great deal of
reading, we like the world to know it. But as Paul Zweig demon-

strates in *Walt Whitman: The Making of the Poet*, we have in Whitman an omnivorous and obsessive reader who successfully disguised his literacy.

At the same time, Whitman loves adapting bits of foreign vocabulary and idiom, magpielike, much as the American language itself does, and sticking them in his nest. He likes the notion of poetry as universal solvent. Zweig (147) cites the naïveté of the notebook: "No two have exactly the same language, and the great translator and joiner of the whole is the poet. He has the divine grammar of all tongues. . . ." The "Song of the Answerer" elaborates on the idea that the poet speaks across class, race, and occupational and ethnic boundaries, enabling all to claim him as their own. He makes his culture over into his own image or vice versa. Expansive, bulky, soaring unbounded or out-of-bounds, he refuses a fixed hegemonic center (just as there is no American cultural equivalent of London or Paris or Rome but only regional cities of diverse character), hierarchy of persons (no king, no nobility, no gentry, no breeding), values (I am the poet of evil as well as of good), and gender (I am of the woman as well as the man). In sum, no privilege. No preference for this over that. He is a poet of space, not time. Or rather, time for him is always the present and future. Cut off from those immensely overpaid accounts of Europe, he offers no valid account of the past. We cannot go to Whitman for a sense of history. The genealogical claim in "Song of Myself" ("Born here of parents born here from parents the same") feels fraudulent both poetically and as effective American mythmaking, whereas the humorous roominess of "I effuse my flesh in eddies" or "I find I incorporate gneiss" feels authentically spacious. Even his bullying is tonally American, the bullying of a huckster. "His crudity is an exceeding great stench," Ezra Pound remarks, "but it *is* America" (184).

Whitman gets to be America because he wants to so badly and tries so hard. Or at least he ties for first place with Emily Dickinson, that dark horse he could not have known was even in the race. Dickinson, who claimed she did not read him but had heard he was disgraceful. Dickinson, who whispers "I'm nobody" at just the moment when Whitman is booming that he celebrates himself and sings himself and that what he assumes, we shall assume. The neutrino Dickinson, who appears to have no mass, moves at the speed of light, and can pass through granite without reaction, might yet survive the mountainous Whitman. But in the century succeeding his death, if poetry's definition of America exists, it is his. He jetted the stuff that makes Allen Ginsberg say, "America after all it is you and I who are perfect not the next world / . . . It occurs to me that I am America / I am talking to myself again" (*Howl*, 31–32). Whitman's egalitarianism in general and his powerful and ironic passages on slavery and the auction block in particular make June Jordan celebrate him as the great progenitor of black, Hispanic, working-class writing:

> What Walt Whitman envisioned we, the people and the poets of the New World, embody. . . . New World does not mean New England. New World means non-European; it means new, it means big, it means heterogeneous, it means unknown, it means free, it means an end to feudalism, caste, privilege. . . . New World means, again, to quote Walt Whitman, "By God! I will accept nothing which others cannot have their counterpart of on the same terms." (xix)

From "All truths wait in all things" it is scarcely the turn of a page to "No ideas but in things" and William Carlos Williams's beleaguered defense of American concretion against European abstraction. More startlingly, Whitman influences mandarin as well as marginal poets. T. S. Eliot, who "had to conquer an aversion to his form, as well as to much of his matter," might conceivably never have come upon the form of "The Love Song of J. Alfred Prufrock," or the donnée of the speaker as the walker in the city, or the address to an indeterminate "you" at the opening and close of that poem were it not for the example of Whitman. The austere genius of Wallace Stevens, as he begins to formulate the idea of order, imagines the bard's presence:

> In the far South the sun of autumn is passing
> Like Walt Whitman walking along a ruddy shore.
> He is singing and chanting the things that are part
>   of him,

The worlds that were and will be, death and day.
Nothing is final, he chants. No man shall see the end.
His beard is of fire and his staff is a leaping flame. (150)

The Europeanized Ezra Pound makes a grudging pact with him and calls himself "a Walt Whitman who has learned to wear a collar and dress shirt" ("What I Feel," 84). For Hart Crane he is of course "Our Meistersinger." But to multiply instances is absurd. One should simply observe that the twentieth-century American long poem, with its fracturing of narrative and of traditional meter ("To break the pentameter, that was the first heave"—Pound, *Selected Cantos*, Canto 81), derives as clearly from *Song of Myself* as all previous European epic derives from Homer. And when we turn, as poets, to the state of the nation and of our common life, the ghost of Whitman turns with us. Adrienne Rich argues that "the true nature of poetry" is "the drive to connect, the dream of a common language" (7). Anthony Hecht, gesturing toward President Kennedy's assassination, can say that "We were there, / We suffered, we were Whitman" (6–7). The poet of the body and the poet of the soul has made himself everyone's proper property.

"There was a child went forth . . ."

Why have I never before written about Walt Whitman? I always identify myself to audiences as Whitmanic, and I have written about Blake and Ginsberg, who are important to me but surely not more important than Whitman. Perhaps it is because I read Whitman earliest and completely outside of school. We must of course have read "O Captain! My Captain!" in school, and I must have hated it. My parents' Untermeyer anthology contained "Afoot and light-hearted I take to the open road" ("Song of the Open Road," 1), and I rather liked the swing of that. How "Song of Myself" fell into my hands I cannot say. What I remember is reading that poem straight through for the first time when I was thirteen, outdoors amid some uncut grass. That same year I decided Poe was mechanical, a puppet of a poet, all theatrical tricks, all indoors. This Whitman was a living creature, someone alive as I felt myself to be alive.

No, the location was not a meadow. I was a city girl. It was some grass and rocks in Manhattan's Central Park, where a scrim of forsythia announced April and the smell of dirt mingled with dog droppings. But the truth is that the girl is mother of the woman; some portion of myself paused ecstatically at the moment when I (when it) encountered "Song of Myself" and elected thenceforth to celebrate itself and sing itself. Obviously those were the instructions conveyed by every line in the poem, for every atom belonging to the poet belonged to me. To read Whitman was to experience self-recognition. Here were the self's not-yet-articulated perceptions of reality, its not-yet-formulated ideological biases, which plainly inhabited me already because I was an American. Or because I was a grandchild of Russian-Jewish immigrants? Or because I was young? The generosity of spirit meant that Whitman's energies could be mine if I chose. Like some improbably open-minded parent, he would permit everything.

He permitted love. That was the primary thing I noticed. The degree and quantity and variety of love in Whitman are simply astonishing. At thirteen I did not yet know the word *eroticism*, much less *auto-eroticism*, but I could tell when I encountered it, how each manifestation was delicately, systematically supporting all the others, like the network of filiations Whitman would later describe as spinning from the poet-spider's essence. Affection for one's own body, "that lot of me and all so luscious," "no sweeter fat than sticks to my own bones," underwrote the will to incorporate material phenomena—"All this I swallow, it tastes good, I like it well, it becomes mine" ("Song of Myself," 831)—the love of the world, the spectacle of other people, but also the love of what Whitman named the soul. Thus it was with ravishment that I read the amazing section 5:

> I believe in you my soul, the other I am must not abase
>   itself to you,
> And you must not be abased to the other.

Loafe with me on the grass, loose the stop from your
    throat,
Not words, not music or rhyme I want, not custom or
    lecture, not even the best,
Only the lull I like, the hum of your valvèd voice.

I mind how once we lay such a transparent summer
    morning,
How you settled your head athwart my hips and gently
    turn'd over upon me,
And parted the shirt from my bosom-bone, and plunged
    your tongue to my bare-stript heart,
And reach'd till you felt my beard, and reach'd till you
    held my feet.

Swiftly arose and spread around me the peace and
    knowledge that pass all the argument of the earth,
And I know that the hand of God is the promise of my
    own,
And I know that the spirit of God is the brother of my
    own,
And that all the men ever born are also my brothers,
    and the women my sisters and lovers,
And that a kelson of the creation is love,
And limitless are leaves stiff or drooping in the fields,
And brown ants in the little wells beneath them,
And mossy scabs of the worm fence, heap'd stones,
    elder, mullein and poke-weed.

Though the temptation is simply to sigh, let me unravel something of what the green thirteen-year-old self must have ap-
prehended in these lines, for the passage is a microcosm of Whitman's poetic method at its best. Outrageously elusive play is its
essence. Describing (inventing) a scene (or fantasy) of masturbation, or of lovemaking with another person, or of mystical communion—if it is impossible to tell which, the point is that such
scenes are equatable, just as "I" and "the other I am" and "you"
stand in poised balance. The point is also that Whitman makes it

humorously impossible to locate the relation of parts to whole, for each takes on the qualities normally assigned to another. "I" in this passage seems at first a kind of genial arbiter between "my soul" and "the other I am" (presumably the body), those famously rivalrous but insecure siblings. But the relationship immediately shifts. As soon as "I" invites an encounter with "you," "the other I am" disappears before it is even defined. If this term was to stand for "body," why was Whitman not more explicit? Was it to make body echo the cryptic self-identification of God to Moses in Midian, "I am that I am?"[2] In section 4 the mysterious entity "I am" was an observing ego. In section 5, if "you" is still "my soul," Whitman is clearly redefining the soul as separable from and equal to the self (instead of a portion of it), as nontranscendant, nonhierarchical, as in fact possessing its own body capable of relaxing and its own throat capable of humming. Whatever western philosophy from Plato through Protestant Christianity has made of the soul Whitman radically bypasses. Nor can one assimilate this image very easily to Emerson's Oversoul. All that remains here of any notion of an immaterial essence is the sequence of cultural negatives which Whitman wishes away and the "stop" he wishes loosed. "Only the lull I like, the hum of your valvèd voice," with its seductive assonances, proposes a soul like the drone of Indian music, a vibrant fullness which is also void; "lull" would be a sound something like a lullaby, along with a cessation of movement.

Further melting takes place during and after the long four lines describing the lovemaking between self and soul. "I mind" seems a relaxed idiomatic equivalent of "I recall" or "I remember," while allowing "mind" to register almost as a substantive noun. The "transparent" morning prepares us for perceptions and acts that will meet no obstacle. The future implied by the ego's invitation shifts to a recalled idyllic scene in which both self and soul are physically embodied, as if "the other I am" were diffused between them or distributed among them. The work of Eros, which is to join whatever is disconnected, requires palpability; vision is not enough. The tacit action behind the described lovemaking resembles that in Donne's "The Extasie," where the lovers mingle ("interinanimate") first their souls, then their bodies:

> So must pure lovers soules descend
> > T'affections, and to faculties,
> Which sense may reach and apprehend,
> > Else a great Prince in prison lies.
> To'our bodies turne wee then, that so
> > Weake men on love reveal'd may looke;
> Loves mysteries in soules doe grow,
> > But yet the body is his booke. (132)

Like Whitman, Donne wants to mediate the quarrel between the body's impurity and the soul's purity. The crucial difference is that soul and body remain logically distinguished and hierarchically conceived by Donne, whose theology requires the inferiority of bodies to souls, even while he boldly compares physical lovemaking to the incarnation. It is exactly that logical and hierarchical conception which Whitman opposes and rejects, in every inflection of his writing, as false.

The ego's penetrability in Whitman's poem provides one element of the passage's sweetness. There is something wonderful, always, in such moments of ecstatic male surrender. One feels it often in Keats and in Wyatt's "They Flee from Me" when the lady enters his chamber:

> In thin array after a pleasant guise, . . .
> [When] she me caught in her arms long and small,
> Therewithal sweetly did me kiss
> And softly said, "Dear heart, how like you this?" (117)

Another element is its musicality, the assonance of "settled . . . head . . . gently" tied to the alliterated "head . . . hips," the p's and b's of "*p*arted my shirt from my *b*osom-bone, and *p*lunged your tongue to my *b*are-stri*p*t heart," the off-rhyme of "shirt" and "heart," and above all the deep sound of "lull" and "hum" transformed to "plunged your tongue." Rhythmically the easy roll of mixed iambs and anapests, with the feminine endings of the first two lines, collects toward the successive stresses of "báre-strípt héart" and the tight, stretched, monosyllabic last line, with its long e's reinforcing the tension: "reach'd . . . beard . . . reach'd . . . feet."

Several particulars are important in Whitman's description of orgasm. "Swiftly arose and spread" marks the contrast after the sequence of iambs and anapests; the long line enacts the sensation of expansive ripples and "of the earth" suggests their extent, while "pass all the argument" conflates the sense of "surpass" with a suggestion that "argument" is static compared with the motion of peace and knowledge. Eros makes waves, but they are halcyon waves. The peace and knowledge that pass all the argument of the earth are what Eliot perhaps alludes to in the triple "Shantih" at the end of "The Waste Land," glossed as "the peace that passes understanding." Yet from Whitman's perspective, Eliot's fear and loathing of sexuality would make samadhi unattainable. We might also contrast what happens in this passage with the climax of Dickinson's "Wild Nights! Wild Nights!," another poem of autoerotic and androgynous fantasizing which uses the idea of a wide space of water but then brings it to closure in contraction instead of expansion:

> Rowing in Eden—
> Ah, the Sea!
> Might I but moor—Tonight—
> In Thee! (249)

For Whitman the pull toward safety and enclosure never occurs. Instead, the rest of this passage dissolves the conventional division between sexual and mental gratification, returning us to a biblical sense of what it means to "know," without sin or grief or loss of self. Knowledge is cosmic and inclusive, then subsides, as the orgasmic sensation gently ebbs, back to perception of the physical environment. That environment is itself emblematic of sexuality, being "limitless" and including phallic leaves ("stiff or drooping") and vaginal earthy declivities ("wells") full of insect life, finally declining to weedy textural particularities.

During this process—as the reader may not notice—time past has returned to time present, and the "you" has disappeared from the description along with "the other I am." The soul as lover, as active partner, has been as it were reabsorbed into the self—did the reaching and plunging begin this reabsorption?—and has emitted waves of peace and knowledge, much as the fusion of two atoms produces radiation. By the close of the passage even the assertive repetitions of "I know" are gone, absorbed in their turn into the living minutiae of what is known.

Section 5 of "Song of Myself" either is or is not an objective correlative for the reader's erotic experience. There I was, a palpitating adolescent, reading poetry to myself in the park as I so often did, with the noises of dogs, children, and a softball game in my circumference and airplanes periodically overhead—and it seemed to me he had it just right. He had me. He was me. Myself in the slippery moment when I was able to fall in love with anything, beautiful boys, hunched elderly women, frisky dogs, cerulean clouds above Fifth Avenue, mica in the sidewalk, softball teams. Writers commonly remain loyal to the enthusiastic creatures we are in adolescence. I hold dear the child who was simmering, simmering, simmering and was brought to a boil, given permission to exist by "Song of Myself." For decades afterward, the activity of writing poetry seemed to me essentially erotic, as Whitman repeatedly insists it is. Poetry aroused me bodily, felt at once passive and active, derived from an unarguable consciousness of the vitality and beauty of the world, and rested on a conviction that what I could feel, see, know in states of excited joy was real. The erotic was not "sex." It had nothing to do with conquest. It was a means of knowledge.

"Through me forbidden voices . . ."

When a girl becomes a woman and discovers her disadvantaged cultural status, Whitman's presence may strengthen her incalculably. Both for my own poetry and for the poetry of many other American women, Whitman has been the exemplary precursor, killer of the censor and clearer of ground. Even his crudest statements on gender, the insistence in "Song of Myself" (425) that "I am the poet of the woman the same as the man" or his equal-time advocacy of male and female bodies in "I Sing the Body Electric," are revolutionary compared to the sentimental conventions of his own time. I suspect they are still revolutionary compared to the psychoanalytic doctrines which pass for

valid utterance about gender and sexuality today. The poet H.D.,
under analysis by Freud in the thirties, struggled painfully uphill
before she could write in "The Master" that "woman is perfect,"

> herself
> is that dart and pulse of the male,
> hands, feet, thighs,
> herself perfect. (455–456)

But Whitman had already considered the topic of anatomy and
concluded, "That of the male is perfect, and that of the female is
perfect" ("I Sing the Body Electric," 10), adding of the female
form that phallic "mad filaments, ungovernable shoots play out
of it," much as he noticed at sunrise that "Something I cannot
see puts upward libidinous prongs" ("Song of Myself," 555).
He had already addressed "You workwomen and workmen of
these States" in "A Song for Occupations." His Adam had already imagined his Eve "By my side or back of me . . . / Or in
front, and I following her just the same" ("To the Garden the
World," 10–11).

But what moves me, and I suspect other American women
poets, is less the agreeable programmatic utterances than the
gestures whereby Whitman enacts the crossing of gender categories in his own person. It is not his claim to be "of the woman"
that speeds us on our way but his capacity to be shamelessly receptive as well as active, to be expansive on an epic scale without
a shred of nostalgia for narratives of conquest, to invent a rhetoric of power without authority, without hierarchy, and without
violence. The omnivorous empathy of his imagination wants to
incorporate All and therefore refuses to represent anything as
unavailably Other. So long as femaleness in our culture signifies
Otherness, Whitman's greed is our gain. In him we are freed to
be what we actually are, in whatever portion of ourselves eludes
society, system, and philosophy: not negative pole to positive
pole, not adversarial half of some dichotomy, but figures in an
energetic dance. His sacralization of sexuality anticipates Audre
Lorde's widely read feminist manifesto, "The Erotic as Power."
The phallic economy of which feminist theorists complain has no
place in a diffuse polymorphous eroticism whereby the aggres-

sion supposedly proper to adult males yields to "that lot of me and all so luscious." Whitman's evocations of touch align him with female celebrants of tactile intimacy—from Anne Sexton, who cries that "touch is all," to Luce Irigaray, who argues that feminine pleasure depends upon touch as masculine pleasure depends upon the gaze. Above all, the woman in Whitman speaks to us through his impulse to question boundaries—to prefer fluidity to fixity, experiment to status quo. If women poets in America have written more boldly and experimentally in the last thirty years than our British equivalents, we have Whitman to thank.[3]

I do not mean to say that Whitman is a man for all feminist purposes. He solves the problem of marginality by denying the existence of a center, transforming the figures of self, nation, cosmos into a vast floodplain of sensations, affections, filiations. For him there is no outsider position, hence no dilemma of powerlessness. High and low, rich and poor, the enslaved and the free are for him all actors in a pageant. Such a solution is beautiful but useless to one who is a slave. Whitman can write splendidly and deeply of death; he can write powerfully and glancingly of pain and doubt; he cannot write at all about chronic fear, anger, defeat, despair. Happily independent of institutions, including that of marriage, he has no sense of what it means to be crushed by them. If we want a nineteenth-century poet in whom the desire for power and the fact of powerlessness remain inescapably knotted, we turn to Emily Dickinson, whose poems are theaters of war, saturated in the language of politics. The poet who writes around 1864, "Peace is a fiction of our Faith" (912).

I write this essay during the first weeks of a war, the Gulf War of the winter of 1991. My primary emotions since it began are gloom, fear, disgust with the stupidity of my species. William James was quite right; people adore armed conflict while pretending not to. It would seem more appropriate to read Ecclesiastes or the Lamentations of Jeremiah than the cheerful Walt Whitman. I think of Virginia Woolf in 1941 loading her pockets with stones and walking into the sea because she believed her sanity would not survive World War II. I think of Edna St. Vincent Millay on the brink of the same war writing a poem entitled "Apostrophe to Man" which begins "Detestable race, continue to expunge yourself, die out" (302). Or Robinson Jeffers's anguished monologue, "The Sword Will Decide." When I read "Drum-Taps" I cannot forgive Whitman's representation of the Civil War as spectacle, as pageantry, as tragic necessity. Six hundred thousand men slaughtered one another because of intransigent male stupidity, male belligerence, male incapacity for patient negotiation; I cannot think otherwise. The bard's vision of a nation sealed in blood seems to me chillingly close to a politician's vision. Dulce et decorum? Wilfred Owen calls it an old lie. The vampiric tenderness of "Vigil Strange," "A Sight in Camp," and "The Wound-Dresser" makes me shudder. I wish that agonies were not merely one of Whitman's changes of garments. I wish, cruelly, that the soldiers dying in Whitman's arms could have driven him mad. I am sorry he said that there "will never be any more perfection than there is now," because today that seems to me intolerable, and I fear it is true.

Only one of Whitman's works seems to me adequate to the reality of America at present. In *Democratic Vistas*, the pessimist whom Whitman aimed always to suppress is permitted sustained voice:

> I say we had best look at our times and lands searchingly in the face, like a physician diagnosing some deep disease. . . . The underlying principles of the States are not honestly believ'd in (for all this hectic glow, and these melodramatic screamings), nor is humanity itself believ'd in. . . . The depravity of the business classes of our country is not less than has been supposed, but infinitely greater. The official services of America, national, state and municipal, in all their branches and departments, except the judiciary, are saturated in corruption, bribery, falsehood, maladministration; and the judiciary is tainted. . . . The magician's serpent in the fable ate up all the other serpents; and moneymaking is our magician's serpent, remaining today sole master in the field. The best class we show, is but a mob of fashionably dress'd speculators and vulgarians. (*Prose Works*, 369–370)

And so on, windily, sadly, believably. As antidote for the "dry and flat Sahara" of American materialism, Whitman hopefully proposes a class of literatuses, "a force-infusion" of the spirit, "or else our modern civilization, with all its improvements, is in vain, and we are on the road to a destiny, a status, equivalent, in its real world, to that of the fabled damned" (424). The fabled damned. Only a man who identified his immortality with his country's vitality could have written that. Whitman's panoramic, spectacular, dynamic America exists. I too love it. I experience surges of Whitmanian patriotism whenever I return from traveling abroad to the welter of Kennedy Airport or walk a crowded city street. His shallow, corrupt, material America exists as well, and I too hate it passionately. Do we contradict ourselves? Very well then, we contradict ourselves.

NOTES

1. Both Keats and Whitman were intensely affectionate men. But there is a curious chiasmus: Whitman's personal character, often described as languorous, matches Keats's poetic style. Keats's personality, social and exuberant, resembles Whitman's poetic style.

2. Coleridge, in a famous passage of the *Biographia Literaria*, offers a similar echo: "The primary IMAGINATION I hold to be the living Power and prime Agent of human perception, and as a repetition in the finite mind of the eternal act of creation in the infinite I AM" (268). Whitman reviewed the *Biographia* for the *Brooklyn Eagle*, December 4, 1847.

3. See Diane Middlebrook's essay, "Making Visible the Common World: Walt Whitman and Feminist Poetry." See also my study of American women's poetry, *Stealing the Language,* chapter 5, "The Imperative of Intimacy," for a discussion of the features of women's poetry which are perhaps most indebted to Whitman.

Letters to Walt Whitman

RONALD JOHNSON

1

I hear you whispering there O stars of heaven,
O suns—O grass of graves . . .
If you do not say anything how can I say anything?

Let us tunnel

the air
(as a mole's green galleries)
toward the ultimate

cornfield
—the square of gold, & green, & of tassel

that rustles back at us—

let us burrow in
to a susurration, the dense starlings,

of the real—
the huge
sunflowers waving back at us,

as we move

—the great grassy world

that surrounds us,
singing.

2

Unseen buds, infinite, hidden well,
Under the snow and ice, under the darkness,
in every square or cubic inch,
Germinal, exquisite, in delicate lace, microscopic . . .

Slant sheen/wrinkled silver.

Foxtail & lace-fly out of the vast organic slough
of the earth,
& the exquisite eye
—as myriad upon myriad of dandelions—

seeding itself on the air.

MIRRORS OF THE DARK WATER.

Poems beginning germinal in the instant
—reeling out, unravelling, tendril & silken, into the air—
ethereal growths,

sudden, & peculiar as mushrooms?
Uncrumpling
as moths from cocoons—

under the darkness,
pale wings,
slight densities out of the breadth of summer nights?

A largesse!

Argus-eyed & insistent.

3

These I compass'd around by a thick cloud of spirits . . .

Solitary, smelling the earthy smell
. . . a handful of sage.

Here, out of my pocket—
twigs of maple & currant-stems,
copious bunches of wild orange, chestnut, lilac!

.　　.　　.

But I have come O Walt
for the interchange, promised, of calamus,
masculine, sweet-smelling root,
between us:

you, who lie in Camden, still waiting for death,
still exuding an earthly smell
—your pockets redolent with sage—

the pond-soil still clinging to your fingers,
aromatic with plucking
calamus.

Calamus, 'sweet flag',
that still thrusts itself up,

that seasonally thrusts itself up for lovers.

4

The press of my foot to the earth
springs a hundred affections,
They scorn the best I can do to relate them . . .

(The moth and the fish-eggs are in their place, The bright
suns I see and the dark suns I cannot see
are in their place . . .)

I see a galaxy of gnats,
close-knit, & whirling through the air,
apparently for the pure joy of the circle, the jocund
inter-twinement.

And through this seethe,
I see the trees,
the blue accumulations of the air
beyond,
perceived
as through a sieve—

& all, through other, & invisible, convolutions:
those galaxies in a head

close-packed & wheeling.

I am involved with the palpable
as well
as the impalpable,

where I walk, mysteries catch at my heels
& cling
like cockle-burrs.

My affinities are infinite & from moment to moment
I propagate new symmetries, new

hinges, new edges.

5

Earth my likeness

.   .   .

I, too, have plucked a stalk of grass

from your ample prairie, Walt,
& have savored whole fields of a summer's hay in it—

I have known your Appalachian length, the heights
of your Sierra

—I have unearthed the roots of calamus
you left at the margin

of many, hidden ponds,
& have exchanged it with the few, select,
lovers.

I have lain in the open night,

till my shoulders felt twin roots, & the tree of my sight
swayed,
among the stars.

I, too, have plucked a stalk of grass

from your ample prairie, Walt.

6

Hefts of the moving world

at innocent gambols silently rising, freshly exuding,
Scooting obliquely high and low.
Dappled concave pulsing to the cricket's scrape:

the scud & mottle of sudden
dilations, divigations & night-jars.
CHURR, CHURR.

Mackerel & Fleecy,

in alternate dusks &
brightnesses,
as restlessness tumbling its

meadows, yeasty,
churning,
its black & white heifers working the cosmic cud

—a moon-humped bulge, as of the sea, swelling, irresistibly—

CHURR, CHURR,
I, too, caught in its strange tussle
its tough, prosy commas

punctuating the surge of me, out, & out,

lifting & proliferating: drifts
elastic, supple,

effuse.

7

A transparent base

shuddering . . .
under and through the universe

rides the brows of the sounding whales

& swells in the thousand
cow-bells.

It undulates under each meadow
to thunder in the hills, the crow's call,

& the apple-falls.

I hear it always, in a huge & earthy fugue,
from inner ear, to farthest owls:

the circulatory music of all things, omnipresent & in flux.

8

This grass is dark
. . . to come from under the faint red roofs of mouths.
Dark as heat-lightning—

mirage of flesh!
—purifying the air electric.

The intimate kernel putting forth final leaf

from The Valley Of The Many-Colored Grasses.
An *Aurora Borealis*

'dawning'
incorporeal.

All day the figures continued to move
about
& to bend over the green mounds

in the warm air.

Shades limned exact in the prismatic spheres
of death.

O SPEARS! TRANSPARENCIES!

9

Landscapes projected masculine,
full-sized and golden . . .
With floods of the yellow gold of the gorgeous, indolent,

sinking sun, burning, expanding the air.

But are these landscapes to be imagined,
or an actual
Kansas—the central, earthy, prosaic core of us?

Or is the seen always winged, and *eidolon* only to us—& never
the certain capture
of great, golden, unembroidered

slabs?

All is Oz.
The dusty cottonwoods, by the creek,
rustle an Emerald City.

And the mystic, immemorial city

is rooted in earth.

All is Oz & inextricable,

bound up in the unquenchable flames of double suns.

10

The smoke of my own breath,
Echoes, ripples,

buzz'd whispers, love-root, silk-thread,
crotch and vine.

I have put my ear close & close to these lips, heard them
to the last syllable
spun out—
respirations of an encircling night
—a cat-bird's ventriloquil
'whisper-song'

interspersing melodics with soft mews, brushing &
teasing my ears with its intimacies
as if surrounded

by many muted birds in the dark.

And ever these nights of 'love-root', sweet
calamus, embrace me, elusive, illusive, their buzz'd whisper
ever
at my ear.

Echoes, ripples.
There are Camerados, Walt—still they come.
And nights yet to come

to whisper you
to the ears of others.

Notes on Contributors

Amitai Avi-ram is assistant professor of English at the University of South Carolina, where he teaches poetry and poetry theory. His previous articles include "The Unreadable Black Body: 'Conventional' Form in the Harlem Renaissance," published in *Genders*. He is currently working on a book on poetry theory, *The Poetic Paradox: The Postmodern Sublime*. He is also a practicing poet.

Susan Margaret Brown teaches English at Rhode Island College in Providence. From 1982 to 1985 she taught in the Department of North American Studies at the University of Coimbra, Portugal. With Edwin Honig she has translated two books by Fernando Pessoa, *The Keeper of Sheep* and *Poems of Fernando Pessoa*, and she is completing a translation of Pessoa's selected letters. She is also at work on a book-length study of Pessoa.

David Eberly is a poet and critic whose work has appeared in many periodicals over the last twenty years. He is a regular contributor to *Bay Windows*, a gay and lesbian paper published in Boston. His collection of poetry, *What Has Been Lost*, was published in 1982.

Ed Folsom is professor of English and American Studies and chair of the English Department at the University of Iowa. He is the editor of the *Walt Whitman Quarterly Review* and has co-edited books on Whitman and W. S. Merwin. His latest book, *Walt Whitman's Cultural Keystones: Native Representations in "Leaves of Grass,"* will be published next year. He was the director of "Walt Whitman: The Centennial Conference," held in March 1992 in Iowa City.

Thom Gunn, a native of Gravesend, England, moved to the United States in 1954. He now lives in San Francisco and teaches at Berkeley. His eighth book of poetry is *The Man with Night Sweats*.

Alan Helms is associate professor of English at the University of Massachusetts in Boston, where he teaches courses on Whitman as well as modern and contemporary poetry. His writings on Whitman have appeared in *Études anglaises*, the *Yale Review*, the *Partisan Review*, and other journals. His memoir, entitled *Damaged Goods*, is due out next year.

George B. Hutchinson is associate professor of English and chair of the American Studies Program at the University of Tennessee, Knoxville. He is the author of *The Ecstatic Whitman: Literary Shamanism and the Crisis of the Union* and of a number of articles on American literature. He is currently working on a book entitled *American Cultural Nationalism and the Harlem Renaissance*.

Ronald Johnson grew up in Kansas and graduated from Columbia in 1960. His books include *The Book of the Green Man, Valley of the Many-Colored Grasses, Eyes & Objects*, and *RADI OS* (an erasure of Milton's *Paradise Lost*). For twenty years Johnson has lived in San Francisco, working on a long poem titled *ARK*. Though now completed, only the first half has been published in book form: *ARK: The Foundations* and *ARK 50*.

Maurice Kenny, a Mohawk poet born near the St. Lawrence River in New York, has been honored by the American Book Award, the Hodson Award, New York Council on the Arts, and National Public Radio for Broadcasting Award and twice has been nominated for the Pulitzer. In 1987, St. Lawrence University cited him with honors for Distinguished Service to Literature. He is the author of some eighteen collections of poetry and fiction; his current books are *Between Two Rivers, Selected Poems, Humors and/or So Humorous*, and *Greyhounding This America*.

M. Jimmie Killingsworth has taught American literature and rhetoric at the University of Tennessee, New Mexico Tech, Texas Tech, and Memphis State University. He is the director of Writing Programs and associate professor of English at Texas A&M University. In addition to numerous articles on writing in the United States, Killingsworth is the author of *Whitman's Poetry of the Body: Sexuality, Politics, and the Text* and co-author (with Jacqueline S. Palmer) of *Ecospeak: Rhetoric and Environmental Politics in America*.

Michael Lynch was a poet, critic, and activist who taught at the University of Toronto. He was deeply involved in the *Body Politic*, Canada's leading gay and lesbian journal, and in the AIDS Committee of Toronto, and he founded the Toronto Center for Lesbian and Gay Studies. Lynch published *These Waves of Dying Friends* in 1989. At the time of his death in 1991, he was at work on a study of male/male intimacy in New York in Whitman's time called *The Age of Adhesiveness*.

Robert K. Martin is professor of English at Concordia University in Montreal. His 1975 essay, "Walt Whitman's 'Song of Myself': Homosexual Dream and Vision," which appeared in the *Partisan Review*, opened a new period of Whitman studies. He is the author of *The Homosexual Tradition in American Poetry* and *Hero, Captain, and Stranger: Male Friendship, Social Critique, and Literary Form in the Sea Novels of Herman Melville*. He is pursuing his interest in gender and nineteenth-century American literature and is at work on a book tentatively entitled *Nathaniel Hawthorne and the Invention of Heterosexuality*.

Michael Moon teaches at Duke University. He is the author of *Disseminating Whitman: Revision and Corporeality in "Leaves of Grass"* and is associate editor of *American Literature*.

Alicia Ostriker, a poet and critic, is the author of seven volumes of poetry. Her most recent works are *The Imaginary Lover*, which won the 1986 William Carlos Williams Award from the Poetry Society of America, and *Green Age*. As a critic she is the author of *Vision and Verse in William Blake* and editor of Blake's *Complete Poems* and has written two books on American women's poetry, *Writing Like a Woman* and *Stealing the Language: The Emergence of Women's Poetry in America*. She is professor of English at Rutgers University.

Ned Rorem is one of America's most distinguished contemporary composers. He is best known for a remarkable body of vocal music, although he has also written orchestral music and organ music. His songs seek to balance verbal lucidity and musical interest. He has frequently set to music works by Yeats, Byron, Blake, Dickinson, Auden, Stevens, Plath, and Whitman as well as contemporary poets Paul Goodman, James Schuyler, Thom Gunn, Frank O'Hara, and John Ashbery.

Maria Irena Ramalho de Sousa Santos is professor of English and American studies at the University of Coimbra, Portugal. In 1991 she was Tinker Professor of Comparative Literature at the University of Wisconsin-Madison. She has written extensively on American literature and culture, poetics and literary theory, contemporary Portuguese literature, comparative literature, and comparative cultural studies. Her essay here is part of her current research project on the ideology of poetic modernism, provisionally titled *Atlantic Poets and the Re-discovery of the West*.

Eric Savoy is assistant professor of English at the University of Calgary. His recent work appears in the *Canadian Review of American Studies*, the *Victorian Review*, and *Open Letter*. He is working on a book on Henry James and gay literary history.

Gregory Woods teaches at Nottingham Polytechnic, England. He is the author of *Articulate Flesh: Male Homo-eroticism and Modern Poetry*. His first book of poems, *We Have the Melon*, will be published in 1992; its title is a quotation from Whitman.

Selected Bibliography

Alegria, Fernando. *Walt Whitman en Hispanoamerica*. Mexico City: Ediciones Studium, 1954.

Allen, Gay Wilson. *American Prosody*. New York: American Book Company, 1935.

———. *The Solitary Singer: A Critical Biography of Walt Whitman*. Chicago: University of Chicago Press, 1985.

———. *The Two Poets of "Leaves of Grass."* Westwood, N.J.: Kindle, 1969.

Arvin, Newton. *Whitman*. New York: Macmillan, 1938.

Aspiz, Harold. "Walt Whitman: The Spermatic Imagination." *American Literature* 56 (1984): 379–395.

Auden, W. H. *The Dyer's Hand*. London: Faber, 1963.

———. *The English Auden*. London: Faber, 1977.

Avi-ram, Amitai F. "Towards a Theory of the Pastoral: The Classics, Walt Whitman, and Hart Crane." *Dissertation Abstracts International* 46 (November 1985): 1270A.

Ballard, G. A. *America and the Atlantic*. London: Duckworth, 1923.

Baudrillard, Jean. "La Précision des simulacres." *Simulacres et simulation*. Paris: Éditions Galilée, 1981.

Bazalgette, Léon. *Walt Whitman: The Man and His Work*. Garden City: Doubleday, Page, 1920.

Bellah, Robert, Richard Madsen, William M. Sullivan, Ann Swindler, and Steven M. Tepton. *Habits of the Heart: Individualism and Commitment in American Life*. New York: Harper and Row, 1985.

Benveniste, Émile. *Problems in General Linguistics*. Translated by Mary Elizabeth Meek. Coral Gables: University of Miami Press, 1971.

Blasing, Mutlu Konuk. *American Poetry: The Rhetoric and Its Forms*. New Haven: Yale University Press, 1987.

Blinderman, Barry, ed. *David Wojnarowicz: Tongues of Flame*. Normal, Ill.: University Galleries, Illinois State University, 1990.

Bloom, Harold. *The Anxiety of Influence: A Theory of Poetry*. New York: Oxford University Press, 1973.

Borges, Jorge Luis. *Discusion*. Buenos Aires and Barcelona: M. Gleizer, 1932.

Bowers, Fredson, ed. "Whitman's Manuscripts for the Original 'Calamus' Poems." *Studies in Bibliography* 6 (1953–1954): 257–265.

———. *Whitman's Manuscripts: Leaves of Grass (1860)*. Chicago: University of Chicago Press, 1955.

Brown, Susan. "The Poetics of Pessoa's 'Drama em gente': The Function of Alberto Caeiro and the Role of Walt Whitman." Ph.D. diss.,
Chapel Hill: University of North Carolina, 1987.

Burke, Edmund. *A Philosophical Enquiry into the Origin of Our Ideas of the
Sublime and Beautiful*. 1757. Reprint. Edited by James T. Boulton.
Notre Dame: University of Notre Dame Press, 1958.

Carlin, John. "David Wojnarowicz: As the World Turns." In
Blinderman.

Carpenter, Edward. *Days with Walt Whitman*. London: G. Allen, 1906.

———. *Towards Democracy*. 1905. London: GMP, 1984.

Cassirer, Ernst. *The Philosophy of Symbolic Forms*. Volume 1: *Language*.
Translated by Ralph Manheim. New Haven: Yale University Press,
1955.

Chopin, Kate. *The Awakening*. New York: Capricorn, 1964.

Coleridge, S. T. *Selected Poetry and Prose*. Edited by Elisabeth Schneider.
New York: Holt Rinehart, 1951.

Cook, Ramsay. *The Regenerators: Social Criticism in Late Victorian English
Canada*. Toronto: University of Toronto Press, 1985.

Coote, Stephen, ed. *The Penguin Book of Homosexual Verse*. Harmondsworth, Middlesex, U.K.: Penguin, 1983.

Craige, Betty Jean. *Lorca's "Poet in New York": The Fall into Consciousness*.
Lexington: University of Kentucky Press, 1977.

Crane, Hart. *The Complete Poems and Selected Letters and Prose*. Edited by
Brom Weber. New York: Anchor, 1966.

———. *The Letters of Hart Crane, 1916–1932*. Edited by Brom Weber.
Berkeley: University of California Press, 1965.

Creeley, Robert. "Introduction." In Perlman et al.

Daniels, Peter, ed. *Take Any Train: A Book of Gay Men's Poetry*. London:
Oscar's Press, 1990.

Davidson, Michael. *The World, the Flesh and Myself*. London: GMP, 1985.

Delavenay, Emile. *D. H. Lawrence and Edward Carpenter: A Study in
Edwardian Transition*. London: Heinemann, 1971.

Dellamora, Richard. *Masculine Desire: The Sexual Politics of Victorian Aestheticism*. Chapel Hill: University of North Carolina Press, 1990.

de Man, Paul. *The Rhetoric of Romanticism*. New York: Columbia University Press, 1984.

Dickinson, Emily. *The Complete Poems of Emily Dickinson*. Edited by Thomas H. Johnson. Cambridge: Harvard University Press, 1955.

Donaldson, Thomas. *Walt Whitman: The Man*. New York: Harper, 1896.

Donne, John. *The Complete Poetry of John Donne*. Edited by John T. Shawcross. New York: New York University Press, 1968.

Downey, Fairfax Davis. *Indian Wars of the U.S. Army: 1776–1865*. New York: Doubleday, 1964.

Duncan, Robert. *Fictive Certainties*. New York: New Directions, 1985.

Edel, Leon. *Henry James, the Master: 1901–1916*. New York: J. B. Lippincott, 1972.

Edelman, Lee. *Transmemberment of Song: Hart Crane's Anatomies of Rhetoric and Desire*. Stanford: Stanford University Press, 1987.

Eliot, T. S. "Introduction: 1928." In *Ezra Pound: Selected Poems*. Rev. ed. London: Faber and Faber, 1948.

Elledge, Jim, ed. *Frank O'Hara: To Be True to a City*. Ann Arbor: University of Michigan Press, 1990.

Ellmann, Richard. *Oscar Wilde*. London: Penguin, 1988.

Emerson, Ralph Waldo. *Essays and Lectures*. Edited by Joel Porte. New York: Library of America, 1983.

———. *Selections from Ralph Waldo Emerson: An Organic Anthology*. Edited by Stephen Whicher. Boston: Riverside, 1960.

Erkkila, Betsy. *Walt Whitman among the French: Poet and Myth*. Princeton: Princeton University Press, 1980.

———. *Whitman the Political Poet*. New York: Oxford University Press, 1989.

Folsom, Ed. "Talking Back to Walt Whitman." In Perlman et al.

Forster, E. M. *Maurice*. Harmondsworth, Middlesex, U.K.: Penguin, 1972.

Foucault, Michel. *The History of Sexuality*. Volume 1: *An Introduction*. Translated by Robert Hurley. New York: Random House, 1978.

Frank, Waldo. *Our America*. New York: Boni and Liveright, 1919.

———. *The Re-discovery of America: An Introduction to the Philosophy of American Life*. New York: Charles Scribner, 1929.

Ginsberg, Allen. *The Gates of Wrath: Rhymed Poems, 1948–1952*. Bolinas, Calif.: Grey Fox, 1972.

———. *Howl and Other Poems*. San Francisco: City Lights Books, 1959.

———. "Allen Ginsberg on Walt Whitman: Composed on the Tongue." In Perlman et al.

Goffman, Erving. *The Presentation of the Self in Everyday Life*. Garden City: Doubleday, 1959.

Gorham, Deborah. "Flora MacDonald Denison: Canadian Feminist." In *A Not Unreasonable Claim: Women and Reform in Canada, 1820s–1920s*, edited by Linda Kealey. Toronto: Women's Educational Press, 1979.

Grünzweig, Walter. "'Collaborators in the Great Cause of Liberty and Fellowship': Whitmania as an Intercultural Phenomenon." *Walt Whitman Quarterly Review* 5 (1988): 16–26.

Gunn, Thom. *Fighting Terms*. 2d ed. London: Faber, 1962.

———. *Moly* and *My Sad Captains*. New York: Farrar, Straus, 1973.

———. *The Occasions of Poetry: Essays in Criticism and Autobiography*. London: Faber, 1972.

———. *The Sense of Movement*. London: Faber, 1957.

Hahn, Walter F., and Robert L. Pfaltzgraff, Jr., eds. *Atlantic Community in Crisis: A Redefinition of a Transatlantic Relationship*. New York: Pergamon Press, 1979.

Harwood, Lee. *Crossing the Frozen Rivers: Selected Poems*. London: Paladin, 1988.

H.D. (Hilda Doolittle). *H.D.: Collected Poems, 1912–1944*. Edited by Louis L. Martz. Manchester: Carcanet Press, 1984.

Hecht, Anthony. *Millions of Strange Shadows*. New York: Atheneum, 1977.

Helms, Alan. "Whitman Revised." *Études anglaises* 37 (July–September 1984): 257–271.

Hobsbawm, E. J. *The Age of Empire: 1875–1914*. London: Weidenfeld and Nicolson, 1987.

Hockney, David. *David Hockney by David Hockney*. Edited by Nikos Stangos. Introduction by Henry Geldzahler. London: Thames and Hudson, 1976.

Hollis, C. Carroll. *Language and Style in "Leaves of Grass."* Baton Rouge: Louisiana State University Press, 1983.

Horovitz, Michael, ed. *Children of Albion: Poetry of the "Underground" in Britain*. Harmondsworth, Middlesex, U.K.: Penguin, 1969.

Hughes, Langston. "The Ceaseless Rings of Walt Whitman." In Perlman et al.

———, trans. "Fate at the Wedding [Bodas de sangre]." By Federico

García Lorca. Typescript. Theatre Collection. New York City Public Library.

———. *Fine Clothes to the Jew*. New York: Knopf, 1927.

———. Introduction. *I Hear the People Singing*. Edited by Langston Hughes. New York: International Publishers, 1946.

———. Letter to Carl Van Vechten, May 17, 1935. Langston Hughes Papers. Beinecke Rare Book and Manuscript Library, Yale University.

———. "Tell It to Telstar." Langston Hughes Papers. Beinecke Rare Book and Manuscript Library, Yale University.

———. "Old Walt." In *Selected Poems of Langston Hughes*. New York: Knopf, 1959.

———. *The Weary Blues*. New York: Knopf, 1926.

Hughes, Langston, and Arna Bontemps, eds. *Poetry of the Negro, 1746–1949*. Garden City: Doubleday, 1949.

Humphries, Martin, ed. *Not Love Alone: A Modern Gay Anthology*. London: GMP, 1985.

Hyde, Lewis. *The Gift: Imagination and the Erotic Life of Property*. New York: Vintage, 1983.

Jaen, Didier Tisdel, trans. and ed. *Homage to Walt Whitman*. University, Ala.: University of Alabama Press, 1969.

Jakobson, Roman. "Linguistics and Poetics." In *Style in Language*, edited by Thomas A. Sebeok. Cambridge: MIT Press, 1960.

———. "Poetry of Grammar and Grammar of Poetry." *Lingua* 21 (1968): 597–609.

James, Henry. *The American Scene*. Introduction by Irving Howe. New York: Horizon Press, 1967.

———. *The Golden Bowl*. 1904. Reprint. Harmondsworth, Middlesex, U.K.: Penguin, 1978.

———. *Literary Criticism: Essays on Literature, American Writers, English Writers*. Edited by Leon Edel and Mark Wilson. New York: Literary Classics of the United States, 1984.

———. *Literary Criticism: French Writers, Other European Writers, Prefaces to the New York Edition*. Edited by Leon Edel and Mark Wilson. New York: Literary Classics of the United States, 1984.

James, William. *The Varieties of Religious Experience*. 1902. Reprint. New York: Mentor, 1958.

Johnson, James Weldon. *Along This Way*. 1933. Reprint. New York: Viking, 1968.

——. *God's Trombones*. New York: Viking, 1927.

Johnson, Ronald. *The American Table*. New York: William Morrow, 1984.

——. *The Book of the Green Man*. New York: Norton, 1967.

——. *RADI OS I–IV*. Santa Barbara, Calif.: Sand-Dollar Press, 1977.

——. *Southwestern Cooking New and Old*. Albuquerque: University of New Mexico Press, 1985.

——. *Valley of the Many-Colored Grasses*. Introduction by Guy Davenport. New York: W. W. Norton, 1969.

Jordan, June. *Passion: New Poems, 1977–1980*. Boston: Beacon Press, 1980.

Kaplan, Justin. *Walt Whitman: A Life*. New York: Simon and Schuster, 1980.

Karjala, Irene. "The Subversive Seed: The Aesthetics of Auto-Eroticism in Walt Whitman." Master's thesis, Concordia University, Montreal, 1987.

Katz, Jonathan Ned. "The Invention of Heterosexuality." *Socialist Review* 20 (January–March 1990): 7–34.

Keats, John. *The Poetical Works of John Keats*. Edited by H. Buxton Forman. 1914. London: Oxford University Press, 1929.

Kenner, Hugh. *The Pound Era*. Berkeley: University of California Press, 1971.

Killingsworth, M. Jimmie. *Whitman's Poetry of the Body*. Chapel Hill: University of North Carolina Press, 1989.

Kleiman, Robert. *Atlantic Crisis: American Diplomacy Confronts a Resurgent Europe*. New York: Norton, 1964.

Krieg, Joann P., ed. *Walt Whitman: Here and Now*. Westport, Conn.: Greenwood Press, 1985.

Kugel, James L. *The Idea of Biblical Poetry: Parallelism and Its History*. New Haven: Yale University Press, 1981.

Lawrence, D. H. *The Complete Poems of D. H. Lawrence*. London: Heinemann, 1972.

——. *Studies in Classic American Literature*. London: Heinemann, 1964.

Locke, John. *An Essay Concerning Human Understanding and a Treatise on the Conduct of Understanding*. 1689. Reprint. Philadelphia: Day and Troutman, 1847.

Los Angeles County Museum of Art. *David Hockney: A Retrospective*. New York: Abrams, 1988.

Lourenço, Eduardo. *Pessoa revisitado.* Pôrto, Portugal: Inova, 1973.

————. "Walt Whitman e Pessoa." *Quaderni Portoghesi* 2 (1977).

Lozynsky, Artem, ed. *Richard Maurice Bucke, Medical Mystic: Letters of Dr. Bucke to Walt Whitman and His Friends.* Detroit: Wayne State University Press, 1977.

Lynch, Michael. "The Lover of His Fellows and the Hot Little Prophets." *Body Politic* 67 (October 1980): 29–31.

Mailer, Norman. *A Fire on the Moon.* London: Pan, 1971.

Martin, Robert K. *The Homosexual Tradition in American Poetry.* Austin: University of Texas Press, 1979.

————. Review of *Manhood and the American Renaissance,* by David Leverenz. *Walt Whitman Quarterly Review* 7 (Winter 1990): 143–146.

Matthiessen, F. O. *The American Renaissance: Art and Expression in the Age of Emerson and Whitman.* New York: Oxford University Press, 1941.

Merwin, W. S. *The Lice.* New York: Atheneum, 1967.

Middlebrook, Diane. "Making Visible the Common World: Walt Whitman and Feminist Poetry." *Kenyon Review* 2 (Fall 1980): 14–27.

Millay, Edna St. Vincent. *Collected Poems: Edna St. Vincent Millay.* Edited by Norma Millay. New York: Harper and Row, 1956.

Miller, Edwin Haviland. *Walt Whitman's Poetry: A Psychological Journey.* New York: New York University Press, 1968.

————. *Walt Whitman's "Song of Myself": A Mosaic of Interpretations.* Iowa City: University of Iowa Press, 1989.

Miller, F. DeWolfe. "Before 'The Good Gray Poet.'" *Tennessee Studies in Literature* 3 (1958): 89–98.

Miller, James E., Jr. *The American Quest for a Supreme Fiction: Whitman's Legacy in the Personal Epic.* Chicago: University of Chicago Press, 1979.

————. *A Critical Guide to "Leaves of Grass."* Chicago: University of Chicago Press, 1957.

————. *T. S. Eliot's Personal Waste Land: Exorcism of the Demons.* University Park: Pennsylvania State University Press, 1977.

Mitchinson, Wendy, and Janice Dickin McGinnis, eds. *Essays in the History of Canadian Medicine.* Toronto: McClelland and Stewart, 1988.

Moon, Michael. "Disseminating Whitman." *South Atlantic Quarterly* 88 (1989): 247–265.

————. *Disseminating Whitman: Revision and Corporeality in Leaves of Grass*. Cambridge: Harvard University Press, 1991.

O'Connor, William Douglas. *The Good Gray Poet*. New York: Bunce and Huntingdon, 1866.

O'Hara, Frank. *The Collected Poems of Frank O'Hara*. Edited by Donald Allen. New York: Knopf, 1971.

————. *Standing Still and Walking in New York*. Edited by Donald Allen. San Francisco: Grey Fox, 1983.

Ostriker, Alicia. *Stealing the Language*. Boston: Beacon Press, 1968.

Pearce, Roy Harvey. *The Continuity of American Poetry*. Princeton: Princeton University Press, 1961.

Perlman, Jim, Ed Folsom, and Dan Campion, eds. *Walt Whitman: The Measure of His Song*. Minneapolis: Holy Cow! Press, 1981.

Pessoa, Fernando. *English Poems*. 2 vols. Lisbon: Olisipo, 1921.

————. *The Keeper of Sheep*. Translated by Edwin Honig and Susan M. Brown. New York: Sheep Meadow Press, 1986.

————. *Obra em prosa*. Edited by Cleonice Berardinelli. Rio de Janeiro: Nova Aguilar, 1982.

————. *Obra poética*. Edited by Maria Aliete Galhoz. Rio de Janeiro: Nova Aguilar, 1981.

————. *Páginas íntimas e de auto-interpretação*. Edited by Georg Rudolf and Jacinto do Prado Coelho. Lisbon: Ática, n.d.

————. *The Poems of Fernando Pessoa*. Translated by H. Edwin Honig and Susan M. Brown. New York: Ecco Press, 1986.

————. *Sobre Portugal: Introdução ao problema nacional*. Edited by Maria Isabel Rochete and Maria Paula Morão. Lisbon: Ática, 1978.

————. *Ultimatum e páginas de sociología política*. Edited by Maria Isabel Rochete and Maria Paula Morão. Lisbon: Ática, 1980.

Plante, David. *The Catholic*. London: Chatto and Windus, 1985.

Pound, Ezra. *Literary Essays of Ezra Pound*. Edited by T. S. Eliot. New York: New Directions, 1968.

————. *Selected Cantos*. New York: New Directions, n.d.

————. "What I Feel about Walt Whitman." In *Walt Whitman: A Critical Anthology*, edited by Francis Murphy. Harmondsworth, Middlesex, U.K.: Penguin, 1969.

Ramage, Edwin S., ed. *Atlantis: Fact or Fiction*. Bloomington: Indiana University Press, 1978.

Rampersad, Arnold. *The Life of Langston Hughes.* 2 vols. New York: Oxford University Press, 1986.

Rich, Adrienne. *The Dream of a Common Language: Poems 1974–1977.* New York: W. W. Norton, 1978.

Reade, Brian. *Sexual Heretics: Male Homosexuality in English Literature from 1850 to 1900.* London: Routledge and Kegan Paul, 1970.

Rodriguez, Richard. "Late Victorians: San Francisco, AIDS, and the Homosexual Stereotype." *Harper's* (October 1990): 57–66.

Rukeyser, Muriel. *The Life of Poetry.* New York: A. A. Wyn, 1949.

Rusk, Ralph L. *The Life of Ralph Waldo Emerson.* New York: Columbia University Press, 1967.

Sandoz, Mari. *The Battle of the Little Bighorn.* Lincoln: University of Nebraska Press, 1978.

Santos, Maria Irena Ramalho de Sousa. "A hora do poeta: O Hyperion de Keats na Mensagem de Pessoa." Paper presented at the 4th International Symposium on Fernando Pessoa, New Orleans, November 1988.

———. "A ilha incontinente o atlantismo de Walt Whitman e Fernando Pessoa." Paper presented at the conference Um Século de Pessoa. Lisbon: Fundação Calouste Gulbenkian, December 1988.

———. "An Imperialism of Poets: The Modernism of Hart Crane and Fernando Pessoa." Paper presented at the American Studies Association Convention, New York, 1987.

Sedgwick, Eve Kosofsky. *Between Men: English Literature and Male Homosocial Desire.* New York: Columbia University Press, 1985.

———. *Epistemology of the Closet.* Berkeley: University of California Press, 1990.

———. "Whitman's Transatlantic Context." *Delta: Revue du Centre d'Études et de Recherche sur les Écrivains du Sud aux États-Unis* 16 (1983): 111–124.

Senghor, Léopold Sédar. *Oeuvre poétique.* Paris: Seuil, 1990.

Shively, Charley. *Calamus Lovers: Walt Whitman's Working Class Camerados.* San Francisco: Gay Sunshine Press, 1987.

———. *Drum Beats: Walt Whitman's Civil War Boy Lovers.* San Francisco: Gay Sunshine Press, 1989.

Shortt, S. E. D. *Victorian Lunacy: Richard M. Bucke and the Practice of Late Nineteenth Century Psychiatry.* New York: Cambridge University Press, 1986.

Snyder, Gary. *Turtle Island*. New York: New Directions, 1974.

Sommer, Doris. "Supplying Demand: Walt Whitman as the Liberal Self." In *Reinventing the Americas*, edited by Bell Gale Chevigny and Gari Laguardia. New York: Cambridge University Press, 1986.

Spence, Lewis. *Atlantis in America*. London: Ernest Benn, 1925.

Spengler, Oswald. *The Decline of the West*. 2 vols. New York: Knopf, 1945.

Stevens, Wallace. *The Collected Poems of Wallace Stevens*. New York: Knopf, 1971.

Taylor, Charles. *Source of the Self: The Making of Modern Identity*. Cambridge: Harvard University Press, 1989.

Toomer, Jean. *Cane*. Edited by Darwin T. Turner. New York: Norton, 1988.

Traubel, Horace. *With Walt Whitman in Camden*. 6 vols. 1914–1983.

———, Richard Maurice Bucke, and Thomas B. Harned, eds. *In Re Walt Whitman*. Philadelphia: David McKay, 1893.

Webb, Peter. *Portrait of David Hockney*. London: Chatto and Windus, 1988.

Weir, Lorna. "Richard Maurice Bucke and Edward Carpenter: Contacts and 'Cosmic Consciousness.'" Typescript, Carleton University, 1990.

Wharton, Edith. *A Backward Glance*. New York: Charles Scribner's Sons, 1934.

Whitman, Walt. *An American Primer*. Edited by Horace Traubel. Boston: Small, Maynard, 1904.

———. *The Correspondence of Walt Whitman*. 6 vols. Edited by Edwin Haviland Miller. New York: New York University Press, 1961–1977.

———. *Daybooks and Notebooks*. 3 vols. Edited by William White. New York: New York University Press, 1978.

———. *Leaves of Grass*. 1855 ed. Edited by Malcolm Cowley. 1959. Reprint. Harmondsworth, Middlesex, U.K.: Penguin, 1976.

———. *Leaves of Grass*. 1860 ed. Edited by Roy Harvey Pearce. Ithaca: Cornell University Press, 1961.

———. *Leaves of Grass: A Textual Variorum of the Printed Poems*. 3 vols. Edited by Sculley Bradley, Harold W. Blodgett, Arthur Golden, and William White. New York: New York University Press, 1980.

———. *Leaves of Grass: Comprehensive Reader's Edition*. Edited by Harold W. Blodgett and Sculley Bradley. New York: New York University Press, 1965.

————. *Notebooks and Unpublished Prose Manuscripts of Walt Whitman.* 6 vols. Edited by Edward F. Grier. New York: New York University Press, 1984.

————. *Notes and Fragments.* Edited by Richard Maurice Bucke. London, Ontario: 1899.

————. *Prose Works.* 1892. 2 vols. Edited by Floyd Stovall. New York: New York University Press, 1963.

Wilde, Oscar. *Selected Letters of Oscar Wilde.* Edited by Rupert Hart-Davis. London: Oxford University Press, 1979.

Wojnarowicz, David. "Post-Cards from America: X-Rays from Hell." In Blinderman.

Wolfson, Leandro. "The Other Whitman in Spanish America." *Walt Whitman Review* 24 (1978): 62–71.

Wyatt, Sir Thomas. *The Complete Poems of Sir Thomas Wyatt.* Edited by R. A. Rebholz. Harmondsworth, Middlesex, U.K.: Penguin, 1978.

Zweig, Paul. *Walt Whitman: The Making of the Poet.* New York: Basic Books, 1984.

Index to Whitman Poems Cited